Juli Flintoff is an English artist from West Yorkshire. Initially studying drama, she later obtained a Bachelor of Arts degree from Sunderland University. For several years, Juli was a successful community arts development worker facilitating workshops throughout the Bradford, Calderdale, Leeds, Wakefield and Halifax areas. After exhibiting five large banners at the Bradfords International youth event attended by delegates from all over the world, she became involved with projects for young offenders. This led her to train as a prison officer and later a drugs dog handler.

For the past 13 years, she has dedicated her life to caring for her elderly parents. *Blame, Shame and Guilt* is a prequel to Juli's first publication aptly named *The Secret Back Door*—an inspiring book depicting the struggles of living with dementia.

I dedicate this book to my amazing, handsome, funny, intelligent and well-grounded boys, Coban and Corai. You encompass everything in this world that is good holding the ability to inspire me daily and without your love, trust, support, belief and integrity. *Blame, Shame and Guilt* would never have materialised. Love you guys always and forever xx.

Juli Flintoff

BLAME, SHAME AND GUILT

AUSTIN MACAULEY PUBLISHERS™
LONDON * CAMBRIDGE * NEW YORK * SHARJAH

Copyright © Juli Flintoff 2024

The right of Juli Flintoff to be identified as author of this work has been asserted by the author in accordance with sections 77 and 78 of the Copyright, Designs and Patents Act 1988.

All rights reserved. No part of this publication may be reproduced, stored in a retrieval system, or transmitted in any form or by any means, electronic, mechanical, photocopying, recording, or otherwise, without the prior permission of the publishers.

Any person who commits any unauthorised act in relation to this publication may be liable to criminal prosecution and civil claims for damages.

The story, experiences, and words are the author's alone.

A CIP catalogue record for this title is available from the British Library.

ISBN 9781035835904 (Paperback)
ISBN 9781035835911 (ePub e-book)

www.austinmacauley.com

First Published 2024
Austin Macauley Publishers Ltd®
1 Canada Square
Canary Wharf
London
E14 5AA

Thank you to the team at Austin Macauley Publishers for their outstanding appraisal of *Blame, Shame and Guilt*; it is one thing to have your work validated but to have it recognised so descriptively literally blew me away. Thank you for affirming its potential and for your continued support, guidance and expertise along the road to publication.

Thank you to my beautiful boys, Coban and Corai, who provided much support, positive encouragement, the time and space to write, along with numerous cups of tea and hot water bottles. A massive appreciation to Mary Dolan and Emma Wilson who eagerly proofread my manuscript and avidly encouraged me to pursue its publication.

Thank you to Tony Paul Gibbens and his computer wizard abilities for wiping and restoring my laptop, enabling me to write this book, and lastly thanks to you for choosing to share this journey with me.

Table of Contents

DECEMBER 2022	**11**
Chapter 1: Lois	*13*
Little Lois	**19**
Chapter 2: Moving Day	*21*
Chapter 3: The Pushchair	*27*
Chapter 4: The Predator	*30*
Chapter 5: The Confrontation	*36*
Young Lois	**41**
Chapter 6: All an Act	*43*
Chapter 7: Life Goes on	*48*
Chapter 8: "Has He Ever"	*53*
Chapter 9: "Well?"	*56*
Growing up	**59**
Chapter 10: Finding My True Self	*61*
Chapter 11: Joe	*73*
Chapter 12: The Picnic	*80*
Chapter 13: The Plot Thickens	*84*
Chapter 14: Evans and Rathbone	*89*
Chapter 15: Promise Me!	*102*
Chapter 16: Mother Nature	*113*

Chapter 17: Treacle Sponge — 117

Chapter 18: Making the Call — 127

Chapter 19: Maya and Samuels — 132

Chapter 20: Dreams — 143

Chapter 21: The Monster — 149

Chapter 22: Cliffe House — 160

Chapter 23: Visiting the Suite — 164

Chapter 24: Making a Statement — 173

Chapter 25: Dad's Birthday — 189

Chapter 26: My Worst Nightmare — 194

Chapter 27: "We've Got You, Grandad" — 198

Chapter 28: And I Smiled — 205

Chapter 29: On Autopilot — 215

Chapter 30: Singing Lessons — 225

Chapter 31: Saying "Goodbye" — 238

Chapter 32: The Final Farewell — 247

Chapter 33: It's Not My Fault — 258

Chapter 34: Pressing Forward — 268

Chapter 35: No More Shenanigans — 271

Chapter 36: The Shield of Faith — 277

Chapter 37: A Poor Show — 286

DECEMBER 2022

Chapter 1
Lois

Loud tick, low tick, loud tick, low tick that infernal noise penetrates my mind and my thoughts like a rhythmic drum. Loud tick, low tick, loud tick, low tick until it fades into insignificance and my brain dwells on a new focus. Like an antenna, I pick up the low raspy breathing of Poppy my blue roan spaniel crashed out on the settee opposite my bed. I had always been the kind of person that didn't allow dogs onto furniture; you know what I am saying, 'Feet are for the floor.' However, after 11 years of loyalty, I think she has earned the right and now deserves all the comfort in the world. Suddenly, she expels a little whimper from her deep sleep of some dream she's having, which brings an involuntary smile to my face. As I lay in the stillness of the night, I am unexpectedly captivated by the shapes cascading across the ceiling of the lights created by passing cars, driven by the people on their early morning commute to work. And so, it begins, another sleepless night.

A counsellor once told me that to get a good night's sleep, you need to allow the events of the day to pass through your mind. To allow them to gently wash over you, to not focus on any one thing in particular for too long just to allow them to float by, like a cloud. She told me to smile at the things that I had achieved, that I had done well and had found pleasure in. However, this never worked for me as I would wrestle over each decision like the wind battling against washing clamped to its line on a blustery day.

You see, I tend to hold on tight for dear life fearful, questioning whether I could have managed elements better? Had I even done the right thing at all? Or worse still was the dissecting of a conversation then mulling over the ins and outs of it focusing upon how I wish I had responded or stuck up for myself. This is a direct result of always living on eggshells and the concern that if you say or do the wrong thing someone somewhere will blow up. It also makes a massive impact when you actually feel as though your life is not your own or you know that at some point everything you do or have done will be scrutinised. You live in a paradox of confusion knowing that unfounded accusations may be thrown at any one time and all you're really trying to do is your very best.

This is not some layperson's "very best"; this is way beyond the stratosphere of "very best" and it is not for any personal gain, it's actually at a great personal cost to yourself. And so, I continue to stare at the ceiling, a familiar anxiety beginning to circulate my body culminating in the sickness now rising and only being held back by the pulsation of my heart in my throat.

I latch on to the high tick, low tick, high tick, low tick desperately, attempting to block the panic attack from reaching its crescendo, but my attempts are futile. As if to mock me of my earlier annoyance, the distraction technique merely reminds me that I have no control, either now or what future mud will be thrown. The clock continues to tick regardless. It goes on and on, breaking into the silence. I frantically switch to the mindfulness technique of concentrating on your breath but again I am unsuccessful. I try to breathe in deeply to then exhale slowly but I am only able to achieve a count of three before my breath rushes out like a newborn child whose lungs have just been cleared. The urgency increases rapidly as I fight with the overwhelming sensation of having an elephant laid across my chest. I try to calm the impending panic fighting with my focus to concentrate on my chest lifting yet it seems impossible.

Gently counting amidst the explosion, attempting to ignite, I clench my teeth to further ground my attention. I cannot breathe. It feels like I am wrestling for control with an imaginary spirit trying to prevent its possession of my body. Eventually I am able to declare to myself that I am beginning to win the battle and I subconsciously feel my body relax not realising its previous rigid state. Finally, I can just be, at which point time really does stand still as I settle into the limbo of my nightly physical and mentally exhausted state.

As I lay there in the aftermath, a single tear escapes the corner of my right eye and slowly trickles to the crevices of my neck. I do not allow myself the indulgence of another, somehow that still gives *HIM* control but he will never have that privilege again. So, I take a moment to reassure myself that I am ok and for now, Little Lois has gone.

The sense of loss is overpowering, so with limited choices I turn the hatred inward and there the cycle of my form of self-abuse, continues to revolve. I know that the blame, shame and guilt are not mine to bear but I endure the onslaught of my own negative words piercing my mind like an automatic rifle firing its insults. I question myself, why didn't you speak up? Surely there was someone who would have listened. I actively search my memory banks desperately hoping to find the long-awaited answer but instinctively I know there isn't one. Inside I screamed it out so many times, begged them endlessly with my pleading eyes, demonstrated it through extreme changes in my patterns of behaviour and inward turmoil. I didn't say the words for there were no words I could formulate to effectively communicate what was happening to me or the level of fear that had been induced within me.

At the time, it had seemed that everyone around me had lives to live, a purpose to fulfil, places to go and friends to see. I was half the size of everyone else, in a place where no one cared, no one listened, and I had no control or say about anything. This was my family home where a traumatic experience occurred that would change me forever and that would manifest into a lifelong reoccurring nightmare of self-hatred and anger.

A sense of sadness and deep loneliness fell upon me. I am unsure whether it is for the little girl who still screams out from within me for help to soothe her pain or for the person I was destined to have become had she not been violated. A familiar tingling sensation tickles the inner parts of my nose, radiating, beginning to prick at my face as the tears accumulate and threatened to overspill my eyelids. I do not afford myself that luxury as it absurdly feels like HE wins if I succumb. Maybe my harsh inability to comfort myself reflects the consistent lack of comfort that I was given as a child. A reflection of the stunting of my early emotional development caused by childhood trauma, the affects lasting a lifetime and resulting in years of therapy that will never remove the blackness from within.

Despite Daniel lying beside me, my experience creates a cavity of loneliness from deep within. Some people may find this inexplicable, but I have found a way of filling the void by retreating into it. Here I am no longer overwhelmed but are now strangely comforted. You see if I am alone, I have no other responsibility it is only to myself. There are some people who only feel whole if they are part of something or someone else's world yet for me, my strength is in solitude. This is my safe place where no one can get close enough to hurt me. If truth be told, I fantasise about cutting everything away and locking everyone out. A little bit like the character in Shirley Valentine, walking out to some foreign land where no one knows me.

Here, no one judges me, no one ridicules me nor criticises or bullies me. I am the truest version of myself with no false images created by people who never took the time to even care enough about me to really get to know the real person. The damaging aspect is that by locking everyone else out I lock myself in and therefore I am alone to continue my torturous self-hate campaign. This really is the perfect catch 22 of a most imperfect perfect situation.

As I lie there staring into the darkness, I am again just left with my breathing where the emphasis now is that I am actually alive, not just existing. For me, one of the worst experiences in life is to feel invisible to all those around you. I can tend to their every waking need, yet no one notices the needs I require meeting. I know I am a good person, I'm a selfless person an honourable person. I have great integrity and I give so freely and unconditionally yet I don't love myself with the same measure as the quality and quantity that I bestow on others. Why?

The answer is simple, I was taught at a very early age that I am here to fulfil the selfish wants of others. My thoughts, feelings, needs or dreams are secondary at best, but generally speaking, non-existent to others. I am the runt of the litter, the person scorned, looked down upon, belittled and drilled into that "no-one loves you", "you're not wanted". As we grow up these early teachings are not eradicated with time, they are like seeds that grow and manifest into mental illnesses, self-hatred, a lack of self-esteem, poor relationships, etc. Some people self-abuse with drugs or drink to silence their inner voices or practice the act of self-mutilation just to see the blood flow to feel alive.

For me, the worst sense of self abuse is the cycle to continually give in to the hope that you will at last be seen, cherished and loved for simply who you are. Here you physically exist in the presence of other people, but it is like you're so insignificant you're taking up valuable space and using oxygen better suited to someone more worthy. You may be in other people's company, but you become so self-conscious that you don't feel you have anything meaningful to offer or worse still, that no one is interested in anything you have to say, and you are just being tolerated.

The price you pay for this type of existence is a deep sense of nothingness where you continually feel on the outside looking in, alone without feeling. I think that's the worst part for me, I have become the master of disconnection taking out the emotional element and running on my default mode of autopilot. To some degree it can be an emotionally mature stance to adopt when dealing with conflict, as you can step back to effectively evaluate, assess and manage situations. However, used incorrectly it has the power to deny you a positive connection with loved ones as it renders you devoid of true emotions. This regurgitating sequence is like an untrustworthy internet connection, the inconsistency affects the solidity of relationships. Therefore, I persistently retreat back into my safe place of solitude locking myself in and others out on the pretext of protecting myself when in reality it's this pattern that causes me the greatest distress.

One of the keys to unlocking this skeleton closet is to recognise the fact that you are not alone, as the majority of people also suffer from this untruth. I concur I may not be better than anyone else, but I am an equal and as such I go out of my way to make an effective difference to the lives of those around me. I remember my friend Hazel telling me that renovating Grey Gables would be a good form of therapy for me as I would be forced to recognise my efforts and hopefully would celebrate my success rather than casting it aside and moving on to the next challenge.

She was right; in this case, I had nowhere to hide so it has been instrumental in much of my recovery although it has also caused me to face the demons of my earlier years. I recognise how far I have travelled in that I will now not hide my truth even if I have to keep on taking my rightful place at the table called life, I tell myself. You see that is the difference some people have a sense of entitlement where only their rights matter whereas I try to do what is morally right for everyone else around me. Yet no matter what I do, I am still seen as weak. It may not be the easiest of paths I concede but the humble approach with gratitude, I am convinced is more in tune with my character and the only one that I could ever comfortably walk.

I glance behind me to the clock and sigh deeply when its hands display the truth. Originally, I had woken up at 01:50 a.m. and then again two hours later; now, it's 06.30 and I am wide awake. As the world outside continues to evolve and the world inside my home continues to sleep, I venture downstairs to make a comforting cup of tea. The glare of the kitchen lights assaults my eyes, so I take myself off to the twinkling lights of the Christmas tree. At least the clock in the lounge is softer, so here I can breathe effortlessly and await the breaking of the new day.

Little Lois

Chapter 2
Moving Day

It is May 1971 and we have just moved across town to this enormous house called "Grey Gables". We arrived in a small open back truck to see it for the first time. A large white wooden gate is set back to allow our entrance. There is a smaller one, this has been left swinging on the hinges it sits upon, firmly fixed into the stone, walled perimeter. The house is also made of solid stone a stark contrast to the red brick council house we have just left. The roof of the house is shallow unlike the detached built garage that sits beside it. An overlapping dilapidated dark brown fence separates us from our new neighbours. I will soon get to know them very well, they are an elderly couple who own a jewellery store in town, Mr and Mr Cronin are their names. My dog Sandy will become so accustomed to them that he will get chastised for entering their kitchen and stealing a loaf of bread.

Like everyone else, I want to run in to explore my new abode, to find my room and accept this change but I feel nervous in its presence. I have good reason to be, yet I cannot help being energised by the excited buzz of my siblings. I tentatively let go of Mum's hand as she tries to break free in order to grasp armfuls of our belongings from the back of the truck. I instantly notice that the drive is flat at the top which then sweeps down to the left. I already know that I am going to enjoy riding my new 3-wheeler bike down there just as I had done at my old house. A tinge of sadness enveloped me as I think about my friends Neil, Karen, Carole and Louise whom I've had to leave behind. That is the problem, when you are a child, you have no say or choices, the adults in your life make all the decisions that affect your life and there is nothing you can do about it. Just 4 weeks and 5 days ago I had been opening my birthday gifts without the knowledge it would be the last one I would spend at the only home I had ever known.

I remembered having been led into the front room known as, our "best" room and there before the fireplace was a huge square, neatly wrapped present. Everyone was sat around it awaiting my arrival to open this amazing present. In trepidation, I carefully peeled back the paper to reveal a square box. Mum helped me to open the lid but as I peered in to reveal its contents, I was devastated to see the remnants of what appeared to be the broken parts of a bicycle. I was absolutely devastated and to everyone's astonishment immediately burst into tears. There were mutterings of my being a "spoilt brat", of being "ungrateful" but I chose to ignore them, as I always did.

After her initial surprise, Mum began taking the pieces of the bike out of the box, but I couldn't look, I was so convinced my present was smashed beyond repair. It was only when they started putting the bicycle together did someone explain that it had been transported in pieces so that it would fit into the box. To my relief a sparkling, bright red 3-wheeler bike soon sat before me complete with a foot plate between the back wheels and a grey elephant sticker upon its white plastic seat. I was now as restored as my new bike and couldn't wait to join my friends on the street to hurtle our way down the foot path this time using my very own bike instead of having to take it in turns between my friends. Yes, I would enjoy doing figure of eights on the flat part of this drive before peddling as fast as my little legs could go, then freewheeling down the side of this house.

I followed Mum as we entered this new place through a thick robust wooden door into what could only be described as a humongous kitchen. From the outside, this part of the house which was visible from the road was an L-shape. The cupboards in the kitchen were a pale-yellow set in a white surround, the surfaces had a grey and white Formica top. My eyes fell upon a bulky beige apparatus on the far wall which had little doors on the front of it. It was like nothing I had ever seen before. On seeing my confusion, Mum explained it was called an Aga and that it was the oven and cooker for the house.

To the right was a window overlooking the drive where our little truck was parked, with the street beyond. Straight ahead were two little steps leading up to a door where a laundry, a toilet and a pantry were, at the back of the house with a pretty little courtyard outside. To the left of the entrance was another door, deep set demonstrating the thickness of the walls of our new home, this was the door Mum led me through. As she stepped to one side to allow my entrance, I was suddenly overwhelmed by the sheer sense of space.

In front of us was a huge bay window with an outside door to its right, at the bottom of a white staircase. This sweeping, open staircase had spindles running its entire length which were secured by a thick set banister leading to the upper level. The ceiling had two exposed beams running the full width of the room. To both my left and right were further doors leading to more rooms both having their own bay windows and with the beams continued throughout. There was a stale, smell of something old and forgotten that had been contained for far too long lingering in the room. I was therefore only too pleased to follow Mum towards the outside door which she opened to allow the room to "breathe" she told me. In return, the light flooded the room and brought with it a well anticipated breath of fresh air. I could not help thinking that it was not a fair exchange, although both of us were glad for it to be released out into the warm spring day.

As I step through the door, situated almost centrally to the front of the house, I am overwhelmed by the breath-taking view before me. There is a kind of storm porch held up with two posts, mounted on a terracotta tiled platform that is inlaid with white tiles displaying a thick black diamond pattern. Two steps take me down to a flagged, wide patio stretching the entire length of the house. Running parallel to this were 4 large flowerbeds displaying an abundance of coloured blooms. The beds were surrounded and defined by thick, grass borders these were then partitioned further, two on each side by a smaller flagged area sitting directly opposite the door. This will be an area I will use for hopscotch with a girl I am yet to meet. Her name is Tracy, and she lives on the crescent. We will spend hours together in sparrow park and when this is dug up and a road takes its place, we will make up games together on our bikes. She will be an important person throughout my childhood and when I am older, I will enjoy long walks with her dad.

As I explore further, I find 5 stone steps leading down to a huge lawn the size of a tennis court with mature trees surrounding it. Tracy, Ruby and I will spend our summers devising gymnastic routines here and our winters making snowmen and snow horses. We will never master the art of making igloos though we will keep trying. On this lawn, we will play "British Bulldog", "What time is it Mr Wolf" and other games with friends from around the area. These times will be fun, but my favourite memories will be when my parents join in with us and play rounders. This week I will meet my very first friend, he will be called David and we will remain exceptionally close, he will be the only person to ever really know me and to love me unconditionally. We will spend hours climbing these mature trees, race down the hill on our bikes together, play football on the lawn and be free to explore. We will fight and fallout as children do but the invisible cord of friendship will never be broken. He will join the army at 16 and be transferred to many dangerous zones but he will take the time to ring me wherever he goes. I will later realise at these times it was when he was going out on patrol, and he didn't think he was coming back. We will have a deep love and respect for one another that will last our whole lifetime supporting each other throughout the many ups and downs that life brings, because we are true friends.

As I turn my face towards the sun, I am instantly captivated by the sense of peace and focus on its warmth. I don't realise how long I am transfixed to this spot lost in the hypnotic rhythm of birdsong and my inner wellbeing, but this was abruptly severed by the jolting of my siblings rushing past me knocking me to the floor. I already know it is useless to cry despite the welt forming across my buttocks and back courtesy of the steps I now lay across. Crying would not serve any purpose for there would be no offer of comfort, there would be no kind words there never are, nor will there ever be.

I am the youngest of five children and I may as well be invisible. I have two older brothers and two older sisters. Kelly is 14, *HE* is 12, Nick is 10 and Ruby is 8. I am Lois and I am 4. I am the child that nobody wants around, I am the child who is made fun of, belittled, put down and scorned. I learn early the art of trying to please but this is very destructive to my early emotional development, and I will soon recognise that I do not matter. As we settle in to this large, new house the bullying will intensify, because my parents cannot supervise me in all areas. I will be called "Skivvy" because I am the only one who recognises the magnitude of the work Mum does to keep this excessively large house. I will want to help her, feel a duty to do my bit despite my tender years.

I will be told persistently how much I am hated and that no one wants me around. That I was adopted because even my own, "real" mother didn't want me. I will have it drilled into me that I was "found behind the bins" and that my last name is really "Smith". I do not belong anywhere, I am not wanted or cared about. I will even be tormented by Ruby and Kelly that one of them has been flushed down the drain. To substantiate their claim, they will go to the extreme of taking loose hair from their brushes and will place it around the plughole. I will be plagued and tormented, it will go unnoticed, and it will be relentless. If I become distressed, I will be mocked, scorned and laughed at. If I dare to retaliate or to stick up for myself, I will be physically attacked by Ruby. Any friends I make, she will take over to exclude me because she hasn't the ability to make her own. This will last until my mid-forties until I finally recognise my own self-worth and put a stop to it.

Maybe that's why *he* chose me because *he* didn't see me as a human being with feelings, thoughts, emotions or that I had any needs to be met.

I will come to enjoy their school days the most because I will be at home with Mum where I will have the freedom to play age-appropriate games. Jeff my dad will continue to work really long hours in order to pay for our extravagantly large new home. He will take the time out of his busy schedule to telephone us in the middle of the day. I will get into a new habit of racing to the phone whenever it rings as "I am a big girl now" so I will be allowed to answer it. I am also faster and more alert than Mum who will usually be in the "middle of doing something". I know this because she will always say to Dad 'what do you want, I was in the middle of doing something?'

I will grow accustomed to him popping in for lunch or when he gets in after work and bounces me about on his knee. It will not be very comfortable, but it isn't nearly as bad as when he will give me some of his "chin pie". This is where he will hold me really tight, then rub his face on mine after he hasn't shaved for a few days. It will always leave severe red marks on my neck and chin because it feels like coarse sandpaper, but I won't mind a bit because he seems to enjoy it laughing throughout. So, do my brothers and sisters, I have yet to learn that they are happy to see me hurt but also grateful that they are not receiving Dad's "chin pie".

My mum, Emmeline, will adopt the role of persistently doing chores as she will now have little time to herself. I realise much later in life these are not as pleasurable for her as they will be for me. On Mondays, she will spend the whole day doing the washing, Tuesday it's the ironing, Wednesday the accounts, Thursday the wages for Dad's company and Friday the grocery shopping. She will be "fit to drop" at the end of each day so she will sleep soundly. She will be totally unaware of my distress.

Throughout the day I will eagerly assist and love helping her to do all these things because I love being around her as this is where I feel at my safest. We will strip the beds together, I will dust, hoover and help to make meals. I will never be sure how much real help I am providing but I will believe that I am making a valid contribution. I will enjoy it the most when we do the laundry together, it will be hard work, but I will find it satisfying when I take everyone's things to their rooms clean and neatly folded.

We will even iron together because for my birthday I received my very own ironing board. It is made of wood, it has a long, flat thin panel to drape the clothes over with a metal plate at one end, where I will put my own little iron. My mum's iron will be plugged into a socket, I will believe mine is too but really it has a little black sucker on the end that Mum will lick and stick to the wall. I don't notice any difference, but sadly it is not the only thing that she deceives me with, and I am not just talking about the fictional fat man, with a white beard in a red suit. I trust in her completely, because I love her, and she makes me feel secure. However, she will not protect me, no one will. These are the days that I will spend in ignorant bliss. These are those carefree days that only a child who has not yet begun school knows. The days I will spend embedded in a false sense of security in what should be the safety of my own family.

I was yet to learn that this new house wasn't going to be a safe place for me. Here I would soon be isolated, submerged into a living nightmare, no longer carefree but where I would become a diluted version, changed forever, no longer me. I would be condemned to simply exist in their world, to suffer silently, living in a parallel universe to everyone else's reality. I would soon come to realise that because I am the child that nobody loves, the one that nobody wants and is forever in the way, that my fate has already been sealed and I will become the target. My invisibility will make me vulnerable; my tender years will bring with it the ease to coerce, manipulate and render defeat. The lack of love, the isolation, and my age will all work against me, yet in contrast will give *him* a vast sense of power. *He* will use these facts to orchestrate situations to quench *his* sordid desires because I am the child without a voice.

However, children have a habit of growing up and somewhere in the future a course of events will cause a friction where a fuse will become ignited. An invisible clock will start ticking and consequently a countdown will begin. This will propel itself along until the momentum takes it to its final destination, culminating in an explosion into the adult world. Bizarrely enough, this will be created and plotted by Ruby, but she will fail to take any responsibility and will even invent accountability. The true success in giving someone else the bullets to fire is in the skill of first mastering the puppets to dance to any tune you choose to play. Like the strategic game of chess, we all had varying strengths and weaknesses, we were valued differently and although there had been an unfair disadvantage in size things would change. The clock would always be ticking.

Chapter 3
The Pushchair

It is hard to say when I first became the focal point of *his* attention, I guess that is something I could never have known as there were no warning signs at least to me. By the time it became apparent, it was too late. I remember parts of my first Christmas spent at Grey Gables and my initially having a bed in my parents' room. The frame was nondescript, and it had a plain dark wooden headboard and I think a smaller footboard, though of this I cannot be sure. I was so excited at the prospect of seeing Santa that I had knelt up onto my pillows leaning over the headboard gazing out into the night sky.

I remember watching with wonder as the minute star-like crystal, particles fell from the sky. They seemed to dance this way and that my little fingers absentmindedly flickering with an imaginary tune they performed just for me. I was captivated and charmed by their mesmerising dance until my eyes grew tired and the cold from the old sash windows began to swarm around my thin cotton nightwear. Its power demanding my return to the warmth of that old wooden bed. As I snuggled down the blankets tightly clenched beneath my chin, I soon drifted off into a peaceful sleep believing totally that Santa himself would land on the tennis court sized lawn outside and I would find his footprints in the snow the next day.

To my absolute joy, I was woken to shouts of 'He's been.'

I instantly sat upright scanning the room like an FBI agent on high alert, searching for that all important evidence to detect whether an intruder had infiltrated the area. To my left on the floor and leaning against the bottom corner of the bed was a pillowcase, filled to the brim with parcels wrapped in brightly coloured, printed Christmas paper. I sprang out of bed like a gazelle with a lion on its heel's adrenalin surging through my veins forgetting my parents in the bed that was positioned at a right angle to that of my own. Mum sleepily raised her head, blinked a few times then resettled herself and continued to remain in the comfort of her bed.

I took a deep breath and as deftly as is possible for a 4-year-old I climbed down from my bed and began noisily removing paper. I was momentarily distracted when a few minutes later Dad's covers were thrown back, then he was up, out of the door and off down the corridor to use the bathroom. I couldn't tell you what I got for that Christmas although some of the childhood gifts I did get over the years ranged from various art products, to dolls, etch-a-sketch, board games, diaries, tonka toys and finally my prized possession of an Evil Knievel.

Christmases kept the same format throughout my childhood with Dad's works party on Christmas Eve starting the celebrations and a visit from Mum's sister and family in the evening. On Christmas morning, we would open our gifts then be taken by Dad to visit his sister, brother and mother. Nana and Grandpa would be collected by Dad around noon when he would then take his father for a Christmas Day pint whilst Ruby and I kept Nana occupied. Mum would spend the entire day in the kitchen prepping, cooking, serving and tidying up afterwards. We would set the table and do the washing up although it was always a fight because Ruby never wanted to dry the crockery. These were the early days when nothing mattered other than Santa and his amazingly deep, magical sack that carried all the toys for girls and boys for the whole, world-wide.

Then one day a decision was made that would have a profound effect upon me and which would seal my fate for the rest of my life. A naive decision without due care, thought or attention to the consequences that it would have on an innocent little girl, who trusted her parents to keep her safe. That decision was to move me out of my parents' bedroom, not into a room of my own but into a room sharing with two adolescent boys. My bed was dismantled and rebuilt, situated centrally in a juxta position between *HIS bed* and Nick's.

Now, this decision may have been forgotten by other family members but that is hardly surprising as there wasn't anything remotely attached to it for them to warrant it so resolutely embedding itself into their memory banks as it was for me. For instance, I bet they also don't remember the day my pushchair was sold to one of Dad's employees whilst we still lived at the old house. I do, I remember Mum was stood on the doorstep at the side of the property talking to said worker when I joined her outside. With arms wrapped around her leg, I was half-hidden behind her skirt whilst balancing myself between the top step and the door threshold when money was exchanged and he started walking up the path towards the gate, with MY pushchair. I screamed blue murder as she wrestled with me to drag me back inside, embarrassed the Chambers, our next-door neighbours, might hear.

It was a defining moment for me, I loved that pushchair, and the trade-off was that I would now have to walk everywhere. No doubt my siblings will have memories about their own childhoods and decisions that were made that equally had some cause and effect for them, but which were not important enough to resonate with me, but it mattered to them.

Losing that pushchair was a milestone, as it is in any toddler's life it symbolises freedom, independence and propels you to the next stage of life, attending nursery. It should be about the ability to get out and explore the world around you whilst also being able to interact properly and make new friends. However, it is also the loss of your safe space, of being guided through your environment, having direct contact with your navigator and the ability to just take a nap whenever you require.

Being moved between those two beds was ironically a contradictive representation of that pushchair where its imagery was to parallel the abuse that took place. I would soon become a prisoner of my thoughts, a victim of control, robbed of my individualism, isolated, living in fear with no understanding of where I was safe, or who I could trust, violated and just like a Freddie Krueger movie forever terrified to fall asleep. That decision would present a young, sexually inquisitive teenager the opportunity to freely investigate and explore his desires which in turn would create an adult monster who would continue to rob children of their innocence.

Chapter 4
The Predator

At first, it had felt a bit like an Enid Blyton adventure, occupying a different room in that big old house especially being with my two older brothers as I somehow felt stronger, protected and safe. I was also regularly being told that I was "a big girl now" so being away from Mum and Dad kind of reinforced this phrase. I guess with having such a large house now there was no longer any reason for me to occupy their room and I am sure they would have been glad to regain their private space. This arrangement was only going to be a temporary solution as a large room at the back of the house was being prepared for Ruby and I to inhabit. A new window was being put in, fitted wardrobes installed, carpet tiles arranged and twin beds with brown triangular studded headboards. In the meantime, I was being prepped to surrender my attachment to my parents in favour of forming the new habit of becoming accustomed to going to bed alone. Therefore, I really must have been "a big girl" now.

I have no way of accurately defining the first moment things changed but I can share the vivid memories that still plague my brain matter. It all started with my waking in desperate need for the toilet and climbing out of bed to clumsily feel my way around Nicks bed in order to reach the door.

The darkness was impenetrable for my squinting eyes due to the thick, blackout curtains hung at the windows. I fiddled along the edge of the yellow ochre candlewick bedspread tracing my fingertips over the embossed swirly pattern. The fringe along the bottom of its edge tickling my toes as I cautiously made my way towards the exit. I tapped gently around the frame of the door moving my hand inward at height level to where I knew I would discover the handle, then equally as carefully, I forced it down to reveal the crack of the door. Onto the landing, I stepped discovering that the gentle pale glow of the outside light by the front door had cast some of its radiance along the bottom of the stairs.

Above me was the dome, a deep indentation of around 4 foot and 2 foot wide that was set within the ceiling, and which revealed itself onto the outer part of the roof.

During the day it provided much needed daylight but now it was as dark as the room from which I had just vacated. I tentatively stretched up high on to my tippytoes managing to both locate and finally flick on the switch to at last illuminate the corridors of the upstairs. To my relief I could now see my parents' door at the end of the corridor in front of me and to my left under the archway the toilet door at the end of that corridor. I deftly made my way down to the toilet and once relieved proceeded into the bathroom to wash my hands.

On my return to the top of the stairs, I no longer wanted my old wooden bed as I succumbed to the call of comfort and closeness that only my mum could provide. So, I crept down to the end of the corridor and quietly released the door from its surround. I first scanned the room to imprint its layout in my mind so I would be able to successfully negotiate the beds distance and shape before turning the landing light out at its other switch by their door. I padded gently across the room until I was finally at Mum's side. I touched around the pillow with my tiny fingers until I located her ear and, in a whisper, called her name, 'Mum, Mum.' With no response and beginning to feel the cold biting, fear started to envelop me with a fight or flight response shaking my confidence. I tried a second time, 'Mum, Mum' with a little more urgency but yet again without success. I knew I was unable to retrace my steps so with little else at my disposal, I began to gently tap her forehead until she groaned and then with faint recognition, she opened up the bed covers and I was able to slip in next to her. Relief swarmed me and I was soon able to fall into a deep relaxed sleep generated by the warmth of her body snuggled around mine.

This pattern became an almost nightly occasion much to my father's annoyance when each morning he awoke to find his bed occupied by a little person who hadn't been there when he'd fallen asleep the evening before. But one night this course of action was abruptly changed when I was intercepted by *him* on my escape from the boy's room. That first night *he* followed me out on to the landing and waited at the top of the stairs until I returned, then *he* urged me back into the bedroom from which I had come. The next time *he* returned me not to my own bed but to *his* and just as Mum had done, *he* wrapped himself around me until in a false sense of security I was soon drifting off into slumberland.

However, this was abruptly percolated when I felt his hand taking mine and tugging it behind my back in an unnaturally awkward position. Inevitably, I started to stir at my discomfort though not sensing any danger I shifted to my back and then it was too late. My tiny little hand was securely gripped as if in a vice and forced upon what I was later to establish was the hot, clammy hardness of his penis. I tried in vain to retract my hand with my body equally recoiling at the repulsion that my hand had detected. But I couldn't break free. He began to whisper and hush me as if to coerce me into submission his hot breath upon my neck as he struggled to ensure my hand stayed exactly where he wanted it.

Nick did not stir, I was alone, pinned in this position no longer with my adolescent brother but with a sexual predator. I tried to scream out, but no words would escape my mouth instead they choked themselves somewhere in the back of my throat and dispersed into the air with each breath. In the true style of a child, I closed my eyes tight shut believing if I couldn't see him, he couldn't see me. There was no rationality of the fact that I was in a dark room just an attempt to escape the reality of this living nightmare that I was finding so hard to comprehend.

The next day, I was wary of him and so kept my distance, but he acted as though nothing had happened, so I was confused as to whether this had been normal behaviour. That night I did everything I could to regain my position with my parents but with little tolerance nor understanding I was persistently returned until scared to even move I fell asleep only to wake wet through. I had no option but to try and make my way to the bathroom the nylon of the nightdress clung to my naked body and the pungent smell of urine filling my nostrils. The corners of my mouth arched themselves down forming dimples at either side of cheeks, my lips beginning to tremble at my disgusted state.

I wanted my mum, but she had turned me away and I didn't know where to go or what to do I just wanted to run away and cry. I tried to take my pants off but they awkwardly rolled in their wetness and then I heard a noise behind me which made me want to cry all the more. *He* was stood at the bathroom door surveying the scene before *him* and I instantly knew I needed my mum. A tear ran down my cheek as the whimper of a wounded animal escaped my mouth. Why was I here all alone with *him* where were everyone else? Why hadn't they been disturbed by the landing light or the sound of creaking floorboards of movement along the corridor. I gulped not knowing what to do, trapped there in the bathroom with no means of escape like a rabbit in a car's headlights alone on a country lane. One thing I was resolutely sure of was that I did not want to be made to touch *him* again.

He stepped forward and in response I tried to step back but couldn't for the sink unrelenting of any movement, so I froze eyes wide and fearful. *He* moved nearer reassuring me all was ok and that *he* would help get me cleaned up, I had no choice but to trust *him*. *He* bent down and took the edges of my nighty and pulled it up over the entire length of my body, the wetness peeling itself off my skin in quick succession as it moved swiftly upwards. The small button at the nape of my neck tugged at the strands of hair gathered at its edges extracting wisps as it was dragged over my head. I did not wince as I didn't even notice it because more importantly and for the first time in my young life, I was suddenly aware of my nakedness. I stood there stripped bare, so small and defenceless against this boy 8 years my senior examining me greedily with his beady eyes. I knew I was in trouble like an animal caught in a trap and I felt sick at my helplessness.

'Please,' I managed to utter. 'I am cold.' I trembled.

'It's ok, we just need to wash you and then we can get you back into bed safe and warm,' *He* lied.

He took the sponge that was resting upon the sink, wet and soaped it before very carefully and deliberately slowly wiping it over my entire body performing it extra slowly over my private areas. I stood rigid at his mercy internally begging for the moment to end so that my body could be covered by the towel and once again my dignity restored. I was beginning to shake with the cold, but this seemed to amuse *him* and energised *his* facial expressions. I didn't know it at the time, but this was called lust and I was *his* prey.

I was then led back towards the bedroom, my nakedness completely exposed so once we reached the archway, I tried to pull free to run towards my mum's room, but *he* had other ideas. *He* chastised me with a sudden aggressive jerk of my arm, his face contorted with distain at *his* prize attempting to break free and literally dragged me to *his* side of the bed. Nick did not stir, I was alone, not with my adolescent brother but with a sexual predator. I remained rigid, unable to close my eyes, unable to relax for fear that I would be subjected to what I would later know was sexual abuse. This time when *he* tried to take my hand, I kept my fingers in a tightly balled up fist and attempted to stiffen my arm to prevent *him* moving it.

However, this was a futile bid as *he* easily gained submission through *his* sordid desire to overcome and *his* yearnings to be satisfied. On this occasion, *he* roughly prised my fingers open and placed them around his hardened willy and maintaining his grip over my hand *he* forced it to move up and down gathering momentum in an attempt to satiate *his* arousal. This was the first time I experienced the new habit of zoning out by gritting and grinding my teeth, withholding myself, being able to disappear somewhere deep within me, locking myself there by avidly counting. This became my only coping mechanism to block out the degrading outward trauma and enabling me to detach from the inward explosion of emotions.

It is difficult to know how many times this happened though I do know I began wetting the bed almost every night fearful to get up for the toilet in case it alerted *him* and again my fate would be guaranteed. Nick never stirred; it was always me left alone at *his* mercy. On one occasion when I was ill, Mum left me alone with *him* after school so she could get some medications from the chemist. I was laid at the far end of the brown, corduroyed material settee with a blanket over me. *He* came over to me and knelt on the floor beside me, but I was too ill to take notice.

The next thing I knew, *his* hands were under the blanket and *his* fingers were exploring the privacy of my innocence. Confused, crying and needing the protection of my mum, I whimpered. My discomfort at his violation seemed to pleasure him all the more until the door to the kitchen could be heard opening and with the creaking of the floor indicated the presence of another person. He shot up quickly fleeing to the door to which Nick opened and walked through.

'What are you doing?' he demanded.

'It's ok,' he said, grabbing at Nick's arm attempting to guide him towards me, 'come in, she will let you do it too.'

Nick pushed him off and marched out. I was left alone at the mercy of the predator powerless to fight him off, utterly forsaken, abandoned and incapable of fathoming out this new state of play. Nick had not only stirred but he had actually caught him in the act with my pants down and been invited to take part like it was some pretend game of "Mums and Dads". In effect, I had just been thrown to the wolf to be devoured as Nick did nothing to uphold appropriate boundaries or stop him. So, in *his* head, *he* had just been granted permission to continue, this being further reinforced when Nick did not divulge *his* secret, deviant behaviour to our parents.

Subsequently, it gave *him* licence to continue committing his abhorrent acts against me. One thing I did find strange though was that directly after this episode, Nick no longer had freedom in his own nakedness and whenever he shared our bath times, he suddenly started to cover his private parts with the flannel.

Also, around this time a photographer came to take a photograph of the five siblings which was displayed for many years on top of the pianola in the far room that thankfully we rarely used. Mum was really pleased at the new portrait but all it captured for me was the fear upon the face of a child with no voice, the one no one wanted around, the one who had been violated by her adolescent brother, the predator with the smug grin on his face. The face stamped on my eyelids whenever I shut them.

Chapter 5
The Confrontation

The abuse stopped as abruptly as it had started; whether this coincided with the time he began his first age-appropriate relationship is unclear, but it would certainly explain his sudden disinterest. I do know that the coercive nature of the abuse *he* displayed towards me along with the power it continued to yield over me, undermined me in a very destructive way. I became insular and self-conscious rendering me an easy target for Ruby to take out all her frustrations upon. Then came the secret chats with Mum. Every time I entered a room, they would suddenly whisper something, look at me and then one or both of them would walk off in the opposite direction.

It began to make me really paranoid that they were talking about me and coupled with the sexual abuse it made me believe that this was their topic of conversation. I had continually needed my mum but at this point I felt that she was laughing at me too and that together they were sharing some secret at my expense that I wasn't privy to. I started to think that perhaps they were thinking what I believed that I was a dirty little girl and it was all my fault.

One day this came to a head when initially in a good mood I had come running down the stairs in response to Mum's call, I was possibly around 8 years of age at the time. The look on her face sent shivers through me and fear overpowered me reducing me to an immediate stop. It was the look only a mother can give her child. You know the one, where you are more than aware she already knows the answer to the question before she even asks it, and she is taunting you to dare to lie. Naturally, I deduced that I was in big trouble with no way of escaping it. An overpowering sense of defeat flooded through me as I waited for the declaration but to my surprise, she grabbed my elbow quite roughly.

'I want to know if *he* has ever done anything to you?' she demanded in a stern tone unlike I had ever heard from her before. Immediately, I was terrified and rooted to the spot. 'Come on,' she persisted, demanding an answer. 'I want to know, and I want to know right now.'

Inevitably, the anger in her voice, the sternness of her facial expression up so close to my face and the accusatory manner in which she had confronted me rendered me mute. I was so afraid to say anything in case whatever I said was the wrong answer and my very real consideration of whether she would attack me too? My eyes were wide, my mind scanning for possible potential answers all within a split second, but nothing was forthcoming. Just as alarmingly she loosened her grip, returned to the kitchen for further secret chats with Ruby. The moment may have passed but the incident was palpable and had a catastrophic effect upon me leaving me scarred and unable to ever broach the subject with her again.

If only she had set a different scene instead of reacting through her own fears. If only she had taken a different approach one that was less threatening and nonconfrontational then maybe, just maybe I might have had the courage to speak up. Unfortunately, cornering me the way she did reenforced his words that it was my fault and I had better not tell, otherwise I would get the blame and be sent away. Inside I died even more that day as my one and only opportunity to get the emotional and physical support I required was lost because my mother had the compassion and understanding of a sledgehammer.

I was left dejected and further isolated from my family members with an imaginary hand hovering above me pointing down over my head like the lottery adverts. It was me; it was my fault; I was the problem child and right now I could also understand why nobody wanted me or loved me. Right now, I didn't love me either but unlike everyone else who could walk away and find other things to occupy themselves I was stuck with me and couldn't escape this self-made prison I was creating. Inevitably I now felt that I was completely alone and on the outside with absolutely no sense of hope or that I belonged anywhere. Many years later I will find a green, diary from this time depicting my utter helplessness and devastation. There it will record my attempt to use a penknife to cut my wrists and the alarming note that the blade was "too blunt" to have any effect. I dread to think what course of direction this could have careered down had the blade been sharp enough to cause significant damage. Either way the level of misery is unmistakeable for a child who was not trying to be difficult but trying to communicate her deep hurt and sadness at the world around her.

As the days, months and years went by so with it came an unnerving level of anger a result of being denied the right to grow up in a safe, loving, non-abusive home heightened by my inability to flee. Meanwhile, *he* went from relationship to relationship apparently enjoying life to the fullest and so with it grew my utter distaste and resentment towards *him*. It was an impossible situation with my only release being a walk with my dog to the green hill at the top of Pildacre overlooking Chickenley, Thornhill and in the distance Emily Moor mast. I would sit between the eight trees set in a row at the top of the hill sobbing until I had expelled the measure of my heartache. Only when I felt I had got every ounce of my misery out and was able to cope with more of the same would I finally return to Grey Gables.

It was a place I came to hate; I was trapped in the misery of childhood trauma being forced on a daily basis to have the abuser in my company. If that wasn't bad enough, Ruby suddenly intensified her hate campaign against me whether it was in front of my friends forcing me to retreat indoors or through violence behind closed doors. I remember having problems with my back at one point so if I upset her in any way, she would drag my head forward by my hair and pound her fists down on it.

In my early teens, I was diagnosed with a condition called Osgood-Schlatter disease which is "the inflammation of the area just below the knee where the tendon from the kneecap attaches to the shinbone". (https//orthoinfo.aaos.org/en/diseases-conditions/osgood-s-disease-knee-pain/)

Inevitably, if I said or did anything that contradicted or challenged Ruby in any way, my knee would be the first place her shoed foot would connect with. Not only was she a bully prone to violent outbursts but she had no empathy nor human connection to me at all. In fact, throughout my lifetime, I will continually attempt to gain her favour only to be persistently cast aside with some humiliating or degrading retort. All I ever truly wanted was for her to be a sister to me, but that is something she would forever deny me. Equally she will never get over her sibling rivalry maybe because I never allowed her to know she had ever affected me. That became the only power I had being the youngest, the ability to detach and hide my real feelings from them. Never did anyone do anything to protect me or attempt to gain insight to help and support me so eventually after being battered, belittled and broken for so long I started to fight back.

Over time these buried emotions brought with them the rumblings of a volcanic reaction and when suppressed for too long, either Ruby or Kelly would push it one step too far and with it an eruption as destructive as a tornado would follow. Unlike their pleasure that ensued when I was on the receiving end, I hated myself for allowing them to push my buttons to the point that I had lost control. This negative energy embedded itself further and deeper within my psyche to the point it had a massive impact upon my mental health and well-being thus spilling over into my school life too. Yet still no one did anything to delve into the problem whereas nowadays teachers would be alerting social services to identify potential issues within the home.

My one and only opportunity had been extinguished to a puff of smoke leaving a blazing fire to continue to rage within me. I knew I needed help but with the only adults in my life appearing to be of authority I was mystified how and who to reach out to. I didn't know it yet, but I would be 26 before the subject would be broached again; only this time my mother would be forced to listen and a surprise revelation would be in store for me.

Young Lois

Chapter 6
All an Act

I went through my early teens shutting people out not wanting close friends but equally yearning for them too. At school, I had no respect for authority and lashed out at anyone who tried to enter my personal space, so not surprisingly I soon got a reputation for being a bit of a hard nut. By the time I was 16 and leaving school with no idea of my next step, I suddenly realised that school had actually been my only safety net all along. To leave created a sense of being open to the elements, existing alone in the big bad world, to feel exposed.

I remember joining the queue for students who wanted to sign up for the 6th form college that Ossett Comprehensive School offered only to be told by the deputy head that she'd 'had me there for 5 years and I needn't think I was staying for another 2 years.' Then she promptly sent me back to class. That didn't matter to me, what did though, was the personal torment going on inside and hating every minute of having to be in the same house as *him*. *He* would sneer, be really cocky about everything like *he* was so untouchable that just being in *his* company made my skin crawl as vivid memories would scream out at me. *He* would use ridiculous made-up words like calling everyone "wammel head" or overexaggerate Yorkshire phrases like "Tha'nose" or addressing people with "ows t'doin mucca".

The most embarrassing by far was calling my friend Leanne "Booberella" due to her large chest or asking if she'd 'like to go upstairs with *him* to see *his* brackets.' Leanne was a shy, unassuming girl during puberty so to have this kind of unwanted attention, it must have been horrific for her. I am ashamed to admit that I did laugh along perhaps just glad that the negative spotlight was not shining on my face for once. The most damaging and ingrained belief was that I couldn't do anything about it because to speak out would split the family unit and bring my mum's world crashing down, so this fact continued to reduce me defenceless for decades.

Then one night a turn of events I could never have been predicted suddenly sent a curve ball to remind me that the past was still very much a depiction of my present. The disclosure that the strangleholds of my childhood still had me in their clutches would fragment my already fragile mind and would render me totally incapacitated. I arrived home late one evening to find Mum in an agitated state regarding something to do with *him*. As the story unfolded, I was informed that *his* latest relationship had failed and that the girl *he* had been seeing was having an affair with someone else. Apparently, *he* had caught her in the new house they shared together. There had been some kind of a kafuffle where *he* had become violent and thrown her out. The problem *he* had was not wanting her to gain access to the property after *he* left in the early hours of the next morning for work. No idea what it had to do with me or why I should be interested, the next verbal blow sent me sideways.

'So, you are going to have to go down there,' Mum stated.

'Whoa hold on a minute, what has it got to do with me?' I quizzed.

'Well, everyone else is out and there is only you here, so you will have to go,' she delivered.

'But I do not want to go down there, it has nothing to do with me and I am not getting involved. If you're that bothered, why don't you go?' I protested.

Just at that moment, the house phone rang, it was *him*. As she replaced it in its cradle, she adopted that tone that told me there was no use arguing and I would have to do as I was told. 'It's organised, you're staying there tonight to keep the house secure so he can get off to work.'

Very reluctantly, I gathered some essentials together and Mum dropped me off not even bothering to come inside. The house was cold and damp but not as miserable as me. He was in the kitchen in a heightened sense of despair that actually I quite enjoyed witnessing. Over the years I will glimpse this side of him many times which will assist me to realise that he is actually a very poor coper in times of distress, he is weak, inadequate and not as powerful as I had imagined. In the future, it will help me to confront the sordid behaviour of his past and put measures in place to become the person I was always meant to be. In the end, I will overcome it all and I will walk free from the chains of misbelief. However right now I was stuck so there was only one way forward to grit my teeth and pray for tomorrow morning to arrive so I could get out of here.

He told me that as *he*'d be getting up around 02.30, *he* would sleep on the settee and I could have the bedroom so at least I'd get a good night's sleep. In order to ensure *he* didn't disturb me, *he* collected *his* clothes and belongings and thankfully I could shut the door behind *him* in blissful ignorance to *his* presence downstairs. It had been approximately 11.15pm when I had arrived, so I made my way upstairs to give *him* the chance to get at least a couple of hours sleep. The bed was comfortable enough although I had to make a concerted effort not to think too deeply about the fact *he* had slept in these sheets. The streetlight outside the front of the house radiated a warm comforting glow through the thin cheap curtains but it didn't prevent sleep falling over me.

Somewhere between the doors of reality and dreamworld I subconsciously became aware of movement but in the hazy state of sleep my image was of a dog at the bottom of the bed. But then the covers around my feet seemed to lift causing a draft to seep in and I vaguely detected weight and movement as though someone was in the bed under the covers and climbing their way up towards me.

Before my brain had a chance to engage, *he* was on me, *his* weight pinning me to the bed, *his* manhood primed for sex. I tried to scream to tell *him* to get off me but that pathetic little girl resurrected herself at the worst possible moment and I was rendered absolutely useless. *His* hands greedily began to maul my body as *his* pelvis grind against me attempting to shift my legs apart. However, unlike that little girl, I wasn't giving up without a fight and forced myself into the present, to stay alert, to not mentally flee and so I compelled myself to confront the beast.

There was no whimper this time. 'Get off me!' I managed to scream out with all my being.

He sniggered like it was some kind of "cat and mouse" game which seemed to fuel his sordid intention further.

'I said, get the fuck off me!' I screeched with more anger than panic this time. 'I am your sister, for fuck's sake!'

Somewhere within *his* brain an alarm bell must have sounded that what he was doing tantamounted to attempted rape but that this was also incestuous. I detected the slightest shift in *his* body weight slide a tad to my left. That modification was all I needed to change the state of play and much more alert now I wrenched myself from *him*. I was then up and out literally screaming at *him* and calling *him* all the names under the sun. Being confronted with the uncontrolled temper of a rabid dog *he* was suddenly the one who was reduced to submission as *he* sat passively and inactive at the end of the bed. What a pathetic sight to be sat there in his nakedness, no longer hungry for sex, flaccid and so inadequate unable to even acknowledge his gross misdemeanour.

'What the heck?' I began.

'Shhh, you will wake the neighbours up,' he said, 'I couldn't sleep downstairs; it was too cold.'

'Is that really your only excuse, you were cold?' I was beyond baffled as he must have been downstairs pleasuring himself beforehand. To think that he had not only had unholy thoughts, but that he had made his way up the stairs, opened the door, seen that I was fast asleep yet was still intent on actioning his plan was outrageous.

'Well, I was letting you have the bed,' he said sulkily as though he was doing me a favour.

'The last thing on earth I ever wanted was to be left alone with you again but sharing a bed with you? Are you for fucking real?'

No answer!

'I am NOT that scared little girl and I no longer need someone here to help me,' I lied trying to sound stronger than my shaking legs felt. 'Don't you ever come near me again or I will wait until you are asleep and cut that pathetic dangly bit of shit off!' I raged.

He got up without even looking in my direction, walked solemnly out of the bedroom and downstairs. I pulled my jeans on and sat tentatively on the edge of the bed until I had heard the front door shut and his car drive away and only then did I burst into tears. I sat there shaking, rocking backwards and forwards trying to comfort myself in the aftermath of what could have been a whole different scene. I was angry, hurt, scared and alone having been violated again. Then I wondered if he had orchestrated the whole thing just to get me there. Let's be honest; even if he hadn't, he was guilty of taking advantage of the situation without any care or concern for me or the long-term consequences his actions would have. In shock, I mused over the events and reached the conclusion that now being in his mid-20s, he was a very sick and dangerous man.

At that moment, I promised both myself and Little Lois that this would never happen to us ever again and then I was left with a very worrying and sombre thought. I had been placed in this position because my mum had forced me to be here with him all because his wants were more important than my need to be safe. I felt sickened and disturbed as I knew yet again that I had been let down and I still had no one with whom I could approach for help to process these events. In effect, he would get away with it again as it was my word against his so it was just going to be yet another skeleton to bury in the ever bulging cupboard.

This was one of those dates and memories that would inadvertently embed itself into my soul whether I wanted it there or not. You know the ones they are like the formation of wormholes one see's left behind on the sand, you know they are there under the surface because they have left their imprint upon you. Sometimes the physical scars are obvious but the psychological warfare that runs like an undercurrent and affects you in later life is not as obvious, either to the sufferer nor to their loved ones.

These unresolved traumas can play out at any time and without notice, often ignited through some unbeknown trigger that can create explosive consequences. Through forced silence, isolation and the inability to escape my environment my inner torment would have no way to expunge itself. So, within me it created a kind of system overload causing a flood of fragmented emotions and experiences to be scattered and divided into several compartments. Over time these compartments became subconsciously sealed to afford myself a self-protective coping mechanism. However, the downside was the development of intense, deep-rooted anger. My conflict was always whether it was my fault, and did I do anything to deserve being abused? Surprisingly, I never dreamt of confronting the failures of those around me who neither noticed my responses to the abuse nor stood in the gap to protect me from it.

The haunting truth would have meant that I would have had to hold my parents also accountable whom I trusted and the siblings who mistreated me the way they did that isolated me to become a victim. This concept was too difficult to comprehend so the destructive self-hate campaign continued to reign unchecked because as a child you are not able to cognitively understand the complexities of either relationships or the meaning of life. Nor are you psychologically mature, enough to be able to regulate your emotions to adjust them accordingly to fit into the concept of "normal" behaviour.

So, for the time being I had to do the only thing that had worked for me to date and that was to push it all down, compress it all and try to maintain some form of my own normality.

Chapter 7
Life Goes on

Having been turned away for the opportunity to go into the 6th Form, I decided to look at the option of going to a real college and applied for the Performing Arts course at Wakefield College. Luckily, I attained the four O-level entry requirements so in September 1983 I dived into my new chosen domain. I welcomed the opportunity to reinvent myself, able to reveal parts that had been long buried through the portrayal of characters on stage. At last, I felt confident in the knowledge that my peers accepted me for who I was not an image traced over me blotting the real me out. I no longer felt suffocated by the strangleholds of the past nor controlled by remnants of emotional trauma. These had been comfortably sealed in their boxes whilst I explored my new world and experimented with my physical image. I encountered differing musical cultures, had my nose pierced and dressed as a punk which looking back now was probably another subconscious effort to ensure others maintained a safe distance. I had developed serious trust issues which was hardly surprising however I began to progress from having rigid barriers firmly set in concrete, to being able to formulate appropriate, healthy boundaries.

The brilliant aspect of attending a community college was interacting with people from a wider geographical area rather than just my hometown. It presented varying experiences in the form of parties, nights out and the development of new friendships which promoted an essential sense of belonging. With the isolation element eradicated along with the primary reliance upon only the family unit and the gateway to new experiences opened, I was finally able to grow as a person. I was no longer sat up in the air on my end of the seesaw because these new elements suddenly realigned something within me. I loved those early college years as they provided a feeling of escapism both mentally through the therapy of drama and physically by being absent from the house.

After excelling in the performance art course, I was destined to follow my dreams and attend university to study at degree level however my confidence was suddenly shattered when my grandfather suddenly passed away along with my beautiful Labrador Sandy. A year later my grandma also died, the only bedrock of my childhood had collapsed and with it my confidence and ability to make the best-informed choices and decisions for myself along with it. My friends seemed to be steadfast in the paths they were taking and resolute in the journey they were about to embark upon. I was suddenly like the builder who hadn't built on solid ground the unforeseen movement shook my house of cards and it came tumbling down.

I suddenly became the same 16-year-old pupil leaving school, again not knowing which way to turn and feeling completely exposed to the uncertainties of life's direction. I knew I wasn't ready to repeat a move to an unknown destination, so I chose to stay within the arts at Wakefield college. Here I submerged myself in varying forms of self-expression finally concentrating on mixing the art of sculpture with photography. I progressed immensely artistically speaking, though socially I became more introverted submerging myself only in my art as a therapeutic vehicle to soothing my inner being.

At the end of the course with my confidence reinstated, I was ready to flee my external environment to further extinguish those inner demons. What I was finally ready to do was to embrace who I really was as a person and to do that I needed to go it alone away from those who had persistently dripped their poison into my ear. Any counsellor will tell you that in order to really kick a habit you have to be removed from the environment in which you circulate otherwise your sobriety will inevitably be compromised.

For the next 3 years, I welcomed the many facets of what made me whole as a person and I liked them, despite it not being an easy personal growth period. Although I had embarked on my first proper relationship during my Performance Art days, I still was not comfortable being with a man. I did try a couple of times but knew I was more suited to having relationships with women as here I was a lot more relaxed, loving and I felt in control because we seemed to sync naturally without a power struggle. Inevitably in the late 1980s, same sex relationships were taboo, with gay men and women being subjected to disgusting abuse both physically and verbally.

I remember my partner and I travelling to Manchester for the pioneering Clause 28 March where I met Sue Johnston and Ian McKellen and for the very first-time life was really good. We started a group for other students at the college and arranged trips to the Newcastle gay scene and to Leeds where my friends all had nightclubs. I even gave a speech in front of hundreds of other undergraduates who were apposing gay rights for students and won. A new position was created to assist the integration of young gay students into campus, and I was earmarked for the role despite nearing the end of my 3rd year degree there.

However, the breakdown of my long-term relationship brought with it a devastation and heartache I had never realised existed. It was the catalyst that sent me spiralling into a mere version of my former self as I became withdrawn, alone and hurt. I felt so angry with myself for daring to believe that things could ever be any different for me. Worse still I ended up back at "Grey Gables" which compounded things further, echoing my failure to escape. I felt so alone and black inside that I didn't even have the inclination nor motivation to attend my own degree presentation. My heart was broken and like a finished jigsaw puzzle that always has that one piece missing my heart has never been the same since.

For years, I didn't come close to even loving another person because the shutters had well and truly come down with a brick wall erected so high that no one had a chance to scale it never mind knock it down. It hardened me and I am sad and disappointed to say resurrected my old friend called anger. Around this time, I also heard a chance remark from Nick to his friend Keith about *him* which spiralled me further out of control. Nick had said that '*he* was going to get himself into bother with the police as he had been "fettling" schoolkids.'

I seriously couldn't believe my ears, apparently there were two 15-year-old girls who were truanting from school in favour of going to his house. Seemingly, he was giving them cigarettes and drink whilst trying to coerce them into sexual acts. I felt so powerless yet deeply angry at the world, the past, the reoccurring present that didn't seem to offer any escape from *him* and the future which felt equally as bleak. I was helpless in a hopeless situation and began battling bouts of deep depression hating my very existence and believing fully that the world would be a better place if I wasn't in it.

Over the next few years, I kind of drifted working in the arts but not really building any significant personal connections just predominantly focusing on surviving each day. There were so many family gatherings where I was forced to tolerate the obnoxious retorts, the loud attention seeking behaviour, the constant put downs in my ear. Whether it was a party, a wedding, the local pub or at home there was no way to escape what can only be described as verbal diarrhoea, but I had to sustain it. Worse still was the fact that *he* seemed to be popular and all the young girls liked *him* because *he* put on a façade of being this likeable character buying everyone drinks. I later realised *he* did this to hide the truth and that it gave *him* a "way in" providing them with a false sense of security.

The most humiliating experiences were *his* acts of exhibitionism like the time we were out for my birthday. *He* had just met *his* new girlfriend and both her and her mum were at a small nightclub called Thirtysomething in Ossett. Some of my siblings were out, my friends and also both my parents. There had been some fun and frolicking going on with a charity mud wrestling event then as we enjoyed drinks a raffle was being offered. Inevitably to support the cause we bought tickets not knowing what the prizes were. However, I knew the manager exceptionally well, so I think he rigged the draw because low and behold mine was the winning ticket and here I was on my birthday. I was then being called forward to supposedly get into the mud bath with these 2 beautiful, scantily dressed women.

Well, that was never going to happen, I like to sit in the background at the best of times so despite the chants from the crowd I declined. He then grabs the ticket from my hand neon runs down to the front, strips to *his* undies and drives in much to the crowd's delight though not *his* new girlfriend nor her mum's. The girls in the pit basically dragged *him* under, rolled around a little then ripped *his* pants off *him*. Most people would be embarrassed, concede defeat and gladly wait for their clothes or a robe to cover their modesty. But no, he stands up, legs wide apart shouting 'way-ay' swinging *his* privates back and forth as though *he* was some kind of porn star.

My father was absolutely disgusted and left thoroughly embarrassed. Here he was a well-known businessman out with his wife and family being subjected to crude, sexually explicit behaviour and from his own son. They promptly left. *He* did not bat an eyelid it was all in good fun and so you see why *he* makes my skin crawl because this is what I have constantly had to put up with throughout my life. The abuser, the exhibitionist, the façade, the tormentor, the predator, the rising anger, the inability to escape and the lack of accountability for *his* actions.

I knew the shame, the blame and the guilt were not mine to carry but the continual effects of witnessing such outrageous, narcissistic and attention seeking acts did make me question my own responsibility, as there was no culpability as far as *he* was concerned. It made me sick to the stomach to the point I couldn't abide being anywhere near *him* and resulted in my hating myself more every time I was forced to accept *him* in my presence.

Chapter 8
"Has He Ever"

Not long after the birthday incident, I was at the same club with friends and Ruby was also there, so at the end of the night, we inevitably walked the short distance home together. We'd both had a few drinks but not to the point that either of us were particularly drunk, just in good spirits so to speak. I cannot say why the subject of *him* came up maybe *he* had been out as well I don't recall but as we walked down the back lane towards Grey Gables, she suddenly stopped dead.

'Has he ever done anything to you, Lois?' she initiated.

I had kept on walking, not remotely aware that I had said anything to rouse any form of suspicion. I turned around not fully engaging in what she had said more that her voice seemed further away. The look on her face told me that all was not well and sensing a sudden shift in the atmosphere and with her tone it also confirmed this.

'Tell me, has *he* ever said or done anything to you Lois?' she persisted.

'What are you on about, who?' I said trying my hardest to sound nonchalant, vague and unaffected. It didn't work.

She marched over to me and directly asked, 'Has *he* ever done anything to you that a brother should not do, to *his* sister?'

'I don't know what you mean,' I faltered, 'like what?'

'You know what! *He* has, hasn't *he*, Lois?' she urged.

I didn't want to get upset because any form of emotion in front of Ruby was viewed as a vulnerability on my behalf, one that she had constantly taken advantage of. The other issue I was finding equally difficult was the parallel of the confrontation I'd experienced all those years ago with Mum. I'd always longed for someone to be available for me to confide in, never in a million years would I have expected nor ever have chosen Ruby and now was no different. Despite my years of desperation, I didn't trust her so I was not about to open my inner most self to the one person who had spent my entire childhood destroying me.

'Don't be silly,' I said trying to sound as nonplussed as possible turning to continue on our route home.

'No,' she said sternly. Then grabbing my arm and talking up close to my face she continued, 'I can tell there is something and I won't ignore it so if you won't tell me, you can tell Mum.'

'What the hell, I will not!' I panicked.

'You either tell me now, Lois, or understand this, Mum will get it out of you,' she said firmly standing her ground.

This was a living nightmare, one minute I was enjoying a night out and the next I was being accosted on Back Lane about my personal childhood trauma's. My head was in a swirl, I was trying to repress the emotion building up and select my words very carefully, but I was becoming too self-conscious. Through momentarily trying to scrutinise each word, sifting through it and analysing its content prior to verbalisation she was too quick and immediately picked up on the slightest hesitation.

'Ok, then we will have this conversation in front of Mum,' she affirmed and began to walk off in front of me.

'Ok, ok,' I conceded, 'yes, it is true; *he* abused me as a child,' I admitted and that was it the words were finally out there sat in the air unable to be retracted. I can honestly say I never imagined having this conversation after a late night out under these circumstances.

There was no time to recover nor respond because Ruby was off on her heel ultrafast in a determined pursuit of Mum.

'Wait,' I called, horrified at what I was witnessing and terrified of the outcome that opening this can of worms would create.

But she was no longer listening and had now turned the corner at the bottom of the lane intently striding her way towards our gate. I did not want to follow if anything I wanted to say, 'Beam me up, Scotty' and be transported as far away from here as possible. I couldn't face another interrogation nor the disappointed face of Mum or her disgust at me. Equally, I did not want to have to deal with the aftermath this revelation would cause, everything was such a mess.

Why did Ruby even bring this topic up in the first place? And why was she pushing me so much to get an answer? I felt utterly wretched, but I knew there was no escape I had nowhere else I could go so I had to continue home and somehow cope with whatever the situation delivered. So, I walked the short distance home like a condemned man on the green mile on death row to find out my fate.

Chapter 9
"Well?"

The short distance up the hill seemed to take a lifetime as the muscles in my legs suddenly tightened and threatened not to support my decision. The door was open, the stark fluorescent light of the kitchen completely illuminated the room a stark contrast to the star lit sky from where I had just come. It took a moment for me to acclimatise. The house was eerily silent with none of the anticipated chaos I had been expecting. I decided against making a hot drink as that would only serve to delay the inevitable. Instead, I chose to down a glass of water the coldness alleviating my thirst and sharpening my cognitive awareness. I was ready, not to go into battle but to tackle the situation once and for all. It had plagued my whole existence for as long as I could remember and there was no point delaying it any longer.

I opened the door to the middle room the one Mum had led me through on that first introduction to the house, it was in darkness but I could hear the low rumble of quietened conversation. I was unsure if this was due to the hour or the topic that was being discussed. Nevertheless, I turned to my right towards the lounge and from the slight crack in the door assessed correctly that there was only Ruby and Mum present. I tentatively opened the door, stepped in but kept the door ajar and stood awkwardly to evaluate my reception. Mum was sat on the settee to my left and Ruby was stood opposite her leaning on the mantelpiece.

'Well?' Mum started like a prosecutor pushing for that pertinent answer to win the trial and my stomach instantly fell to my knees. Here we were again; the exact replica of 18 years ago with a confrontation rather than understanding, support and loving kindness.

'Well, what?' was my poor and unrehearsed response.

'Is it true what Ruby has just told me?' she asked.

'Well, I don't know, because I don't know what she has said,' I inadequately retorted. I was dying here, I felt like a kid caught with their hand in the sweetie jar with nowhere to hide and no reasonable explanation that I could find to offer.

'Lois, just tell her, for goodness sakes,' Ruby pleaded.

'Why, Ruby, it's not like it's going to change anything. And why is what happened to me so important to you all of a sudden?' I asked her.

'Please just tell her,' she pushed me.

It was one pressure too many and I literally crumbled sobbing, releasing the years of pent up hurt, anger, despair, guilt, loneliness and secrecy of the situation. There was little else that needed to be said as the spontaneous outward expression was communicated to the fullest. It was the complexity of a grief-stricken cry culminating from the loss of my innocence as a child and the person I was destined to become had I not been robbed of it by *him*. So profound was the release that I would not experience this depth or gravity of pain for another 20 years until the day my father passes away.

I then had the indignation of having to go into the sordid details, squirming with each revelation but nonetheless it all slipped out as easily as a body bag over the side of a boat. Once I had purged myself, I then had a new issue to deal with the embarrassment that they both knew, and the fear Ruby would somehow find a way to use it against me at some inappropriate moment in the future. That was an unbearable thought however I was stronger for the release and dared to hope that at least Mum would have my back should the situation occur. How wrong I could be.

Growing up

Chapter 10
Finding My True Self

I went to bed that night feeling completely exhausted emotionally and mentally so I slept quite soundly for once. The next day when I got up it was as if nothing had occurred or been said the night before as not a word was even mentioned. There were no reassurances, no queries about whether I was ok or an offer to sit and chat anything through it was life continuing as normal. I was baffled. I had been cornered and forced to admit the worst memories of my childhood, I had absolutely poured my grief-stricken heart out, given my all and for what purpose? It seemed that they had got what they wanted, an admission, but clearly, I was still going to be the same nonentity in this family that I had always been.

I had constantly felt alone before but now I felt like that lad on *Diary of a Wimpey Kid* who everyone points to screaming "cheese touch" and the playground scatters to leave him isolated. It was safe to say that life was going to roll pretty much the same as it always had so I kept myself to myself the exposure of the truth clothing me like the invisible man.

At the time, I had been working for a banner making company in Huddersfield and, not having access to a car, I was taking a bus to Dewsbury each morning, walking up to the train station and on to Huddersfield. It felt good to have the monotony of this routine; it was safe, and it gave me time to be alone and think. The work could be anything from painting huge banners for the opera house in Wakefield to assisting with workshops within school settings, The Hospice, festivals or within shopping centres. It was perfect for me because I could cut myself off and use my art therapeutically.

Then I secured a job as a community arts development worker in Wakefield for a local charity where I organised and facilitated workshops throughout the West Yorkshire region. This gave me the opportunity to thrive as an artist and to engage with people from differing social and cultural backgrounds, of varying abilities and from an expansive geographical area. I worked hard and began to save every penny I could until 1995 when I was able to put a deposit down to buy my own house. I was 28, independent and were finally able to break free once and for all.

I am unsure whether my siblings were jealous or whether it was just their hatred for me but there were many cutting comments dismissing my attempts at independence. Despite the house being brand new and my funding every penny myself, they still found time to demean my efforts and criticise my choices. Even when I offered my new home to Kelly and her family for the night so they could attend a wedding and save on hotel costs she ridiculed it for being too small. No matter how much I tried to help any of them whether it was babysitting or lending them my new car to tour France there was never any gratitude or a good word shared. Therefore, I learnt to totally depend on myself and didn't ask any of them for anything.

Over the next 2 years, I worked intently to make that little house a home taking great pride in each and every one of my achievements. I also enjoyed the freedom of working throughout Calderdale, Wakefield, Bradford, Huddersfield and Kirklees. I even found a lovely little church that I started to attend spending much of my spare time there. I was soon combining my work and leisure running a youth club on the Peacock estate along with a group of friends from the church, so life was good again. In 1996, four of us took aid to Belgrade the capital of the then Yugoslavia. We met with refugees from the war-torn areas of Slovakia and Slovenia distributing aid, contributing to meetings with the church leaders and reaching out within the communities.

I still vividly remember some of the conditions within which they were forced to survive like a 91-year-old lady in one of the bottom beds of numerous bunks crammed into a community centre. One bombed and abandoned school had the classrooms partitioned with old broken pallets to divide areas for whole families to live in. The building was similar to an office block with about 4 floors to it and all the families were sharing 3 horrendous showers to wash themselves and their clothes in. Outside were remnants of rusty cranky old swings and a slide yet despite the state of their conditions the children with whom I played "Tig" were happy and giggly. Maybe that was only due to the silly English girl chasing them and having fun regardless of our language barrier.

One person I could never forget was a lady whose home was a mere shack on the other side of town. She shared this one room with her husband, 2 children, mother and a brother. Although we had seen her in the doorway on our arrival, she would not come out to be formally introduced to us. I was later informed she felt unworthy through embarrassment for her living situation. Her 96-year-old mother sat knitting slippers all day for anyone passing by which needless to say I did buy some and still treasure them today. I was enthralled by her character and the deep lines upon her face depicting the story of someone who'd had a wealth of a lifetime of experiences. This elderly lady was as equally amused by the attention her new visitors afforded her and happily posed for a photograph. Many years later I painted that portrait onto canvas simply called "The Seated Woman" which was chosen for the third Outdoors Gallery exhibition held in Nafplion, Greece, in September 2022.

A couple of days later, I was attending the church in Belgrade where a queue four deep and as far as the eye could see had formed to collect provisions and worship God, I saw the elderly ladies, daughter in the crowd. My heart broke for her lost in the sea of faces so I beckoned furiously for her to join me as I walked through with our guide, but she was too ashamed. So, I fought my way through the crowd, took her by the hand and led her through the front door down the steps and into the area where boxes were being filled with food. I took a box and alongside the other workers I filled it myself with every item available and as I handed it to her, I saw she was weeping.

A little worried I had offended her, I asked one of the workers to ask her what was wrong but what she told them blew my mind. She explained that she had been so embarrassed about her home situation that she had hid from me and today in the crowd she had tried to hide from me again. Then she said she would thank God for not letting her hide because today she had met one of his earthly angels and now, she would be able to feed her family. I put my arms around her and prayed for her, her family and their situation then we stood together in the church's morning service.

We were also introduced to a lady, her husband and 14-year-old son who lived in the basement of a block of flats. It was a bleak route of breezeblock, broken furniture and large industrial pipes to get to the corner they had sectioned off to make their home. As little as they had she invited our party of five to eat soup that she had made specially for our arrival. She told us the story of her life which was one of privilege and great wealth. She had been a very successful bank manager. Her bosses had been so impressed with her abilities, they had provided holidays for her family and had given her a house which she had filled with cut crystal ornaments and vases. She had thrived and taken much pleasure in her wealth and polished the crystal each day with great care.

However, then the bombings had begun, one smashing their home and the cut crystal to smithereens, so they were forced to flee with nothing but the clothes on their backs. She stated that although she now had nothing, she felt that she was far richer than before because now she had God in her life and whilst he was for her nothing, no matter what, could be against her ever again. It was a very humbling experience of faith, hope, love, gratitude and personal growth.

Whilst in Yugoslavia, we decided to venture through to the war-torn areas of Bosnia which was both a frightening and heart-warming experience. Whilst giving out packs of biscuits to children and their parents we were suddenly stopped by soldiers carrying guns. They escorted our party of 2 cars to a large building at the top of the hill near a huge dam. It was apparently the residence of the mayor of the area and within half an hour a film crew suddenly ascended upon us. The mayor wanted to be filmed interviewing one of my friends about the work we were doing. It was a bizarre experience as though it was nothing more than a publicity stunt for the mayor to look good and appear proactive looking out for his people's needs. It made me feel that our efforts were being exploited somehow and I was more than glad to cross the border for the long drive back to Belgrade.

Once our missionary work had been fulfilled in Yugoslavia, we made our way to an orphanage called Caminul Felix in Oradea, Romania to deliver toys donated by our church fellowship and collated through outreach programmes. My friend Debbie was also donating £1200 to support their work that she had raised doing a sponsored slim. It was a heart moving experience and an amazing project where I discovered approximately 8 small houses each housing a number of orphaned children. They had bunkbeds in most of the rooms set around a central dining and living area with each house being run by a married couple who raised the children as their own.

In the summer of 1996, when we visited, the project had only been running for around 6 years and at the time, they were busy trying to establish workshops to teach the children employment skills for when they eventually left Caminul Felix. We met with the children, their parents and the founders Linda and Lars Hornberg who took great delight in sharing their vision for this amazing project. Some of the children had been simply abandoned at the side of the road and then we heard the heart-breaking story of one little girl whose parents had tried to poison her. Inevitably I took numerous photographs which formed the nucleus of the presentation Debbie and I gave of our trip to our home church on our return. (https://caminulfelix.ro/)

It was as a direct result of this presentation and the work that I was involved in on the Peacock estate that a new member of our church decided to volunteer with the youth work. A year later in September 1997 we were married the week before I was due to start my Prison Officer training, a 12-week course at the Wakefield site on Aberford Road. He was a 3rd year physiotherapy student, so finances were very tight especially during that first year though I still managed to provide for all our needs. However, he soon became unsettled in the house that I'd had prior to our meeting as his name wasn't on the mortgage and favoured a move to "our" martial home. We moved to Sandal, but it brought with it many challenges especially when I had to work away having been promoted to drugs dog handler.

I think the ever-increasing pressures of the environment within which I worked and some of the atrocities I witnessed played a huge part in the marriage breakdown along with his persistence to keep getting himself into debt. After suffering a miscarry in May 2000 and then discovering I was pregnant again in Nov 2001, I found out he had taken out even more debt. I did initiated counselling with my associate pastor but then I found out he had been seeing someone at work. Despite my beliefs, the breakdown became irreconcilable, so I had to call time on the marriage for my own sanity and the stability for my unborn child.

Even before he was born, my pregnancy was different to how everyone else's had been. There was no genuine excitement, words of congratulations or baby showers thrown; in fact to say my husband and I split when I was 3 months pregnant you would have thought I'd be given all the support I could want, but no. I was devastated at the end of my marriage and yet I was not able to talk to anyone about how I felt because absolutely no one wanted to listen. I tried once with Ruby, but she dismissed me and said 'oh can't you change the record.'

Yet when she was getting divorced, both Mum and I were forced to live through it with her having the exact same story day after day. It was relentless and mind-bendingly depressive having to listen thread through needle to every word exchanged. In the end, I offered her the keys to my house and for me to move back to Grey Gables to escape the torment of her situation, but the children's school was apparently too far, about a 6-mile drive. A new, three-bedroom detached house rent and bill free but she couldn't afford the petrol money for the school run. In reality, she was just the kind of person who liked to moan and if there wasn't a crisis, she would create one. Like accusing her ex-husband of being a paedophile, accusing her brother and initiating the police investigation, later making unsubstantiated accusations to power of attorney that I was mistreating Mum and misappropriating her funds and researching company's house to see if she could get Nick in trouble for fraud.

Then many years later, she would ruin Sarah's wedding just because her loyalty lay elsewhere, and she was losing her only friendship and later annihilating the family accusing her new husband of being a paedophile. It is amazing how some people allow their rage and bitterness to affect them to the depths that they genuinely what to bring about devastation. I personally find it so much easier to walk away with a glad heart and be thankful for the lessons, trials and tribulations each chapter brings. At least then you can move on to the fullness of what life has to offer you rather than waste your time scheming and plotting vengeance.

In fact, their hatred seemed to intensify when Mum was being very supportive to me and to be honest, I do not think I could have got through most of life's difficulties without her. However, on one occasion I was staying over at Grey Gables and for the umpteenth time *he* had moved back in unable to sustain his latest relationship. I believe it was supposed to have been a temporary arrangement of around 6 months yet years later he was still living off Mum and Dad whilst wasting his earnings in the pub most nights. It was during this time when I was around 7 months pregnant that I had gone into the kitchen to make a cup of tea.

He as usual was not supervising his young children aged about 4 and 6 at the time but outside washing his car. The girls had been left to their own devices and were cuddling up to my passive drugs dog. Not an issue as such she was an exceptionally loving animal however as per protocol, she was not a domesticated animal and so she was always kept separate from their interaction. Inevitably I encouraged them to go to their father and closed the door to Jess nothing sinister or awful about it. I then went back upstairs for something and when I came back down, they were with her again.

'Sorry Auntie Lois,' Sophie ventured in such a quiet almost pleading voice.

'Daddy made us come back in,' Cerys said, the corners of her mouth beginning to quiver.

I couldn't take it out on the children because at the end of the day I knew *him* well enough to know this sick controlling and coercive behaviour of children was his signature. So, I gave them a smile to communicate I wasn't upset with either of them and nodded that I understood. 'It's ok, sweethearts, shall we have a drink and a biscuit?' I asked.

They nodded vigorously in relief that they were not going to be caught in the crossfire and we all went back into the kitchen to get our refreshments. When there were no raised voices nor the children running back out to *him, he* soon came to see why his plan hadn't worked.

'What the hell are you two doing sat there, eating biscuits,' he yelled at the poor loves.

'I gave them to the girls,' I began in order to take the attention away from Sophie and Cerys.

'What the hell has it got to do with you?' he aggressively challenged me.

'Well, as you are so busy doing the essential job of cleaning your car rather than supervise your children when you have access, maybe someone needs to meet their needs.' I was not backing down; both Sophie and Cerys needed to know that someone would stand up for them against their bully of a father. Besides, I had sustained enough of his tantrums, threatening behaviours and aggressive taunts to last me a lifetime.

'Get out,' he screamed at the girls pointing towards the door.

'Don't take it out on them, it's me you have the problem with,' I stated.

'You're just a fucking slag,' he said.

'Wow, well I think it's safe to say it won't be you winning "Father of the Year" again, will you? Such wonderful usage of the English language,' I mocked.

He then grabbed hold of Sophie by the elbow and said, 'Isn't she, she's a fucking slag? Tell her, go on, tell her she's a fucking slag,' he pressured the poor mite.

Sophie was absolutely terrified and couldn't speak for fear, so I smiled gently and said, 'It's ok, darling, don't be afraid.'

'Don't fucking speak to her or I will jump over there (referring to the breakfast bar I was stood behind) and kick that fucking brat out of your stomach,' was the vile threat he spat at me.

'You put one finger on me or either of those children and I will be straight on to the police, and I will have you locked up,' I calmly stated looking straight into his face. I can honestly say I was petrified, shaken and in fear for the safety of my unborn child. I had never felt that my safety had ever been this compromised, not even when working with murderers, terrorists and rapists. He was a nasty man.

Not long after this incident when I was almost full term with an uncomfortable bump too high to even breathe properly as he wouldn't engage, I visited Mum. Ruby was already there but I have no idea what on earth was going on with her, I just remember her mood instantly changing when I arrived. Then for no apparent reason, she went into one of her abusive tirades totally annihilating me verbally rendering me incapacitated. I was sat in Dad's favourite chair sobbing my heart out literally unable to catch my breath; her onslaught was so excessive, yet she just kept going on and on relentless. This is what I mean about Ruby having no human connection with me; she'd had 2 children of her own the youngest being only 7 months, yet she had no compassion to my heavily pregnant condition or mental state. If there was an opportunity to exploit any weakness, she was off like a train careering down the track to abuse me if she observed any vulnerability.

Jack was born soon after via emergency caesarean section in July 2002 which should have been a new start for both of us but unfortunately what ensued was four years of court proceedings so early parenthood was a very unhappy and stressful time. This was another very difficult point in my life one which depleted me emotionally and that reinstated the trauma response to detach in order to cope with the circumstances surrounding me. Eventually my ex-husband stopped his catalogue of unrealistic requests after the judge pointed out that I was actually working with him and not against him. I was then able to organise talks between our pastors so that we could both be supported and to endeavour to give Jack the best of both of his parents.

However, I had been on high alert for so long having to go into battle unnecessarily during those court sessions, trying to maintain a healthy work life balance and provide for the needs of my very young son. A time where yet again I can honestly say I was standing alone without any support from my siblings let's face it with no connection to me there could hardly be any understanding of what I may be going through. So, there were no offers to babysit or to take me out, to pop in for a coffee, no checks on my mental state or anything else for that matter. Although if I was organising any parties, they would all come eat, drink and enjoy my hospitality but there was nothing that they shared in return.

Kelly did invite us for Christmas dinners which was always quite stressful especially as Ruby took pleasure in telling me that the only reason, I was there was to provide the transport for Mum and Dad. It just meant my whole Christmases when Jack was young were spent running around and not being able to just relax and enjoy those precious moments with him. The most distressing and upsetting issues with my siblings was not just their disdain for me but the hatred they showed towards Jack just because he was my son.

Once Jack had been born, I was always mindful of whenever *he* was around him and so became quite overprotective. Then one night Mum and Dad were babysitting for me, where I would bathe Jack, put him to bed at their house, meet friends but then return and stay the night. I was always glad of their help but would never have dreamt of taking advantage of them. Before I had arrived home, *he* had apparently gone back shouting and carrying on about something. Mum had been sat on the settee in the lounge, Dad to her left in his favourite armchair whereas *he* was stood in front of her towering over her in the centre of the room.

Mum replayed the scene of him shouting and swearing about something that had happened whilst he had been out and that he was getting very aggressive and quite animated. So, Mum had simply asked him to lower his voice not only did she not want to be shouted at in this way, but Jack was fast asleep upstairs. A reasonable request under the circumstances however to this individual who was used to getting his own way it was viewed as a rebuke and he went ballistic. He stepped towards Mum calling her all the names under the sun, accusing her of favouring Jack, goading her to dare to stand up and threatening to knock her down if she did. *He* had apparently called Jack some terrible things too and accused Mum of favouring him and mocked her for treating him like he was some kind of prince.

My father had previously had experience of *his* violent outbursts in the past having been punched and grabbed at the throat by him and had his desk overturned in his office, so he was having no threats towards his wife. He told him that the next day he would have to pack his bags and leave, finally they had stood up to him and not cowered down. However, in his uneducated, immature brain he deduced that his predicament was all my fault again and worse still Jack's, so you see no matter what went on I was always the scapegoat!

I remember organising a party at my friend Wendy's house one New Year and as I was hosting the games, I kept noticing Jack who was sat next to Nick randomly jerking. Inevitably I told him off and urged him to sit still but then I also noticed the smug grin on Nick's face. The next day Jack had several little nip bruises down his side. Another time Nick, his partner and daughter called to give Jack his birthday present a week late, but we made them welcome. Again, Nick started winding Jack up when I wasn't looking then feigned surprise when Jack hit back, so again the smug look when I told him off.

Then there were the constant problems with Ruby who absolutely hated jack and always let her children run wild whenever she brought them to Grey Gables much to Mum and Dad's annoyance. Not the children's fault at all but one day when they turned up Mum had gone into Ossett and had left strict instructions, she didn't want them in the piano room. Mum was avidly engrossed in doing her family tree and had got important papers laid out that she was utilising. When Ruby arrived and saw that dad had written Jack's name on the patio with the jet wash, he was using she was absolutely furious and instantly in a bad mood. The children were left to run riot as usual and knowing Mum would be upset, I called them to come out of the piano room as requested. This was just the red flag and excuse Ruby was looking for to blow up, scolding me for Dad writing Jack's name on the patio and not her son's. 'No one should have the highest honour,' she had screeched.

This alone wasn't enough for her to eradicate her anger so she literally continued with all manner of personal insults throwing all kinds of rubbish at me from years before that she had apparently stored up. Personally, I would have been more upset if someone had to step in and correct my child in any way as it would be a reflection on my parenting. If there is anything positive to say about my sibling's constant criticism, it is the fact that I was so self-conscious about my children that I brought them up to be well behaved, good mannered and respectful that they were always a pleasure to take anywhere.

Despite this, my siblings would always do their best to criticise my efforts or antagonise Jack to disregard any healthy boundaries I had set for him, by purposely encouraging him to override what I had said just to cause discord. They took great pleasure at wearing their smug, sly little grins if their efforts bore the mildest of fruits. They continued to scrutinise everything I did and took great delight in sharing their opinions loudly to ensure it was accidently on purpose in my earshot. Luckily, I had witnessed their own parenting standards so theirs was never a yard stick by which I would measure myself. All it created was just another excuse for them to speak negatively about me and resulted in further unpleasantness when in their company. So inevitably when I became pregnant with Joe, I didn't even bother sharing my news with them.

Of course, the parties and the family get togethers continued but I started omitting *his* invites if I was organising anything as I couldn't abide being around *him* nor being embarrassed by *him*. This came to a head at Jack's 4th birthday party in the summer of 2006 when I was holding a garden party at my home and a large number of my church friends were attending. There was one lady in particular called Rachel, she was the head of the worship group I sang with and was quite rotund in stature. As she entered the crowded room, *he* could suddenly be heard over the top of everyone else bellowing 'wha-ay it's Vicar of Dibley, you aw'rite Dawn.'

Yet again with no care nor concern for anyone else's feelings just succumbing to the constant desire to elevate *himself* came yet another pathetic putdown at someone else's expense. I accepted I may not be able to escape *him* with family events but that this would be the last time he was ever invited to anything I could control. I held many get-togethers without him but then I had to contend with the mutterings and snide remarks from Kelly about how sad it was that I had excluded *him*. It has always amazed me how bullies operate, there is never strength to stand alone and be counted, they either hide behind others, give someone else the bullets to fire or bring their gang with them. Yet, stand up to them, report them or call them out on their behaviour and suddenly they give the most amazing performance of being the victim!

He was like a man-child that had zero understanding of any interpersonal skills at all, but this was the turning point for me and when I really saw *him*. That night after everyone had left and I had cleaned up I reflected upon the party and how lucky I was to have such amazing people in my life. I had a good job, I was a prison officer and drugs dog handler, I had a lovely home and although I was a single parent, I had a beautiful 4-year-old son. As I evaluated my life, I had to admit things were hard, but I had done well and I had always done my best in all situations. When I assessed *his* in comparison, the truth revealed itself. *He* had nothing, *he* lived in a caravan in our old yard, *he* had 3 failed marriages behind *him*, no one had any kind words to say about *him* and he had even had to rely on my father to sustain any form of employment.

The only person who had any time for *him* was Ruby. I quickly realised how alike they were, neither had anyone of substance in their lives, they were both explosive in temperament, they had no real friends and simply clung to each other because that's all they had. Seeing the truth that had been in front of my eyes all these years was like the bible chapter in Acts 9:18 'when something like scales fell from Saul's eyes and he could see again.' Like Saul my vision, focus and emotions had been on the wrong aspects of this situation but now that I could clearly see I recognised the power I had, not the insecurity I felt. It was like a switch had been flipped and the tables had most definitely started turning.

From this point on, I no longer allowed derogatory comments to go unchallenged, in fact, I told *him* a few home truths until it got to the point, he either shut up or left in a rage of anger. On one such occasion Ruby later told me, he had rung her effing and blinding down the phone about what a bitch I was and that his tirade had lasted *his* entire walk all the way home! Yes, the tables finally were turning, and they were never going to change back either.

Chapter 11
Joe

When Joe was born in January 2007, I'd had to have another emergency c-section at 34 weeks gestation due to a severe case of Pubic Symphysis Dysfunction. I had been left incapacitated due to a separation of my pelvis and required an x-ray just to ensure there was a safe exit from which to extract him. Giving birth naturally was not an option due to the pressure this would have placed on my pelvic area. On his removal, he was immediately taken to special baby care and within an hour the Dr had arrived to deliver the news they didn't have the provisions for him to stay at the hospital.

Ultimately, he was fighting for his life, and they needed a more specialised hospital to take care of his needs. At this point, they were currently in consultation with Sheffield Hospital however, an hour later he was refused admission there because his condition had suddenly and dramatically worsened. I was then given the news it could possibly be Manchester, Newcastle or even further afield. Five hours after birth I pleaded with nursing staff to assist me into a wheelchair so I could be taken to see my tiny little boy who had pipes and tubes springing out of every orifice. I was beside myself so performed the only option left open to any new parent in that situation which was to pray fervently that he would secure a place nearby and quickly. Then the call came to say a bed had become available for him at the Huddersfield Royal Infirmary, the only problem was that due to my condition I couldn't be moved so I had to stay where I was, which was pretty grim.

At 02.30 hrs when Joe had set off to Huddersfield Royal Infirmary, I was wheeled on to the ward into a side room, an empty cot still sat at the bottom of the bed that staff had forgotten to remove. Once I had been transferred on to the new bed, seven pillows in place to support the infirmity of my pelvis and morphine dispensed, I was left alone to listen to the cry of the newborn babies upon the wards. Throughout the week I worked hard to fight through the emotional anguish at being separated from my newborn baby and the physical agony of the pelvic displacement. I couldn't get to the toilet so was reliant upon a catheter and had the indignity of being bed bathed each day. I was lucky to have many visitors from the congregation of my church to sustain me, along with Mum, Dad, Jack's godparents Mick and Michelle, Leanne who kindly brought Jack and then Kelly came too. Neither Nick nor *he* showed any interest at all which suited me in my weakened and debilitated state and as for Ruby, I still hadn't even let her know about the pregnancy.

The hospital staff at Huddersfield were great at sending pictures for the nurses to print out for me but it wasn't the same as having my baby there and just served to deepen my longing to hold him. I had stated that I wanted to have that first feed and cuddle with him which was fine as they were having to dispense formula milk via a tube. However, little did I know until some years later that Kelly had amused herself by purposefully robbing me of this right at the very first opportunity she could. The same spiteful approach and measure of control that I had always been exposed to and yet another example to exploit my weakness when and wherever they were able to.

I had to stay in a separate hospital to Joe for a full week where each day I would be constantly told a bed had become available for him with promises that he would return only for it to be retracted hours later. Needless to say, if he wasn't coming back to me then I was going to find a way to get to him. I spent days working with physiotherapists to negotiate moving little by little to shuffle to the edge of the bed, then to stand and later to take my first furtive steps with the aid of a Zimmer frame. It was slow, cautious and deliberate work to try to sustain my weight and to manage the pain in order to get approval to be transferred to Huddersfield. It was approximately 21.15 hrs a week after his birth that I was finally wheeled into Huddersfield Royal Infirmary's Special Care Baby Unit to see my little boy. The next day my mother brought Jack to see his brother for the very first time and we were once again complete.

We remained in hospital for a further week, Kelly and her family did come to see me which was lovely although she then started pressurising me for permission to allow Ruby to also visit. Apparently, Kelly had been surprised that Ruby hadn't even known I was having a second child but why would she know given her behaviour towards me when I had previously been heavily pregnant. Then there had been her hatred and exploitation of my weaknesses not to mention her hatred and attitude towards Jack. So, Ruby visiting was never going to be an option never mind the fact that she had not spoken to me for months. As far as I was concerned, I couldn't risk neither mine nor my precious boys, safety or our equilibrium being compromised especially whilst I was in yet another vulnerable position. In fact, if the truth beknown the last people on the face of the earth that I would have wanted anywhere near me was Ruby and *him*.

When we were finally allowed home, I had to reside with the boys at Grey Gables which was very difficult for numerous reasons. It was imperative that my physiology had the chance to repair itself and as I couldn't even bear the weight of Joe on me it was going to be a very long road ahead. Mum was amazing she slept downstairs with Joe in a Moses basket next to her so she could give him his nightly feeds. Both her and Dad provided the transport to school for Jack along with my appointments for the start of what turned out to be 15 months of physiotherapy along with giving me all the support I needed.

I stayed with them for the first three months but knew I had to continue my recovery at home to establish a routine for the boys in our own environment. The level of their help and assistance was unprecedented to that of anything I had ever needed or received before because I had always maintained my independence come what may. In my debilitating struggles and the exceptional circumstances that we all found ourselves in it tightened our bonds and created "our" own little family separate to that of my siblings. Here no one was forsaken, no one was put down, we were all equal, we genuinely wanted the very best for one another, we enjoyed each other's company and we loved and supported each other unconditionally. The flip side to this brought further intense jealousy and nastiness from the others that was unparalleled to anything that I had experienced before. However, I had strength and support now because Mum and Dad had witnessed my helplessness and instead of being exploited, they created a structure of steel around me to protect me in my limitations.

The boys loved their grandma and grandad with such devotion, respect and intensity so happily visited them every day, my dad being their hero and my mum their guardian angel. In return, Mum and Dad were able to develop deep bonds so ultimately enjoyed the benefits of a very close relationship with their grandchildren. Unfortunately, this was a pleasure they had been denied by their other children who only came to visit sporadically and when it only suited themselves. Therefore, Mum and Dad had always felt they were on the periphery of a relationship with their other grandchildren as their interaction was governed by their parents. The difference was that I included them in everything I did and invested the majority of my time and energy into developing a strong, deep and meaningful relationship with them.

That is not to say they loved their other children or grandchildren any less; quite the contrary, they loved each one of us as equal to the next, they were just denied the pleasure of access to spend any quality time in their company. The thing is a relationship is a two-way stream, but it doesn't make sense to invest if the other party is unwilling to input a similar measure. Yet when your efforts are reciprocated and both parties invest into the relationship it is then able to blossom, bear fruit and is more sustainable. Equally if one side is pouring nothing in but nastiness, negativity, hostility and bitterness holding back for their rights to be met there is nowhere to grow. For "our" new little family, life was easy I took care of my parents they took care of my boys. As adults we recognised the value of amalgamating our love, time and energies into nurturing these precious children and we all took great pleasure in watching them grow.

I was soon medically retired from the prison service so spent the first few years of Joe's life assisting with Beavers when Jack secured a placement, helping out in nursery when Joe was old enough and supporting families at Home-start. Despite the physical difficulties of not being able to sustain a pain free existence and the low bouts of depression, I tentatively kept moving forward in the hope I would regain some momentum.

When Joe was 3 years of age, a lovely lady from my church called Wendy accompanied us on a holiday to Tunisia. For us, it was a defining moment where as a family we had regained our independence and all that had been stolen was restored. I was much stronger within myself and Joe who'd had kidney issues from birth was now thriving. We had a wonderful time exploring the countryside on quads, swimming, walking, making sand sculptures and enjoying the benefits that all-inclusive brought with it.

When it was time to fly home, we were suddenly delayed by the volcanic ash situation of April 2010 that grounded our flights for a week. We didn't mind one bit and continued to enjoy our holiday to the fullest. Unfortunately, Mum and Dad had failed to disclose to me that Dad had cancer before the start of our holidays. So, whilst we made plans for our lives on our return pledging to visit many countries around the world as an educational tool for the boys, Dad was preparing for surgery. Initially they had believed I would have a week to come to terms with the news however being delayed for the week resulted in him being admitted for surgery the day after we landed. I then dedicated myself to assist Mum to care for him whilst shielding the boys from the heartbreak and circumstances that we were going through.

I spent many months at his side, liaising with doctors, surgeons, anaesthetists, consultants and nurses to ensure he received the best care possible. If he was ill in the middle of the night, Mum would send for me, I'd transfer the boys from their beds to the car, slip them into bed at their house, assess Dad's needs and make a judgement in his best interests. Whenever he required hospitalisation, I would follow the ambulance to the hospital sit with him in a side room until the early hours, then rush back to get the boys ready for school and once I had dropped them off would return to his side. Nothing was too much trouble at all he wasn't just my boys' hero, he was mine too. Both he and Mum trusted me explicitly because I continuously gave my best and everything was always for their greater good. I never grumbled even when I was exhausted or had other responsibilities to attend to and neither did, I ever seek any praise nor recompense.

During one of the stints when he was in hospital, I had left after a very long day to allow Mum to have some quality time on her own with Dad however other family members suddenly ascended upon them. The next day Mum was so upset about the way Kelly kept talking over her and making barbed, belittling comments towards her. She also stated that Nick, his partner and daughter spent the whole time chatting across the bed to one another ridiculing Tim for living in a caravan and never having any money because he wasted it in the pub. She was thoroughly disgusted at the way they sneered at him and as she stated, 'pulled him through to bits.'

She described there being no care or concern shown for Dad's convalescence or the fact he and Mum may want to chat quietly or privately. They simply bellowed amongst themselves as though Mum and Dad were invisible much to Dad's embarrassment in front of the other patients and nurses. Their worst experience by far was when Kelly appointed herself in charge and would speak quite rudely to the nursing staff about what they should and shouldn't be doing. It was in a superiority tone as though they were her charges, and they should jump to her immediate demand.

When Tim bothered to turn up, Dad had to endure conversations solely about himself; about work, his aches and pains or how busy he had been racing around everywhere. I actually think he believed that what we all knew as the responsibilities of life in general was just applicable to him. I remember on one occasion when Dad had been in hospital at Dewsbury, and I had run myself ragged doing the obligatory afternoon and evening visits for almost three weeks so I rang him to take a turn. He was most put out because he wanted to go to the pub after work, so I ended up going as I hated to think of Dad all alone, only for him to turn up 20 mins before visiting ended! Yet again it was self, self, self-talk! I had to leave otherwise I would have snapped but it was the catalyst to Dad begging me not to let any of them know if he came into hospital again as he 'felt bad enough without them making him feel worse.'

He said, 'Now think on, don't ever ring them again to let them know where I am and don't ever contact them and tell them to visit. Tim made me poorly last night going on and on. I want people to come and visit me because they want to see me and spend time with me not to moan either about each other or their aches and pains. I feel bad enough without having to put up with that.'

'I hear you, but they are your children and it's only natural they will want to know what's happening, especially if you're rushed into hospital,' I told him.

'Maybe they do but I can't do with Kelly here rubbing the nurses up the wrong way telling them what they should or shouldn't be doing. She is not like you who will put it in the right way and acknowledge they are busy but when they have time can they fulfil something. She is rude, abrasive and off-hand so she immediately puts their back up. It's alright for her, she stirs the pot with her nose in the air being clever but then she goes home, and I am still in here at their mercy.'

Not long after these episodes, Dad had to go into a care home for six weeks stay so we could instal an appropriate package of care. Once I had taken the boys to school, I would drop a newspaper in to him whilst he was having breakfast and then I went to assist Mum with Grey Gables. After lunch, I'd visit before collecting the boys from school and then once they had eaten tea and done their homework we'd go back for an early evening visit too.

Before his return home, I managed to accomplish all the jobs that he had previously wanted to achieve but had felt unable to manage at Grey Gables. I arranged for carpets to be laid in two of the rooms, lino for the kitchen and laundry having first to strip these areas and paint them. In order to make it perfect, I required assistance to remove some of the furniture and take up the carpets and lino which was very heavy work. There was also the removal of these items from outside the house to organise so that Dad wasn't alerted before he entered the house. Nick's partner was amazing but when I asked *him* to remove the stuff in his van you would have thought I had asked for the world. My request was for his sick father's benefit, but he slated me for only talking to him when *I* wanted something and decided I would have to pay for any scratches that were caused. It really was unbelievable especially as we only wanted him to drive the stuff to the tip, for goodness sake.

When Dad returned home, he was thrilled to bits with the improvements astounded at the amount of work I had achieved especially as I was also paying him three visits a day at the same time. It ensured he was able to completely relax and enjoy his new environment especially as I had thrown out their old settee and replaced it with a new one, I had just purchased for myself. We had a few good months where Mum and Dad were able to really enjoy each other's company once again and of course the boys were thrilled to have their hero home.

It was at this point that I decided to step back to afford them the space to adopt and establish new routines with regards to carers suddenly coming into the house. I had recently formed some new friendships with other mums whose children went to school with Joe, so I readily accepted their invites for the opportunity to enjoy days out with them during the Easter Holidays. Again, I succumbed to the misconception of the magician's wand, and I surrendered to the belief that life was levelling out onto a more even keel. How could I be so easily and constantly deceived daring to believe in a hope for a better future when my reality was always just one step away from a smack square to the face.

Chapter 12
The Picnic

It was Monday 30 May 2011 and we were at the start of the spring bank holidays. The children were excited as we were busying ourselves for a group picnic to Pugney's near Wakefield. The sun was belting out its rays and there was barely a cloud in the most beautiful cerulean blue sky. My oldest son Jack, aged 8, was dolloping spoonfuls of tuna mayo onto his bread before neatly spreading it out whilst Joe 4 was slapping ham on his in such a haphazard fashion more was hanging over the crusts. They grabbed a bag of crisps each, ready salted the only ones in the variety packs I never liked and neatly packed the sandwiches into their individual Tupperware tubs. I finished chopping grapes, carrot sticks and cucumber chunks before collating everything together and filling our picnic hamper. We made a good team.

'Bagsy I sit in the front,' shouted Jack, a phrase he had heard his friend Martin say numerous times.

'Not fair,' said Joe, 'I want to sit in the front.'

'No one will be sitting in the front, guys, you are not big enough yet,' I reminded them.

'Martin gets to sit in the front of his car, and he is a year younger than me,' Jack said sullenly.

'His mum might let him, Jack, but by law, children should be 12 years or more, or over 135cm (4'5") tall to sit in the front, you are neither so you will sit comfortably and safely in the back until you are,' I reminded him. (https://www.childcarseats.org.uk/carrying-other-peoples-children/child-seat-and-seat-belt-laws/)

Before he had time to argue the point any further, I opened the fridge to reveal their favourite bottles of dandelion and burdock drinks that I'd secretly stored the night before.

'We had better not forget these,' I suggested.

'Ooh lovely, that's my favourite,' said Joe as if I hadn't realised.

'Here Jack put these in the cooler bag with the grapes, dips and sausages,' I said. 'Right, I think we have everything, let's dance.'

The boys looked at each and started laughing as they always did when I used the phrase "let's dance". Years ago, when I trained as a drugs dog handler, I'd had the privilege of meeting an amazing instructor from the Durham constabulary whenever our vans were loaded with the dogs and food for the day he would always say "shall we dance". I had never forgot him he was such a lovely, talented man so every now and then I would use the phrase in memory of him. Another man who stood out to me from those days worked for the Yorkshire & Humberside Area Team (YHAST) his phrase was "tickety-boo" whenever asked if he was "okay". That was an interesting part of my life where I was able to make a positive impact to the lives of those around me and a time when I was probably at my most confident.

I led my little troupe to the car an orange Renault Scenic Conquest where I firmly secured the food bags with our camping chairs in the boot. The boys jumped into the back, slid into their respective seats and secured their belts in place. I was just about to lock the front door when I realised the picnic blankets were still in the hallway. Once I had got everything into the car, it was time to set off. We were meeting Flora with her 3 boys Danny 6, Mark 4 and Paul 3 at Jenny's house who lived around a mile from our house. So, with my sunglasses in place, the music on, a cursory glance to ensure their seatbelts were clicked in, I turned the engine on and shifted the car into reverse. We were off.

When we arrived at Jennie's house, it was a hive of activity, Martin 6 and Luke 3 were fighting over a water pistol, Jenny was on her knees in front of 18-month-old Holly tussling to get her zip fastened and there was food all over the kitchen units. 'Boys, for goodness sake, take it outside!' She screamed as a jet of water hit the back of her long brown hair.

'Have we come at the wrong time?' I asked.

'No, you're here exactly at the right time,' she said, 'will you take these two outside so I can finish up here. It's not as bad as it looks, honestly, I will have it all packed up in a jiffy.'

'Hello,' we heard Flora call from the front door and then the stampede of Danny, Mark and Paul as they flew past us in search of the others.

Little Holly was the only girl of the group and although Jenny always dressed her in beautiful little dresses, she always ended up blacker than any of our boys. I had met Flora through nursery as her son Mark was the same age as Joe, Flora and Jenny knew each other because their eldest children Danny and Martin were also the same age. Jack being the eldest of the group was fast becoming the leader. As an alliance we had only recently become friends and having spent the Easter holidays meeting up at various outdoor pursuits found that our kids got on really well together and so did we. I enjoyed their company although they were very young mums in comparison to myself, Flora was so laid back she was almost horizontal, Jenny was a bit ditzy and reminded me of the actress Miranda Hart.

After approximately ¾ of an hour, we were finally ready to set off and Pugney's was only a 15-minute drive away so we were soon parked up, unloading the cars and making our way to the water's edge. It was still only 10.30 a.m. so there was plenty of space to choose the best spot where we arranged our blankets in a triangular shape to one another's and secured them in place with our heavy bags of food. Jennie had brought various bits to keep the children entertained as she always did a pack of cards, a football, water pistols, badminton racquets with a shuttlecock, colouring books and pencils for Holly.

As we settled in, I took a moment to breathe in the scene before me. There were swans bobbing about the still waters of the lake, insects hovering around the reeds at its edges, the sun shimmering through a little thicket to my right and a dog scurrying along a nearby footpath. I breathed in the deep calmness of all that nature brought with it slipping my sandals off to twiddle my bare feet in the short grass. As I looked down, I noticed the less than attractive scatterings of cigarette butts stubbed out and left in the fine sand. I must have communicated my distaste in my facial expressions as my trancelike state was abruptly interrupted by the laughter of both Jenny and Flora.

'What?' I said innocently and joined them in their laughter. We had a wonderful day watching the children interact, play games and paddle. The day was filled with the ease of just being, enjoyed with people intent on having a good time. It was carefree, fun and pleasurable with the simplicity of just sitting in the sun doing nothing but relaxing, chatting and playing. The varying foods that the three families had brought made a substantial picnic when put together and we were all satisfied and content with our portion.

We stayed until the late afternoon before collecting our things together, bagging our rubbish and making our way to our respective cars. As always some of the children wished to travel in different cars so they swapped their brothers for a friend not thinking we knew their plan was to remain together and reduce the potential of going home early. So, we arranged to meet at Jennie's house where our day had begun due to Holly's needs being the greatest and bid a short farewell until we arrived. My car was very noisy even though I only had Joe and Luke as we had to have their favourite CD playing the songs they had been learning in nursery.

As the children sang, their feet absentmindedly kicking the back of my seat, I glanced in the rear-view mirror with such pride and delight feeling so blessed at how happy we all were. It was one of those moments where you want to bottle up the laughter and deep contentment or to simply press the pause button and stay in that moment forever. I finally felt at peace with my life, the boys were thriving at school they had lots of friends and our social activities were made easier on me with the support and inclusion of my new families. Life felt good but little did I know that the clock had never stopped ticking and the countdown was almost upon me and it was only a matter of minutes.

Chapter 13
The Plot Thickens

My mobile rang but given my pre-distracted state I simply answered it without even glancing at the caller identity still laughing. 'Hello,' I said trying to keep my emotions in check.

The person on the other side of the phone was hysterical and crying, 'They've arrested him.'

'Sorry?' I was confused.

'Lois, they have arrested him.' More sobbing.

I tried to pinpoint the voice, but it was neon impossible to gain any form of recognition amidst the level of despair but obviously the person knew me because they had used my name. 'I am sorry, who is this and who has been arrested?' I ventured again.

'Him, He has been arrested,' she stated.

My blood went cold as I suddenly understood. My face must have reflected my inner thoughts as I tried desperately hard to quash down the bile that was threatening to coarse its unnatural way upwards. The room had instantly become silent, no one daring to breathe, hesitant in that moment of knowing once the information was revealed nothing would ever be the same again. I removed the phone from my ear to identify what was written on the screen but it just confirmed what I already knew. As I held the jaggedly protruded device in my hand staring at it like it was some type of explosive, I knew my thoughts must have been reflected upon my face. I had to think fast before the boys' sense of security was obliterated.

'Sorry I just need to take this in here Jenny is that ok?' I urged, staring wide-eyed at the boys to indicate it needed to be out of their earshot.

She just vigorously nodded and then as I exited, I could hear her attempts to distract everyone, 'Right, who is going to be the first to use the toilet and wash their hands ready for a drink and snacks?' Bless her.

I slipped into the front room and quietly closed the door behind me before I returned to the caller. 'Ruby, what do you mean they have arrested him? For what?' I ventured trying in vain to remain calm. My initial thought was for drink driving or a minor misdemeanour that would easily be cleared up.

'For interfering with his own kids,' she said.

'What?' I screeched aloud. The magnification and ramification of what she was revealing was both totally shocking and alarming beyond all measure.

'I had to tell you because the shit is really going to hit the fan and I have to go to the police station now,' she told me.

I was unable to get my head around why she should have to go to the police station and falsely thought his one phone call had been to her and so she was going to support him or was collecting him or something. So, I remained quiet that bit too long so in her heightened state she reiterated her last statement.

'Lois, I have to go to the police station as they need me to make a statement,' she offered.

'Hold on a minute, Ruby, why do you need to go and what statement are you making, I am confused?' Nothing was really computing in my now frazzled brain.

She was still in a heightened stated of emotion and continued to sob throughout as she explained that the police had to have her statement because she had known what was going on. This absolutely blew my mind and my initial thought was how could she just sit back and allow this to happen. Afterall they were best mates. Little did I know at the time but she was responsible for his arrest and moreover she had actively been part of an 18-month investigation into his offending behaviour. She told me that she would have to go as the police were expecting her to arrive at the station by 8pm. I quickly checked the time it was 18.45, despite it being the last thing I wanted to do I knew I had to support her.

'You can't go there alone, Ruby, I will meet you at the police station,' I told her.

'But it is Huddersfield police station that are expecting me,' she said. Which I guess made sense as it was nearer her location, I had just assumed it would have been the main one in Wakefield. Then I reasoned to myself that if he were being held at Wakefield, then her going somewhere else would make more sense.

'Don't go anywhere,' I told her. 'You cannot drive in this state; I am on my way.' I ended the call.

I nipped into the kitchen where I found Jenny organising drinks for the children, Joe and Luke avidly awaiting the filling of their plastic beakers. Once they had vacated the area, I asked if it was ok for the boys to remain with her as I had a family emergency, it was. Poor Jenny thought one of my parents had passed away from the grave look on my face so respectfully didn't ask. We hadn't been friends long but I appreciated her devotion and I knew without any doubt both my boys would be fine so it was one less thing to worry about.

On the drive over to the small village where Ruby lived, there were an abundance of thoughts raging my troubled mind and I knew I would have to bring them in to check if I was going to get to the bottom of things. When I arrived, she was quick to come out as though she had been waiting at the door. She opened the passenger door and slipped into the seat next to me, it was hard not to notice the ashen pallor of her skin.

'Thank you,' she offered.

I waited for her to pull the seatbelt across her and to fix it in place before I began to manoeuvre the car away from the kerb and then remained silent until she was ready to begin. She shuffled in her seat before settling with her small cross over bag upon her lap then it began. She told me that he had been away for the bank holiday weekend to a vintage vehicle show somewhere and that upon his return the police had been in situ ready to arrest him. In the back of his van, they had found a mattress.

'But why were they ready to arrest him? They must have been conducting a prior investigation to have a warrant issued for his arrest,' I said perplexed.

'The thing is Sarah (his wife) has had suspicions for a while that he has been abusing the kids,' she continued.

'But yet she was still sending them to him for overnight stays,' I argued, knowing full well both Ruby and Sarah had been out a couple of weeks prior and that the children had been with him.

'Well anyway,' she dismissed, 'the police have been looking into many facts and feel they have sufficient evidence to take him in for questioning.'

'So where has all this evidence come from? How many people are involved?' I was anticipating there could be many complaints as he seemed to have had lots of relationships with people who had young children. I felt nauseous.

Ruby went on to say that she knew for certain that he had abused his two young children and due to this she had urged Sarah to contact the police. Wow so she was the one driving the investigation, my mind was beginning to splinter into all avenues of possibilities. She then described being at Sarah's house and witnessing a condemning reaction Elena had displayed when a Social Worker knocked on the door. Apparently, she had become nothing less than hysterical screaming and crying that they were there to take her daddy away and that he would have to go to prison and it was all her fault. Both Ruby and Sarah, had tried to comfort her but she was panic-stricken clinging to the banister and fearful of her own safety. I was absolutely flabbergasted to think this poor child of only 6 years of age had been subjected to any form of abuse was sickening.

I then remembered a couple of years prior when I had been at Kelly's house. We were in the kitchen where I was sat at their table and Kelly was leaning against the units. Out of nowhere, she suddenly mentioned that Sarah had taken Elena to the doctor due to some rash around her face. When the Dr had first examined her, he had diagnosed impetigo but then she had returned where he now discovered the rash was in her mouth and her throat. My initial reaction had been like anyone else's would have been "the poor love that must be horrific for her and very painful trying to eat and swallow".

With a knowing glint in her eye, Kelly revealed what she was really trying to communicate, 'Yes, it makes you wonder what he has been doing to her, doesn't it?'

Once she'd soaked up my facial reaction, she had simply turned with a grin on her face and began doing the washing up as though this was a normal comment. I never knew why she always got such enjoyment out of being the one to deliver catastrophic information, but she positively revelled in it. Needless to say, I had to challenge her at the time regarding her statement as it couldn't just be ignored.

I'd said to her, 'If you even think for a minute he has done anything of that nature to any child, you should be taking action, it is not something that should ever be ignored.' But as far as she was concerned the subject was finished. At the time, I wasn't privy to another essential piece of information thus being Kelly's own daughter Haley had shared details with her about another potentially abused child. Kelly had failed to protect that child too by simply turning the other cheek. In the coming months, she would demonstrate this attitude quite blatantly by challenging Ruby upon 'why she was getting involved in the investigation as they weren't her children.'

Outrageous to think this woman trained as a nursery worker and this is her approach to child exploitation. Knowing first-hand the real threat he was to young children I could neither walk away nor ignore it so had passed the information on to a social worker friend of mine. She contacted the appropriate authorities on my behalf but apparently the girl who took the call knew him and years later we found out that she had failed to act upon the information.

Inevitably it made me wonder what Ruby's intention was right now, so I decided to enquire just so I knew whether I was firmly with her or against her.

'So, when we arrive at the police station, Ruby, what is your plan?' I asked.

'My plan?' she queried, confused.

'Yes, your plan,' I affirmed. 'Is it your intention to stand in the gap for these children and be the voice for them and so divulge everything you know? Or is it a case of tell the police nothing like it's them and us out of some misplaced family loyalty?' I wondered.

'I intend to tell them everything as far as I am concerned; there will be nothing held back,' she said and these were her exact words, 'I am going to get the bastard.'

The bitterness with which she spat out the last seven words was intense, and I got the distinct impression she had a score to settle and nothing nor anyone was going to stop her. Gone was the quivering wreak of a person who could barely speak on the phone now replaced by a venomous woman with revenge on her mind. I let the change sink in and wondered what had occurred between Ruby and him that had caused her to suddenly hate him. Up until recently they had been enjoying nights out together, always seen in cahoots with one another but now suddenly she was intent on "getting the bastard". The plot thickened.

Chapter 14
Evans and Rathbone

I pulled into the car park of the police station which was like every other one in the country about as welcoming as sex just after birth. The gravel crunched beneath my tyres as I inched my way towards the nearest available space. Despite the task ahead, Ruby did not seem fazed, in fact she positively looked like a woman on a mission. Unlike Ruby, I was attempting to suppress the butterflies doing a manic dance within my stomach. As we neared the door, I suddenly considered the possibility of not being able to go through with it, but my heart told me I had no option.

'When you introduce me, Ruby, just say I am Lois who has come along to support you, nothing more,' I said.

She looked quizzically at me but when I offered no explanation she simply shrugged and said, 'Yeah ok, whatever.'

Ruby marched her way in with all the confidence of a seagull darting for a gulp of passer-by's food. It made me feel she had been here many times before though it did nothing to quash my own nerves.

We walked through a glass door to a small, vestibuled entrance which had the customary noticeboard containing a number of ear dogged posters. Some depicting the need to report non-emergency incidents via 101 rather than England's emergency number of 999. Others were of the usual nature offering information where to obtain help for drug related issues and the need to stop domestic abuse. I followed Ruby through to the main entrance which was no bigger than a garden shed it was also cluttered with information. It may as well have been pasted in newsprint as there was too much for the eye to focus on any one item in particular as it was far too busy. Maybe this was the vibe that all stations went for, but the bleakness did nothing to increase my courage.

A lady appeared at the reception hatch to which Ruby was quick to attend whereas I stayed centrally within the room. The woman was dressed in uniform though a tad unkempt like she had just been getting forty winks until she was alerted to our presence. She wore an indifferent expression upon her face until Ruby introduced herself.

'Hi, I am Ruby Williams. I am here to see PC Simon Evans with regards to making a statement,' she declared.

'Ahh, yes,' the woman began, 'we have been expecting you, if you just take a seat, PC Evans will be with you shortly.' She gave us her winning smile. It was hard to gauge if she was happy to see us or not, as it was the kind of fake smile with no feeling behind it, like she'd been practising it in front of the mirror.

We had only just managed to sit our bums on to the hard wooden seats when a man and a woman came through a door to the left of the hatch. I was right to assume he was PC Simon Evans. The lady was a PC Emma Rathbone. Ruby introduced me as I had suggested and then we were led into a shabby little room with a huge table in the middle. There was barely enough room for anything else. I immediately noticed that upon the table was a tape recorder, which unnerved me. To the far diagonal corner of the room was a little hand basin to its right a window and to its left a fireplace with another door directly opposite us next to it. The officers offered us the seats in front of them, so our backs were to the fireplace whilst they took the seats nearest to the door. I suddenly felt hemmed in, it was not a comfortable position.

'As I said earlier, Ruby (pause); you don't mind me calling you Ruby, do you?' PC Evans enquired.

'No that is absolutely fine,' Ruby confidently replied.

'Good, thank you,' he began. 'Due to the sensitivity of the case and also because we have one other in custody awaiting questioning, I have to let you know I will be recording the interview today. Do you understand that Ruby and give your consent to the interview being recorded?' he asked.

'I can confirm I have no objections to the interview being recorded,' Ruby said very formally.

'Thank you, PC Rathbone will be sitting in today and also scribing on our behalf for our records. At our conclusion, you will then have a chance to read through the statement that she has taken, make any alterations or if you agree it is an accurate account of what we have discussed I will then ask you to sign and date it. Is that clear so far?' He said and we both nodded to him in agreement.

'Before we get started, are there any questions or is there anything you're not quite sure about?' PC Rathbone asked.

'No, I am good to go,' Ruby replied a little too enthusiastically for my liking as though she was enjoying herself a bit too much.

'So, for the purpose of the tape I am introducing myself, I am PC Simon Evans I am conducting an interview on behalf of Wakefield Metropolitan District Police in connection with a complaint received regarding Mr Timothy Rodgers. It is Mon 30 May 2011,' he checks his watch 'it is now 20.11hrs, also present are...' And he turns to his left.

'PC Emma Rathbone,' she said. He nodded to both Ruby and me.

'Ruby Williams,' said Ruby.

'I am Lois, Ruby's support,' I spoke.

'Right, with the formalities conducted the purpose of this meeting is to collate a voluntary statement by yourself Ruby with regards to an ongoing investigation about your brother, Timothy Rodgers.'

The mere mention of *his* name sent a shiver down my spine and caused me to swallow hard. Evans gave me a cursory glance then returned his concentration back to Ruby, much to her delight. I couldn't help noticing the way she was intently enjoying their full attention; this was all about her and the information she had for them, and it seemed she was going to be making the most of it.

'So, Ruby, I would like you to tell me in your own words what your relationship is like with Timothy, your brother?' PC Evans enquired.

'We have always had a difficult relationship,' she started.

I had to really concentrate on not reacting as this was news to me. From my perspective, they had always been as thick as thieves and went out together all the time. I had never known a time at all where they did not get on or were not out drinking together not to mention Ruby was best mates with his wife and always at their house. The plot really did thicken, so inevitably I was confused however she had made the statement from the outset 'she was going to get the bastard,' so I was intent on listening carefully to see what I could learn.

'When you say "always", how far back are you talking? Is it a number of years or further back?' asked PC Evans.

'It has been a lot longer than a few years. I would say back to when I was a child,' she stated.

'Was there a time that you remember when you did have a good relationship with Timothy?' he asked.

'No,' she stated adamantly, 'I never liked him, he always made me feel very uncomfortable.'

'Was there anything in particular he did or said that caused you to feel uncomfortable?' he asked.

'It is awfully embarrassing but yes there were several occasions that he made me feel uncomfortable,' she told him.

'I know this is difficult, Ruby, but could you be more specific about how he made you feel uncomfortable,' he urged.

'Yes,' she said but there was a pause as though she was trying to muster up the words.

'In your own time, Ruby,' he gently encouraged.

'When I was young, he would watch me getting dressed,' she blurted out.'

'At what age do you estimate this might have been?' he wondered.

'I was around 12 years of age,' Ruby responded.

'And where were you at the times he would watch you?' he asked.

'I would be getting out of the shower,' she said.

'Just so I have a clear picture Ruby, can you describe in more detail the exact scene of the alleged offence?' he asked.

'At our parents' house, we had a downstairs bathroom, the door has two glass panels in them, at first he used to be looking through there,' she offered.

'You said when you got out of the shower,' he asked.

'Yes, the room layout was with the door being to the far right, the sink to the left of the door with the toilet straight ahead. The shower was after the sink but was partitioned by a wall. So, it was round the corner, so to speak with another window opposite it that had a fan built into it.' She accurately described whilst gesticulating with her hands to further communicate its layout. PC Rathbone made a quick drawing in her notes to further identify Ruby's account.

'So how could he see in to observe you getting dressed, Ruby?' he queried.

'There is a long radiator opposite the sink next to the toilet where I would hang my clothes once I had stepped out of the shower, I would walk into the centre of the room to dry myself and get dressed. Here I would be fully exposed from the position of the door and he would look through the window at me,' she concluded.

'Did you ever challenge him about this behaviour Ruby?' he asked.

'I had no way of knowing how long it had been going on but one day I thought I had seen the outline of a shadow of someone standing there. You see there is a large laundry adjacent to the shower room and I didn't always put the light on in there so he could have been stood there concealed by the darkness at any time watching me. However, one day when I took a shower it had been daytime, and I definitely saw him illuminated there.'

'So, how did you react at seeing the outline of a shadow of someone standing there?' he asked.

'I grabbed my towel to cover my nakedness then shouted out and the figure disappeared. After that, I was more conscious of being exposed so I would hang my dressing gown at the back of the door and only shower with the outer light on. That way I could keep a look at the door, but it made me extremely self-conscious,' she spoke.

'How do you know that the person was Timothy? Surely you could not identify him from a shadow?' he put forward.

'No, I couldn't, you're right but not long after this incident I was in the shower room again when I thought I had heard something in the courtyard at the back of the house. I threw my dressing gown on, stood on the toilet seat and looked through the open downstairs window. He was lurking about right outside the window trying to peer in, so I know without a shadow of a doubt he was the culprit guilty of voyeurism,' she said definitively.

'Did you say anything to him, Ruby?' he enquired.

'Yes, I called him a dirty pig and told him to get lost or I would tell on him,' she said.

'Did you tell anyone else, Ruby?' he asked her.

'Yes, I told my mum,' she said giving me the slightest of sideways glances.

I was horrified with all manner of thoughts pushing their way into my head until it rested on the most horrendous realisation that if she was 12 when this was going on, I would have been 8! Things started to fall into place like the coins in a slot machine, had this been the catalyst that had forced Mum into confronting me all those years ago when I was running down the steps? Instead of carefully looking into the possibilities of what she was being presented with, she had succumbed to her own anger at the horror of her son's behaviour. All along she had only been interested in gaining information to substantiate and give weight to Ruby's claim. It was more about how this had affected Ruby it was never about accusing me but there again nor was it about protecting me either. I had no way of knowing whether she had confronted him like she had me but either way she still failed to take any viable action because here we were decades later dealing with his heinous behaviour. I felt sick.

'How did your mum react to this information after all he was her son,' he asked.

'She was upset and angry. Yes, he was her son, but I was also her young daughter,' she offered.

'So, what action did your mum take?' he enquired.

'She told me to make sure I only got showered when she was at home and that I was to always inform her when I did so she could keep an eye on his whereabouts,' she said.

'Was that all she did?' he asked.

'No (pause), she was really worried that if he had an unhealthy interest in me that my little sister may also be at risk. She was only about 8 at the time. Mum did try to find out if she had encountered any problems with him, but she clammed up and wouldn't talk,' she admitted with another slight sideways glance at me.

I couldn't believe what I was hearing, she tried to find out if there had been any problems. No, she didn't; her confrontation came across as though she was accusing me of behaving inappropriately. I felt so upset at this revelation but had to sit there with a stoic expression on my face, no reaction just to endure it in silence. Then it also dawned upon me that the secret conversations they had been having and I'd assumed were about me causing the paranoia were actually about him! I felt dreadful these shocking declarations should have been revealed so much sooner and at the very latest when the three of us had talked after mine and Ruby's night out. I had been 26 at that time and now I was 44!

They had both held this information but neither one of them had chosen to share it with me, not even when they knew the extent of what I had experienced. I had since undergone years of therapy not only due to the trauma of sexual abuse but the fact that it had been compounded by the lack of protection, the enforced paranoia and more importantly the wealth of blame, shame and guilt that had swarmed me. These dominant, untruthful emotions had overpowered my ability to live a normal, fulfilling and free existence. I had been trapped, lost and alone without any support, love or reassurance to the contrary so this had stolen my informative years, my teens and much of my adult life. My whole family had stolen that from me because no one had ever chosen to stand in the gap for me.

At that moment, my head began to swirl at the depth to which I had been betrayed and the pain and suffering I had experienced. He had been allowed to get off scot-free because they had let him, and I had been the sacrificial lamb nothing more and nothing less. But there was one thing for sure a new Phoenix was about rise from these ashes as no more of my life was going to be stolen, controlled or affected by any of them.

'So, were there any other incidents regarding Timothy that we need to be made aware of, Ruby?'

'Yes, two other major ones that come to mind,' she admitted then paused. I was unsure if it was for dramatic effect, whether she was embarrassed or suddenly uncomfortable because I was sat there.

'Do you need to take a moment, Ruby?' PC Rathbone asked.

'No, I am Ok,' she answered.

'Would you like a glass of water?' Rathbone asked.

'NO, thank you.' Ruby replied.

'It's ok Ruby, I know this is difficult just take your time,' PC Evans reassured her.

'I was about 14 years of age so Timothy would have been around 18,' she began. 'He had a red van with flames painted along the sides and he used to come down to school at lunchtimes. My friends thought he was really cool. One day I had left a book at home that I really needed during the afternoon, so he gave me a lift back for it. We had a quick sandwich and then when we were ready to set off back, he suddenly locked the outside door instead of going through it. It confused me at first, I thought he was just mucking around so I told him to hurry up because I would be late back to school.'

'So, what happened then?' Urged Evans.

'He asked me if I had ever had sex, I was like urrggh why you would even say that and I tried to reach the key to unlock the door to get out,' she said.

'How did it make you feel being alone there with him and his choice of conversation?' Evans asked.

'I felt trapped, uncomfortable and wary,' she responded.

'So, you had made it clear you were not happy with his choice of conversation how did he respond?' asked Evans.

'He was cocky and menacing, he stood in front of the door barring my exit then said if I hadn't had sex yet wouldn't I like to know what it felt like. I was disgusted and did not appreciate where this was going. I wanted to get back to the safety of school and my friends,' she stated.

'So, are you saying you felt threatened by his conduct and the conversation he was having with you?' Rathbone enquired.

'Yes absolutely, I was there alone in a great big house with no one to witness what was going on. I was worried about what he might do which left me feeling unsafe and trapped,' she said.

'What happened next, Ruby,' Evans asked.

'He wasn't leaving it; he knew how vulnerable I was with no one there to help me and tried to coerce and manipulate me into letting him have sex with me on the pretext of me finding out how it felt,' she said.

'Is that what happened, Ruby, did you have sex with him?' Evans enquired.

'No, absolutely not,' she stated adamantly. 'His ploy was ridiculous and only served to gratify himself so I told him not to be stupid and that if he wasn't going to take me back to school I would walk. I then lunged towards the door.'

'So how did Timothy respond?' asked Rathbone.

'He threw his head back and just laughed like it was some kind of a joke,' Ruby said.

'And did you think it was a joke, Ruby?' Evans enquired.

'Absolutely not, he was testing the waters and I have no doubt he would have gone through with it had I agreed,' she said.

'Did he apologise for his behaviour?' Evans asked.

'No, he laughed it off at the time trying to make out he was only joking and mocked me for not wanting to get in his van to go back to school. However due to the time I had no option I had to accept the lift, or I would have got in to trouble,' she said.

'But surely if Timothy had made you feel the things you have just described uncomfortable, threatened and unsafe getting in the van with him could have put you at further risk,' he queried.

'I had no choice. I would have been late back to school and let's face it I could hardly excuse my lateness stating my brother had just tried to have sex with me,' she said trying to sound aloof, but anger was creeping in.

'Did he ever bring the subject up about this incident or ever mention it again?'

'No, it was as though the incident had never occurred,' she said.

'Did you tell anyone else what had happened to you?' Evans wondered.

'I told my friend Sally when I got back to school and I also told my mum when I got home,' she told him. I was horrified; another missed opportunity to take him to task.

'Did your mum do anything about this incident?' Evans asked her.

'Not that I am aware of,' she said innocently.

'So earlier you stated there were two major incidents that you wanted to tell us about, what was the second one?' He delved.

'The next one was when I was about 21,' she began as I was doing a quick calculation in my head. This would have been around 1984 to 1985 and the time he had attempted to assault me when I was asleep. Inside I was beginning to get really angry but for the time being I had to settle for digging my nails into my hands to take the mental pain elsewhere.

'Did this incident also take place at home, Ruby?' he asked.

'No, this time we had been out round the pubs in Ossett and were laughing about something as we made our way back home. We had just crossed the road at the top of West Wells where there is a grassy area, and we were walking down the footpath that takes you along a winding road to Grey Gables. Ahead of us was an old mill where they sold wool and cottons. He suddenly grabbed my arm and said, "come on, me and you now behind that mill, I will give you something to laugh about!" Before I had any chance to react, he suddenly grabbed my hand and forced it towards his privates. I instantly recoiled in disgust as he had an erection,' she told us.

'Was he perturbed by your reaction?' Rathbone asked.

'No, in fact he continued to attempt to gain my submission by trying to lead me towards the concealed area behind the mill,' she said.

'Did you go there with him?' Evans asked.

'No,' she exclaimed indignantly. 'I yanked my arm free and pushed him away. I then began running along the path towards our home.'

'Did he follow you or try to stop you in any way?' Evans enquired.

'He didn't get a chance because I was off like a whippet,' she explained.

'Did you speak to anyone when you arrived home to tell them what had just happened to you?' He questioned.

'No, everyone was in bed and Mum was asleep in the lounge, so I went to my room feeling upset, angry and shocked. Although it had appeared to be an impulsive act, it was still an assault against me that had happened without any provocation. The fact that it was a sexual assault, and the perpetrator was my brother both repulsed and nauseated me.' She spoke.

'Did you speak to anyone the next day?' Evans asked.

'No, I felt ashamed and embarrassed as this was the second time he had attempted to embark upon a sexual act with me. It made me feel bad within myself as though I must be giving the wrong signals to him or something. So, I never said anything and tried to keep my distance from him ensuring I was never left alone with him again,' she stated.

I knew this to be completely untrue as Timothy, Nick and Ruby all went away on holiday together with their partners at the time. Equally many times afterwards I had been out having drinks with friends and they were always together. I could even recall one of the times we had been in a pub at the same times and when Ruby went to the toilet Timothy said to this guy, 'isn't she gorgeous, got a right pair of tits on her.' This guy had uttered in agreement then asked if she was his girlfriend to which I had interjected with disgust, 'no that was his sister!' The guy looked at him with such disdain and walked away not wanting to be near him.

'You mentioned your younger sister earlier Ruby I was just wondering if anything came to light about any inappropriate behaviour towards her that you know about?' Rathbone asked.

'That is something I think you would be better asking her,' she dismissed.

'Is there anything further you would like to add, Ruby?' asked Rathbone.

'No, I think that is everything,' she spoke.

'Ok then, I am concluding the interview,' he checked his watch, 'it is now 21.34.' he switched off the tape recorder and turned to Rathbone. 'Is there anything you want to clarify?' Evans asked.

'No,' she told him then turning back to Ruby, 'would you just like to read through the statement and if you are happy with it sign and date each piece at the top here, and the bottom there,' she said indicating the spots with her index finger.

As Ruby read through the statement, I tried to look nonchalant gazing around the room my eyes not resting on anything specifically. Evans and Rathbone just made general chitchat to pass the time. Once Ruby had finished, she signed it on each part that Rathbone had indicated then she asked to use the toilet. It was situated through the door next to the fireplace that we had seen on our arrival. Once she had disappeared, I took the opportunity to speak.

'Apart from Timothy, Ruby has 3 other siblings so does this mean you will need to speak to them too?' I asked innocently.

Evans looked up as though disinterested but politely answered, 'Yes it would be standard practise to gather information by interviewing other family members. And in a case of this nature, it can prove to be an integral part of the investigation to substantiate the claims made. So, it is imperative that they are not alerted beforehand,' he told me.

'Yes,' I said, 'I can imagine you would want to gain their immediate and true response to the alleged offences he is accused of.' At this point, I felt compelled to come clean so leant in further towards them and said quietly, 'Then I will tell you now that I am Lois, and I am Ruby's youngest sister.'

They both looked at each other aghast.

I went on, 'I am prepared to give you my statement because he did sexually abuse me as a child, but I cannot do this tomorrow as I need to take my dad to the hospital for his chemotherapy treatment,' I informed them.

'Right ok,' they stammered. At this point, Ruby re-entered the room from the toilet area giving Evans and Rathbone the cue to stand up simultaneously to end their discomfort at this new declaration.

'Actually, there is one other thing,' Ruby began as she reached the table, 'Mum knows all about this investigation.' She revealed.

'When you say all about it, what exactly do you mean?' Rathbone asked.

'All the evidence we collated and provided about Timothy during the investigation, I discussed it with Mum throughout,' she stated.

Now it was my time to look aghast!

'Right, I will make a note of that Ruby and if that is everything, I would like to thank you both for coming in this evening and to wish you both a safe journey home.' He then guided us back through the reception area and corridor to the outside door holding it open for us to walk through.

The journey back to Ruby's was tense to say the least she had expunged herself, but I still had a million questions with one major one that I would not be able to ignore.

'When you say Mum knows about the evidence "we collated and provided", what did you actually mean?' I asked her.

'Sarah was suspicious that things were not right when the children went to stay with him, because afterwards they started behaving differently. Then she was called into school because little Danny was playing kiss catch but he was trying to pull the girls skirts up and kiss their pants. He also tried to slip his finger down the top of Elena's bottom. When Sarah confronted him, he innocently said "well Daddy does it." Then there was the issue with Elena and the social worker she was absolutely hysterical not to mention the sores in her mouth and throat,' she said.

'So how long has this been going on?' I wondered.

'For about 18 months,' she revealed.

'And you're saying that all this time Mum knew all about it but said nothing!' I said incredulously.

'I swore her to secrecy,' she started, 'we couldn't let it get out in case he found out what we were doing.'

'So, all this time you have been working with Sarah to as you say, "get the bastard" and Mum knows all about it?' I queried.

'Yes.' She had no remorse which was understandable but also, she had no insight in how that could have affected Mum or the hurt I felt that this had been going on behind my back and I was only just hearing about it now when she was going in to provide a statement.

It was safe to say I was shocked but just as equally I was puzzled. I still could not understand why Ruby had chosen to ring me. I knew her well enough to know she did not do things by half measures she was calculated so there would have to be a specific reason for her decision. After all, she had persistently made me aware that she couldn't bear being in my company for more than ten minutes and absolutely loathed me. So, was she just taking advantage of my good nature knowing that I would drop everything and be there for her? No, it was more likely that she was in some way manipulating me and the situation to orchestrate a particular outcome. That was her usual game manipulating people for her own amends.

What I could not understand was why any of the information she had just sworn to be the truth to the police had never become known before. Her and Timothy had always been like best buddies and yet she was telling the police that she had never liked him, and they had never had a good relationship. Something just didn't add up like why she was she so adamant she was 'going to get the bastard.' Was she using me because she knew my evidence would be crucial to securing a conviction if it came to it. Or was she using what had happened to me to make her claims seem viable to add weight to the investigation. I felt sick at the thought that I could be being exploited for her benefit to bring about his downfall. But more nauseating than that was finding out Mum had been a part of this whole charade yet had said absolutely nothing about it nor tried to warn me in advance. I could not comprehend that I'd had to sit there in front of the police and listen to the things Tim had allegedly done to her without my having any prior knowledge.

My mind was shattering into shards of glass causing splintering wounds within my own brain just trying to take in these astounding admissions. I could scarce believe that my light-hearted picnic with the boys and friends laughing, singing and enjoying ourselves had been earlier on today. What a stark contrast my thoughts and feelings were now that I had been given a harsh reality check.

There were a lot of things unclear right now but one thing I did know was that I needed to get away from here, to get away from her and to scrub the remnants of this evening off me. Yes, I needed a long hot soak to absorb my thoughts, but little did I know the full extent of the explosion that she had just ignited. The countdown was getting ever closer, and the clock was forever ticking. Tick tock, tick tock.

Chapter 15
Promise Me!

Once we had left the police station and I had dropped Ruby off, I was grateful for the solitude of my car once again though I continued my journey on autopilot. It was late, I was tired and glad to be able to go home without having to explain anything to anyone or to take back the responsibility for the boys. Jenny had turned out to be a good friend immediately stepping in when I had needed her, of that I was most thankful I mused as I lost myself in the winding country roads towards home. The spell was abruptly severed when my mobile rang so I clicked the button on the steering wheel to answer.

'They are at the garage,' Ruby screeched hysterically.

'What, who are?' I asked.

'The police!' she stated.

'Why, what is going on?' I asked alarmed at this new piece of information not feeling that I could actually take in anymore.

'They are searching it for evidence, there are loads of them all over it, you need to get there,' she pushed.

'Hold on, how do you know they are there?' I asked.

'Sarah has just told me,' she said.

I was perplexed, why would Sarah, Timothy's wife, be informing Ruby that the police were at the garage? It didn't make any sense, it was late at night, she didn't live in the vicinity, she had 2 small children so it was not like she would have been passing by at this hour. Also, I had only just dropped Ruby off and was a mere 15 minutes down the road and yet she suddenly knew this was happening right now. It did not make sense and I was beginning to feel there was a bigger picture happening here to which I wasn't privy. I was feeling like some kind of pawn.

Unless both Ruby and Sarah were working in cahoots and as soon as Id dropped Ruby off, she had rung her to let her know how it had gone with the police. Perhaps they had known in advance that the garage was going to be raided and maybe Sarah had arranged a babysitter so she could keep a close eye on it, whilst Ruby was simultaneously at the police station. It would certainly explain how she had come by the information so quickly. I was beginning to think that I was right and my strings were being pulled in yet another one of Ruby's orchestrated performances. I concluded that I would have to be very careful how I trod, or I could potentially be used as their scapegoat. After all, Ruby loved giving other people the bullets to fire whilst she stood back and watched the fireworks.

In the meantime, although I was unsure what was going on I knew I would have to go and check out what was happening at the yard just to satisfy my own curiosity. Then it struck me that if Ruby did know about this all along and it was just another card, she was playing to feign innocence. Let us face it there was no better alibi of innocence if you were at a police station being interviewed at the same time. Is that why she called me, to feign innocence or worse still, was it possible I was merely her gullible witness. Nevertheless, I swung by the garage to see it lit up like Blackpool illuminations with a number of police personnel all over it.

As I sat there at the top of the yard, I felt overwhelmed, it seemed there definitely was a much bigger picture than I had been led to believe and there was a lot more going on that was yet to be revealed. My concern at that moment was for my poor father a retired businessman, an upstanding man in the community loved for his humour, integrity, honesty and excellent work ethics. I couldn't help thinking that as he slept soundly tonight, tomorrow could be a whole different story. I knew it would devastate his world to see the police swarming all over what was both his and his father's business, their pride and joy. I had no idea of the magnitude of what I had just been dragged into but knew that tomorrow morning I would have to put it aside to support him at his hospital appointment. As I chewed over the number of skeletons buried in this ever-increasing graveyard I suddenly wondered if Mum had ever enlightened Dad or had he been kept in the dark too. What a blow that would be for him.

I made my way home, the tension peaking along my shoulders and neck, deciding on a quick shower as I desperately yearned for the comfort and security of my own bed. Inevitably sleep did not come easy and when I finally succumbed, it was to being chased by the police, helicopters overhead monitoring my every move until I was cornered in some abandoned building. When I woke, it was with the dread of capture to find myself alone at home in my room.

I tried to play through the events of the night before noting how composed Ruby had been. The confidence in which she had marched into the police station the way in which she had enjoyed the interview and the definitive answers. Then there were the sideways glances at me. Was she really embarrassed or just attempting to observe my reactions knowing full well I was hearing the account of her experiences for the very first time. Why had she initially telephoned me? Afterall the last time she had called would have been a couple of years prior and this had only been to attempt to ruin my wedding and to cause stress and discord between Kelly and I.

In true Ruby style, she had then not spoken to me for around 18 months not even when Joe had been born or when we were in the same room together. Yet she chooses to contact me when in apparent desperation and needing support. It seemed that there was something a little too convenient almost premeditated about her choice especially as I am the one, she knew he had abused. There had also been something almost sinister in the determination of her phrase 'I am going to get the bastard.' Things definitely did not add up and now I had no choice but to see how this was going to play out. Whether I wanted to be in it or not, I had just been dragged into a mighty shit show. I knew I would be forced to walk over hot coals; I knew it would be uncomfortable and perhaps dangerous and that someone was going to get burnt I just hoped it wasn't me this time.

I got myself showered and dressed then messaged Jenny to tell her that I was on my way and set off to collect the boys. Inevitably she was intrigued to find out what the emergency had been to cause me to drop everything and go. I gave her a very brief explanation without wanting to say too much as there was little, I knew at this time and then the boys and I went on to Grey Gables. Mum was busy in the laundry whilst Dad was sat, teacup in one hand the newspaper in the other in his favourite chair in the bay window.

'Grandad,' the boys shouted as they went in to greet him.

'Now then, you little rascals, I was beginning to think you two had fallen out with me,' he cheerfully chastised.

'Us?' said Jack, 'never!'

'Never,' Joe copied.

'We went to Pugney's yesterday for a picnic, but we are here today, Grandad,' Jack said earnestly.

'I am only kidding,' Dad said to Jack as Joe scooted up on to the arm of the chair to be as close to his grandad as he could possibly get.

'He is only kidding, Jack,' repeated Joe, feigning prior knowledge.

'Now then, you little scallywag,' Dad said to Joe as he put his teacup down on to the little table next to him, then in one swift move grappled Joe on to his lap to tickle him. Joe squirmed and wriggled but was no match for his grandad who had hands the size of shovels whilst Jack jumped about energised by the infectious screeches escaping Joe's mouth.

Mum came through the door to see what all the commotion was about giving Joe the opportunity to break free of Dad's grasp with his momentary lapse of concentration. 'I think it's time you were setting off for the hospital,' she declared as Jack swung around and threw his arms around her waist.

I glanced at the time on my mobile thankful that it was nearing the time to go as right now I really could even look at Mum never mind be in her company. Ashamed as this made me feel it wasn't as heavy as the weight of the secrets her and Ruby had been engaging in nor the hurt that radiated through me right at that moment. She had failed to protect me again with a replica of all those years ago keeping Ruby's secrets whilst exposing me to the elements of last night. I was angry and knew we would have to leave swiftly before Dad picked up on the sudden change in the atmosphere. Joe scooted off into the kitchen to get Dad's shoes whilst Jack ran upstairs for his suit jacket and flat cap then we said our goodbyes and I assisted him into the car.

'You ok? How are you feeling about the treatment today?' I enquired glad to normalise my situation.

'Alright but it's not me I am worried about,' he began.

'What do you mean?' I asked tentatively unsure whether he was aware of the occurrences at his old premises the night before.

'It's your mother, I am telling you she has that dementia,' he said.

'Dementia, why would you even say that?' I was shellshocked.

'I am telling you she is at me all the time and she doesn't make any sense,' he told me.

'Like what?' I queried.

'Well, in the TV room I am allowed to walk in with my slippers on and I can eat in there,' he started.

'Right…' I said not too sure where this was going.

'In the dining room, I am allowed to sit in there and have a cup of tea but I cannot wear my slippers,' he continued.

'What?' this was beginning to sound bonkers.

'Exactly, in the piano room I am allowed to eat and wear my slippers, but I cannot take a drink of tea in there,' he concluded.

'But that's ridiculous, why does it matter where you eat, drink or wear your slippers?' I asked stunned.

'It doesn't or it shouldn't, but she has suddenly put all these restraints on me and I don't know if I am coming or going,' he explained.

I began to laugh not knowing what else to do at such an absurd statement.

'It's not funny, Lois, each day it changes what I can and can't do in each room, so she is at me the whole time and it's making me poorly. I am telling you she has got that dementia.'

I pondered the thought for a moment and the fact that Mum was on the waiting list to see a specialist due to other healthcare professionals raising concerns about her ability to retain information. It was possible that she did have the early stages of dementia however what Dad was describing was quite extreme. Then I had quite a disturbing thought maybe Mum was experiencing these symptoms due to the stress and anxiety of the situation Ruby had put her in. Let's face it if she was sworn to maintain Ruby's confidence regarding some very serious charges against Timothy, her son, which would be enough to cause Mum serious distress.

Over the years, Mum and I had managed to develop a very strong relationship that was initially carved out during my time at university. She had sent food parcels to me and had written 2 to 3 times a week, so I had succeeded in viewing her differently. I had not just seen her as mum, wife, sister or friend but I had gained valuable knowledge and insight of who she was as a person and how she thought and felt about her environment. When I had returned to Grey Gables, she had become a person I would confide in and go to in times of trouble or to ask for advice. I had trusted her, looked up to her even admired her which is why it hurt like hell now to think she hadn't talked to me about what she was going through. I would have described us of having a really close relationship, having enjoyed several holidays abroad, in England and Ireland together and generally we had spent most of our days together over the past 20 years.

When Jack came along, she was at the hospital with me, she supported me through my divorce, and we told each other everything. Therefore, it was hard not to feel that she had let me down again. I really hoped it had not been a replica of the past where she had been secretly plotting with Ruby especially knowing the sensitivity of the situation. No matter which angles I chose to view it from I could not escape the fact that she had chosen not to say anything to me about it. I could not accept that she would wilfully put me in this position and not forewarn me.

At that point, my mobile phone rang. As I momentarily glanced at the screen, I noted it stated, "private number". Wishing to distract myself from the disturbing thoughts I was having and Dad from the conversation we were engaged in I answered it via the handsfree on the car. We were on the M1 going North about to exit at junction 41 to then take the dual carriage way towards Wakefield and to Pinderfields Hospital our destination. I wasn't ready for the voice that came through the loudspeaker especially as I had told Evans and Rathbone that I couldn't give them a statement today as I was taking my father for chemotherapy treatment.

'Hello, is that Lois Rodgers?' the person enquired. It was the unmistakeable authoritarian voice of a police officer, so I quickly reacted before they said anything in Dad's earshot.

'Yes, it is Lois Rodgers, but can I ring you back please or request you contact me after 1pm as I am driving at the moment with my father in the car on our way to hospital,' I responded.

I had hoped that to say I was driving; the police of all people would not want to distract me and that due to the sensitive nature of Timothy's case they would not want to discuss it in the presence of anyone else. Not to mention this was my dad whom they could potentially want to interview independently. Also, the mention of being on the way to the hospital could insinuate an emergency so I really was pulling out all the stops. It worked but not before it had roused Dad's suspicion.

'That's absolutely fine,' the voice agreed, 'I will endeavour to contact you after 1pm, thank you.'

I clicked the button on the steering wheel to end the call as I pulled out of the slip road on to the roundabout to turn right towards Carr Gate. When I was required to change lanes, I inevitably glanced over my left shoulder to ensure no vehicle or bike was on my inner side and that's when I caught Dad's glare.

'What was all that about?' he asked quizzically.

'Not sure yet but no doubt I will find out this afternoon,' and then I purposely changed the subject talking incessantly until we pulled into a disabled parking bay at the hospital. I removed his wheelchair set it up for him at the passenger door and assisted him into it before locking up and pushing him through the hospital entrance. I had brought him several times before, so I knew exactly where I was going and made my way along the winding corridors to the department where staff were avidly awaiting our arrival. I wheeled Dad to the receptionists, desk, gave his details and left him in their care.

I had too much surplus energy to sit in the waiting room twiddling my thumbs, so I chose to take a walk along the passageway to a little portacabin that sold coffee. It was staffed by volunteers who cheerily greeted me as I stepped inside. I managed a painful tight-lipped grin unfortunately I was unable to muster anything greater. The coffee was poured into one of those thin white plastic cups the type that immediately lose shape when you try to pick them up and burn your hands when you hold them. This one was no more than tepid having been depressed from a large cylinder type flask. It looked depressingly weak and as we say in Yorkshire more "like witch piss" so I decided to buy a piece of plain flapjack so the sweetness would take the taste away. Although there was a vacant table in the cabin to consume your refreshments, I knew I wasn't able to tolerate the chirpiness of the two volunteers excitedly chatting about their bank holiday weekend. I walked halfway back along the corridor and just stood gazing out of the dirty windows on to the car park feeling completely miserable.

There were doctors, nurses, visitors and patients streaming up and down this thoroughfare all focused on their given destinations either heads down or faces in phones unaware of anything else around them. A sudden wave of hurt and upset came over me as I realised how invisible we all are to each other. We go about in our own little worlds unless something sends us careering off course into the path of someone else's orbit. Maybe that's how deviants find it so easy to fly under the radar because no one is paying attention to anything or anyone else around them. My thoughts were abruptly halted when I noticed a nurse beginning to wheel Dad out of his treatment room and into the open waiting room, my signal to re-join the rat race.

I greeted him with the deep genuine love, care and consideration only afforded to an elderly parent who has given you the best years of their lives and to whom it is a pleasure to give yours to them. He was jovial and giving the nurses a good old laugh with his dry sense of humour.

'Right,' I said, 'where to now?'

'We're going home, aren't we?' he asked.

'We could if you're really tired and that is where you want to go,' I teased.

'Really tired? I am not past it yet, you know!' he said indignantly.

'I guess it will be a trip to McDonald's for an ice-cream and then we can go sit and eat it in the park if you like.'

'I guess you're right, it will,' he said.

I wheeled Dad back through the corridors and out into the car park where I assisted him into the passenger seat and relocated the chair into the boot before driving on to McDonalds. It was easier for me to go via the drive-through than mess about going inside so we collected our McFlurrys and continued on to Wakefield Park. We had done this so many times before and I knew it was a treat he really looked forward to, it was also an opportunity for him to discuss things with me that were on his mind. Today was no different although I was quite taken aback by the content of his concern. Once we were in our usual spot on the rocks near the bottom of the slide he took a deep breath, turned to me with a pensive look on his face and then paused as if contemplating his exact words.

'What is it?' I asked.

'I want you to promise me if anything happens to me you will look after your mother?' he said earnestly.

'What do you mean nothing is going to happen to you,' I said taken aback by his solemn tone.

'Lois, she is the love of my life and I know I should be there to look after her but what if I go before her?' He said intensely.

'Why are you thinking this way; have you just been given some bad news by the doctor,' I enquired.

'It's not that, I honestly do think she has got dementia, I was reading an article this week in the paper, and it really does sound like her,' he said.

'But Dad, if I was to look up my symptoms on the internet, I am sure I could self-diagnose anything but that doesn't mean it would be accurate or that it is anywhere near the truth,' I tried to appease him.

'I get that, but she is even having trouble making a cup of tea yesterday she gave me hot water and milk forgetting completely about the teabag,' he claimed.

'Really, that doesn't sound good,' I began, 'However we do have her in the system now so let's just see how it pans out and please try not to worry. I think you have enough on your plate with your own health, don't you?' I asked him.

'Yes, but you also have to appreciate that I am having to deal with how she is each and every moment of the day Lois so I cannot help but worry,' he said painfully.

'Fair enough,' I said finishing my ice-cream, but he wasn't finished making his point.

'So, you must promise me that you will take care of her Lois if anything happens to me,' he said suddenly grabbing my hand preventing me from standing up to take my empty carton to the bin.

When I turned back around, the grave look on his face hit me smack between the eyes like a sucker punch there were tears threatening to spill his bottom eyelids. 'Dad?' I began, 'what is it, you're worrying me now.'

'I am just being a silly old fool,' he said trying to push the emotion down.

'No, you're not,' I said moving in as close as the wheelchair would allow.

'I just dread to think what would happen to her if I were not there to look after her. You will make sure she is ok, won't you?' he asked.

'Of course, I will that goes without saying,' I encouraged him.

'Do you promise, Lois?' he asked.

'I promise you that come what may I will step in the gap for her and that I will ensure she is fine,' I declared.

'There is one other thing,' he started.

'Ok go ahead,' I offered.

'At the service, can you make sure she kisses my coffin?' he finally said, now he really was tormenting himself.

'What on earth, why are you talking like this?' I asked getting a bit upset myself.

'Please. Promise me you will make sure she kisses my coffin,' He insisted.

'If anything happens to you and we are in that predicament, I will make sure she kisses the coffin,' I solemnly declared.

'Thank you,' he said. His shoulders seemed to slump ever so slightly the weight of relief falling from his back like leaves from a tree in the autumnal months.

We sat a few minutes each in our own personal contemplation before he went on to explain. 'For over 55 years, I have watched her at every funeral walk up to the coffin at the crematorium kiss her fingers and then touch the coffin. It is her mark of respect for her loved ones I just don't want you to let her forget to kiss me goodbye.'

With that explanation left in the air, there was no more to be said and so we just sat there holding each other's hand staring off in to the distance until the prospect of the warmth of the car finally called me from the cold of the rock. It was a sombre ride home and what with last night's escapade and today's topic of conversation, I was emotionally spent. I ensured Dad was safely sat in his old familiar chair, that he had a warm cuppa, with a teabag in it and a sandwich and left him under the watchful gaze of Mum. Inevitably the boys were glad to be going home having slept at Jenny's the night before so as soon as we got into the car, I put some tunes on and we were already singing before I pulled out of the drive. I had only got maybe 500 yards down the road when Jack said something that literally made my blood run cold.

'I don't like Uncle Tim, Mum,' Jack uttered, my ears immediately tuning in.

'Really love, why is that' I said trying to sound as blasé as I could but inside my stomach was leaping into my mouth.

'He just makes me feel uncomfortable. And he watches me,' he said.

'If it is any consolation, he makes me feel uncomfortable too,' I said trying to normalise things.

'No, I mean he is not nice, and he watches me pee,' he confessed.

Right now, I wanted to scream and shout 'what the flip' but this was my 8-year-old son, so I had to rein in the emotion and not make the same mistake that my mother had made when I was his age. 'How do you mean, love?' I asked softly and calmly.

'The last time we were over here, Joe and I stayed with Grandad whilst you and Grandma went up into town to the market. Uncle Tim arrived as I was going through the kitchen to the toilet. I thought he had gone through to see Grandad. I never thought anything about it so went to the toilet and left the door open like we always do. Halfway through me having a wee, I suddenly got the feeling that someone was behind me, so I turned round. Uncle Tim was stood at the side of the toilet door peering round it at me. I don't like him; he makes me feel uncomfortable.' he told me.

I was absolutely beside myself so apparently, not only is he being investigated regarding an unhealthy interest in both his male and female children and the historical abuse of his sisters, but he is also displaying predatorial behaviour towards his nephew too! I decided to quash down the anger that was threatening to explode my near fragile mental state in favour of placating this situation for my children's sake.

'You're right, love, that is very strange behaviour, darling, and I can see how that would make you feel very uncomfortable. I am glad that you felt you could share that with me it must have been difficult, thank you for being my brave little soldier. Maybe whenever he is at Grandma's or anywhere else for that matter and you want to use the toilet, just let me know. I will make sure he doesn't bother you ever again,' I reassured him.

'I love this song,' Joe suddenly interjected right on cue and that was the end of the conversation though inevitably not the end of my thought process.

When I arrived home, the boys raced inside to see who could get to the fridge first, maybe Dad was right with the thought about Mum and her having dementia as it transpired that she had forgotten to feed them. As I closed the front door, I was alarmed to find a tiny card the size of a credit card clamped into the end of the letterbox. I immediately recognised the police insignia emblazoned upon it and along the front someone had handwritten "we urgently need to speak to you, please call as soon as possible."

I put the remnants of our picnic from the day before on to the floor and perched myself onto the bottom of the stairs. As I scanned the Tupperware tubs with their leftover crusts from Joe's lunch and the browning banana peel in Jack's, I couldn't help thinking what meal the police were going to have with my evidence. Like the waste in front of me, this was all such a mess but could not so easily be disposed of. I took a deep breath, shoved the card into the back pocket of my jeans, collected the leftovers and braced myself before taking them through to the bins.

There was nothing more important right at this moment than having the healing joy of my boys around me and knowing that I had their love. So, I closed the proverbial door shut on the world outside knowing I may not be able to stop the wheels from turning but I could put off the inevitable until tomorrow.

Chapter 16
Mother Nature

When I woke the next morning, it was to Jack and Joe noisily clanking a cup and a plate down onto my bedside table.

'Morning,' they chimed.

'Hello,' I responded. 'What's all this?' I asked yawning and trying to focus my eyes as I raised myself up to rest my back on the headboard.

'We really missed you last night, Mummy, and wanted to let you have a lie in so we brought you breakfast in bed,' announced Jack.

'That's absolutely lovely,' I beamed glancing at the plate and expecting to see toast. 'So, what delight have you made me?' I enquired.

'An egg mayonnaise sandwich,' Joe revealed with absolute delight.

'For breakfast?' I enquired.

'Yes, for breakfast,' said Joe.

'What time is it?' I asked Jack.

'It's 45 past 6,' Jack announced proudly having recently learnt about telling the time.

'Quarter to seven,' I couldn't keep the surprise out of my voice nor stop the raising of my eyebrows at the thought of eating an egg mayonnaise sandwich so early in the day.

'Don't you want it?' Joe asked looking hurt.

'I can think of nothing better for my breakfast than an egg mayonnaise sandwich,' I lied. And they sat there and waited until I had eaten every bit of it.

Once I had showered and got the boys sorted, we decided to take our cocker spaniel Poppy for a walk through Coxley Woods which sits on the periphery of the village of Netherton. There are a number of paths winding through the trees dipping up and down, but we liked to follow the stream much to Poppy's delight who could never resist the opportunity for a quick dip. Joe and Jack stumbled along in their wellington boots despite it being bone dry underfoot throwing sticks into the water encouraging Poppy to jump in and out.

I decided to sit on an old fallen tree stump to give them the space and time to explore, the bark upon the log crumbling through its decay. Tree roots intermittently exposed had caused the earth around it to crack and develop deep ingrained ridges which were now as hard as iron. There was a small bridge to my left where the stream ran into a rumbling little creek. Above it and at the edge of the wood was two open fields looking out towards the villages of Middlestown and Overton beyond, in the distance. The sun tried in vain to push through the overhanging trees but with little success, the shadows of the branches elongated upon the bed of the woods.

It was quite cool in here despite the warming June day with the only sound being the odd bird or the scurrying of animals beneath the cascading ivy upon the steep inclined banks. It was peaceful, calm and serene being surrounding by the quietness of nature a stark contrast to the past couple of days. A loud splash aroused my attention and with it came the damp smell of disturbed stagnant waters. As I gazed at those two beautiful boys the personification of innocence my heart swelled with pride and an overwhelming desire to love, protect and to keep them safe. It was difficult to comprehend a thought process that would contemplate the possibility of intentionally wishing to harm, humiliate or degrade either of them or any child for that matter. It was simply abhorrent and completely unfathomable. They were carefree, energetic, fun, loving, kind, inquisitive, happy, articulate, relaxed, confident, resourceful and adventurous but equally they could also be defined as vulnerable if they trusted the wrong person. The very idea that anybody could view a child only from the perspective of satisfying their own sexual gratification without any thought for the despair and lifelong emotional damage was simply monstrous. It contravened the epitome of what was morally right or ethically decent.

I felt sick and swamped by the blackness of my desperation to protect my boys and that of the heaviness of my past that had suddenly been resuscitated. My heart ached for I knew that just like that stagnant water, the river of my own serenity would soon be obliterated to cataclysmic levels.

I sat for a moment in deep contemplation then forcibly re-steered my thoughts back to the present before I was lost and drowning in an abyss of screaming torment. I purposefully latched on to my environment to help secure an anchor. This is why I loved to connect with nature as to take in the sights and sounds around me it provided a safe space in which to think. However, the artistic side of my brain couldn't help making connections between my vision of the woods and the perception of my life.

For instance, the exposed roots could metaphorically be described as the strangleholds acting like tentacles running to unseen depths. Their partial exposure not unlike the behaviours being investigated with a consideration of what more may come to light given time. Equally as we walked through the woods the roots were causing a stumbling block not unlike past traumas which appear from nowhere. The splash in the stream sending ripples ricocheting outward symbolises the more disturbing affects, on everyone else around him. Once the grounds for his arrest had been confirmed and the momentum of questioning of family members conducted these ripples would cause the unsettled waters never to flow together in the same format again. The misplaced rock now unseen and embedded in the mud beneath, a reminder of drowning, isolation and the unwanted foreign body of sexual abuse.

Then there is the cascading ivy hiding what is concealed beneath not unlike the mask I wear to cover the damage of the psychological and emotional hurts. The elongated shadows of the branches represent the bony skeletons seen but also unseen depending on the exposure of the light. The magnificent trees so strong, shooting up heavenward as powerful and uncontrolled as the explosive rages of anger. The sun in all its glory bringing warmth and growth persistently attempting to push through, to bring light into the darkness, to soothe little Lois and heal me.

The ground as hard as iron represents my coldness, the mental detachment and the walls I have erected. There are many paths in the wood depicting a parallel to the choice of direction through life with the ups and down dips an indication of the peaks and troughs of experiences. The decay of the crumbling of the bark is death to self but then the polar opposite in the cycle of life is that death must occur for life to thrive. So, I am left in deep contemplation to flip the switch determined not to accept what was or even what is and has been but to look for what will be. And at that moment I know that I have to be the master of my own destiny and must no longer idly give those controls to anyone ever again under the guise of wanting to please. Yes, I loved to absorb Mother Nature's resources to unpack and process the complexities of my own thought patterns. She brings with her a clarity and a calmness that defies the gravity of any situation regardless of its severity. She and I are at one with each other maybe due to our early connection pouring my grief-stricken heart out on the Green Hill under the eight trees on Pildacre.

I knew I would have to return to the dysfunctional absurdity of life as a willing participant if I was going to confront the demons of my past life and successfully sever those ever-powerful strangleholds. These had entrapped me in their grip for far too long and the time had come to cast them out forever. Yet, in the wake of our contentedness I just needed to revel a little longer because I knew that once the pin was removed from the grenade it would then be detonated.

Chapter 17
Treacle Sponge

After our walk in the woods, I decided to go see Dad not to discuss anything, but I wanted to absorb his love and interaction with the boys. I felt energised but I needed that one ingredient only my father could instal and that was his assurance that everything would always be ok. He was a strong man spiritually despite his present fragility physically and a resolute character that always provided me with strength and security, I needed that right now.

As we arrived at Grey Gables Mum was at the door taking delivery of the Meals on Wheels service, I had organised for them both. It had proved essential during Dad's convalescence to encourage his intake of food but also to remind Mum that she should eat too, not to mention the social interaction having a meal together provided. I smiled to myself as I recalled Dad's depiction of Mum's absurd impositions upon where he ate, drank or wore his slippers so was intrigued with what I may discover. Dad was sat in the piano room with place settings arranged one in front of him and the other opposite for Mum. He had a cup in his hand so he had obviously been allowed a drink in here although amusingly I did notice he wasn't wearing his slippers. As if he had read my thoughts, he lifted his foot and stuck it out raising his eyebrows at the same time as if to say 'see.' I acknowledge his secret code with a swift nod of my head however it wasn't as deftly as I had hoped for, I caught the ever-vigilant Jack scrutinising the pair of us.

'Where are your slippers, Grandad?' Jack queries.

'They are on my feet,' Dad responds playfully.

'No, they are not, Grandad,' Jack notes.

'Maybe he has his invisible slippers on, Jack!' Joe states.

'Yes, lad that's right, I have my invisible slippers on,' Dad decides to play along knowing full well that Joe will believe anything that his grandad tells him like for instance convincing Joe he is only 11 years of age.

'There are no such thing as invisible slippers,' Jack told them both.

'There is,' begins Joe, 'Grandad had his invisible slippers on the last time we were in this room,' Joe tells us with confidence whilst Dad chuckles remembering that he had inevitably used the same excuse the last time the boys had been there.

'I will go and find your real slippers, Grandad,' Jack says and runs off to make his way through the dining room, up the staircase and along the corridor to Mum and Dad's bedroom in search of them.

'Where are you going in such a hurry?' Grandma asks entering the piano room with 2 foil trays containing the food from the Meals on Wheels delivery man that she has simply put on a plate for each of them.

'He says he is going to look for Grandad's *real* slippers, but he doesn't need them because Grandad has his invisible slippers on,' Joe innocently tells her.

Mum looks from Joe to Dad and then to me but when no explanation is offered, she simply shakes her head and proceeds to place the plates onto the table, one in front of Dad and the other between the knife and fork opposite him. Upstairs, directly above us we suddenly hear a thud which sounded a lot like Jack jumping off the bed on to the floor. Not wanting to be left out of the opportunity of having fun Joe took to his heel and raced upstairs in pursuit of his brother.

Meanwhile, I decided to go put the kettle on as a cursory scan of the table told me that Dad would need another drink to finish his meal and that Mum hadn't got one either. As I entered the kitchen, I noticed Mum's cup was still sat at the side of the kettle and on closer inspection I found it had been half drunk but was now lukewarm and it only consisted of milk and water, no teabag. Perhaps, what Dad had divulged earlier wasn't as absurd as I had first thought and maybe it was also a cry for help because he was finding it difficult to comprehend or deal with. I absentmindedly made the three of us a warm drink and got two beakers out for the boys to have a diluted blackcurrant drink.

'Told you,' Dad said breaking the silence as he walked into the kitchen.

'What?' I asked a little perplexed.

'I told you that she forgets to put a teabag in when she makes a drink and that she won't let me wear my slippers in the end room whilst I can eat and drink in there,' he offered.

'I don't get it why would she place such weird constraints on you?' I asked puzzled.

'Because she has got dementia,' he said.

'Who has got dementia?' Mum faltered, entering the kitchen before we'd had time to realise she was even there. Busted.

'Do you want to tell her or shall I?' I asked Dad. When he didn't answer, I guessed it must be me then. 'Dad was saying that you seem under quite a bit of stress at the moment and that some of your behaviour is very similar to the early signs of someone at the start of dementia,' I tried as tactfully as I could muster given that I had just been thrown under the bus.

'Don't be so daft, I have just got a lot of things going on at the moment what with looking after your dad and getting used to all the carers coming,' she said playing the situation down as much as possible.

'Yes, that must be it,' I agreed trying to appease the situation and not wanting to hurt her feelings.

'That doesn't explain why you're making cups of tea without the teabag in it or you suddenly not knowing how to use the remote control,' Dad stated not wanting to let the opportunity to address the situation go unmissed.

'I sometimes like to have a warm drink without the teabag in, it is comforting,' Mum tried to sound convincing.

'I don't, but you keep giving me a cup of tea without a teabag in,' he said like a dog with a bone.

'Well, if it bothers you that much, you can make your own,' was Mum's swift and final response before walking back through the middle room to the piano room.

As we followed her through Joe suddenly asked, 'Where are the puddings, Grandma?'

Dad and I both looked at Mum who faltered before recognition swept across her face and she retraced her steps back into the kitchen to collect the puddings which is what she had gone in for the first time.

'Told you,' Dad quietly remarked under his breath.

As soon as Mum walked into the room with the puddings, Joe immediately scampered up on to the spare seat at the side of Dad.

'Oh, I love treacle sponge, Grandad, it's my favourite,' Joe declared.

'I thought apple crumble was your favourite,' Jack declared, 'that is what you said yesterday, Joe.'

'I like them both equally,' Joe corrected himself wisely.

Dad loved to toy with Joe, so he deliberately exaggerated each movement of cutting the pudding up, spooning the custard over each part and scooping a dollop on to his spoon. 'I love treacle sponge, it's so moist, soft and sweet especially when it is dripping with custard,' he mused.

'That it is exactly how I like mine, Grandad, dripping with custard,' Joe said licking his lips desperate for a sample.

'Is it, lad,' Dad teased.

'Yes, Grandad, and that treacle sponge looks very tasty,' Joe revelled.

Dad knew Joe was desperate for a bit of his sponge pudding because they went through the same shenanigans every day, hence why Dad loved to string it out in order to torment him to the fullest. His next move was equally unchanged as he lifted his spoon as though about to deposit its contents into Joe's mouth and then at the last-minute Dad redirect it to his own mouth. Joe looked just as downcast as the day before at almost securing the first bite and Jack fell about laughing that his brother had fallen for Grandad's antics yet again. Today was no different. As Grandad continued to tease Joe, I followed Mum back into the kitchen to take the opportunity to chat to her alone. I stood and watched her for a moment as she took her cutlery to the sink and placed them into the bowl. She seemed so deep in thought and I wondered how long she had walked amongst us with the weight of the world upon her shoulders unable to talk to either Dad or myself.

I suddenly felt really sad as I acknowledged that neither of us had even noticed the ordeal she had been experiencing. I had initially been angry at the thought she had failed to protect me again and that by her not telling me she had also betrayed me in some way. Yet as I stood in the doorway and gazed at her what I saw was a totally different scene and it filled me with the overwhelming sense of wanting to protect her. I glimpsed a tortured soul locked away without a voice not unlike Little Lois had been and my heart wanted to reach out and meet her need.

'I know,' was the only thing I could utter.

'Yeah, I know you do, Ruby has filled me in,' she sighed, her entire innards spilling out with that painful breath like one of Poppy's stuffed animal toys.

I couldn't tell if she was relieved, thankful that it was out in the open or whether it was a deflation knowing that the proverbial shit was now going to hit the fan. 'I have so many emotions running through me at the moment I cannot pinpoint them independently but one that upsets me the most it that I am so angry and hurt that you did not tell me what was going on,' I confessed.

'I knew that would be the case,' she said defeatedly.

'But yet you still said nothing?' I asked incredulously.

'What else could I do; Ruby had sworn me to secrecy,' she stated.

'You could have assessed whether maintaining a secret of that magnitude was conducive to our relationship and evaluated what long term affects it may have had. I come here every day to maintain both yours and Dad's needs, yet you have so blatantly ignored mine and failed to protect me again,' I accused her.

'I didn't tell you because I was protecting you, Lois, surely you can see that,' she implored me.

'How have you protected me? I would have thought forewarning me would have been protecting me, not tittle-tattling behind my back with Ruby yet again. I feel utterly betrayed; both of you knew full well what he did to me but you both chose to keep me in the dark again.' I was so hurt I couldn't see past it nor could I grasp the point she was trying to make or maybe I just needed to sound off right now.

'Lois, I never asked to be held in Ruby's confidence and just for the record it has caused me immense anguish at not being able to talk it over with either you or Jeff. Every single day when you have arrived, I have busied myself with anything to steel myself to face you. I have literally ached to tell you, I have been desperate to tell you, but I simply couldn't,' she said fading off.

'I am sorry, but I really don't understand why you couldn't talk to me about something that is so important especially if it was upsetting you like you say it has. I mean, I thought we told each other everything. How is it possible to have kept your emotions so deep rooted that neither Dad nor I even suspected anything was bothering you.' I was becoming unreasonable.

'If only you knew the depth of despair that this has forced me to plummet to with the images of what he has done plaguing my sleep and the conversations with Ruby that have imprisoned my thoughts. If only you had a measure of that, Lois, then you would understand,' she said utterly deflated.

'I think I had a small measure of what you may have felt as I sat in her interview and learnt about what he did to her as a child,' I spluttered tears streaming down my face. 'That's another major topic you failed to communicate or what should have been revealed in, oh let us say, anytime in the last 30 years!' I told her.

'I can see you're angry, Lois and I appreciate why; I would be furious if I was in your shoes but honestly, I was trying to protect you,' Mum tried.

'After what he did to me, don't you think I should have been the first to know then at least I could have prepared myself rather than having it exposed to me at the very last minute on his arrest. Really, it is a bit too late to put your protective coat around me now don't you think?' I asked.

'I didn't tell you, Lois, because I know you,' she said.

'Know me, what is that supposed to mean?' I asked.

'If you knew that Ruby and Sarah had gone to the police and that they were conducting an investigation into him regarding the sexual abuse, you would have dived straight in,' She revealed.

'If you mean I would have done anything to protect those children, then yes, your right of course I would have stood in the gap for them, every single day of the week and without any apology. I know what it is like for a child to have no voice so why would I allow him to harm anyone else?' I almost screeched.

'You're missing my point, Lois,' she said with a sigh.

'Ok then explain it to me,' I urged.

'I was protecting you by not telling you, Lois, because I knew that once you found out you would have gone straight round to the police station and reported what he had done to you. Ruby would then have stood back having orchestrated it all and given you the bullets in which to fire. Whatever the outcome of the police enquiries, you would have been the scapegoat again whilst she would have assumed her usual position of innocence,' Mum affirmed.

I could scarcely take in what Mum had just said, but ultimately, I knew she was right and then the pennies started to fall like into the slot of a one-armed bandit. My suspicions about why Ruby had contacted me to unveil his arrest was because she knew I would drop everything and go straight over. I would then be in a position where I would be forced to support her by having to sit in on her interview thus hearing the revelation of the whole sordid affair. Also, the phone call from Ruby immediately after the interview whilst I was still on my way home regarding the garage. Of course, she had wanted me to attend because it would further enhance *his* guilt if I saw the magnitude of the operation and I would inevitably divulge the pièce de résistance, my evidence.

There was no concern about how it may affect me or how difficult it would be to disclose the facts of the abuse to a third party I was just a pawn within her plan to "get the bastard" and nothing more. I needed time to think away from here and I knew just the spot to clear my mind the only place that would help me put things into perspective.

At that moment, my mobile rang, and it was none other than Ruby, 'Hello,' I said walking outside not really wanting to talk about the subject in front of Mum.

'I wanted to let you know I have just got off the phone to Kelly, I rang her to let her know what has happened with regards to Tim,' she said all matter of fact.

'Ok, so what has her highness said?' I asked although I am sure I could have guessed.

'She is sitting on the fence on this one,' She delivered.

'Surprise, surprise,' I said.

'You know what she is like, she doesn't want to get involved,' Ruby said.

'Oh yes, I know what she is like alright; never there to do the right thing or be supportive when it matters,' I dismissed.

'Yes but get this; she then had the cheek to ask me why I was getting involved, as—and quote "it wasn't like it was my child that had been abused,"' Ruby announced.

'You have got to be joking, she actually said that?' I questioned, outraged.

'She actually said those words! I was like oh so if it was my daughter Aleigha that had been abused, are you saying that you wouldn't get involved because it wasn't your daughter?' Ruby told me.

I had to let that sink in, it was a callous, irresponsible and immature attitude that I found utterly deplorable.

'The other thing she said was that you had better not start telling what she should think or feel about the situation either or she would just cut you off,' Ruby delivered without feeling.

'Wow! I think she is actually judging me by her own yardstick, maybe she should be careful that she doesn't get splinters in her arse from sat so high up there looking down on everyone,' I stated.

'Don't shoot the messenger,' said Ruby.

I thought about that for a moment no doubt Ruby had taken pleasure discussing the case with Kelly revealing all the nitty-gritty including how he had sexually abused me and of her knowing about it all these years. My mind went back to the occasion in her kitchen with her suspicions of him abusing Elena not to mention her daughter Haley who spoke of his abuse of Sophie. So, she had known of these incidents, had done nothing to protect either child and here was Kelly still comfortable sitting on the fence. Her arrogance and lack of responsibility astounded me but then again, she had always been exceptionally superficial depending on what audience she played to. It wasn't her failure to stand in the gap for me that bothered me. I mean why would I expect anything else from her she had never assumed the role of protective older sister in her life. It was the get out clause she had installed of the threat to cut me off if I so much as questioned her about it.

Obviously, this excessive remark was borne out of guilt at being in the wrong and not wanting to have to face the fact a bit like a child throwing her teddy out of the cot. A clear case of I will not like what you have to say about my decision because deep down I know that it is neither fair to you nor honest.

'As far as I am concerned, she can please herself what stance she takes that is for her conscience not mine,' I was done with this rubbish.

'I just wanted to tell you that she knows and to warn you of the threat she had made,' Ruby stated.

When I returned to the kitchen, Mum was still stood at the sink her back to me, shoulders slumped as if in defeat not even able to turn round and face me. I walked over to her and put my arms around her waist. 'I am still hurt but thank you for clarifying your position,' I told her. 'I am sorry you have had to go through this alone, but you should never have been put in that position.'

'But don't you see, Lois, that was the whole point, she put me in this awkward position because she was relying on the fact that I would tell you. Possibly hoping you would jump straight in and take the fall so that was the sole reason I kept it to myself because I knew her intention was to hurt you. She didn't care about what she was doing, she had no remorse or concern for anyone else at all she just revels in causing devastation to other people's lives,' Mum explained.

'Does Dad know anything about *his* perverted behaviour or have any inclination that his son has been arrested?' I enquired.

'No,' Mum said, 'it would kill him.'

'Well, it is going to get out sooner or later and when it does, we will all be living under the cloud of disgust for keeping it a secret for so long,' I offered.

'I know, unlike Ruby I have been dreading this moment for months along with having to tell your dad what has been going on,' she admitted.

'Maybe we need to sit tight and see what the investigation throws up first but there is one thing for sure, the clock is ticking,' I told her.

I gave Mum another little squeeze having received answers to some of the questions that had been careering around my brain. Before I did anything else, I knew I required a moment in the expanse of the green hill and that afterwards I would be making the phone call to the police that they had been awaiting. I called the boys to come put their shoes on whilst sauntering into the room to see what they were up to. Joe was now sat on Dad's lap with treacle round his mouth and drips of custard decorating his jumper not unlike a Jackson Pollock painting. Jack was sat upon the piano stool readily making plink plonk sounds much to Dad's entertainment.

'Come on you two, I want to take Poppy along the Greenway to the top of Pildacre hill,' I told them.

Amidst their groans and grumbles that she had already had a walk they still made their way into the kitchen where Mum happily bent down to assist them into their corresponding footwear. As I removed the remnants of food waste from the table and collated the coated foil cartons, Dad also decided to take the opportunity to have a quiet word.

'Did she say anything to you?' he queried.

'About what?' I asked.

'About whether she thinks she has dementia,' he said.

'No, I think she has just had a lot on her mind,' I said truthfully.

'Oh' he said sounding disappointed, 'I thought when you were in the kitchen for such a long time you must have been having a word with her about it. I was trying to keep the boys in here to give you the privacy to broach the subject,' he continued.

'I did mention about the cup of tea situation as you heard but she was passing it off with an excuse so maybe she isn't ready to face it yet,' I said, 'don't worry I will keep my eye on matters and take notes so that when we see the doctor I can be specific about the relevant changes. Ok?' I asked.

He nodded in agreement though this was not really what he had anticipated and then followed me into the kitchen where I disposed of the foil cartons into the bin and Dad's cutlery into the sink.

'Do you want me to put the kettle on before I go?' I threw out to them both.

'Yes, you had better do, it might be the last one I get with a teabag in it until you come back tomorrow,' he jibed.

Mum shook her head, gave the boys a hug and kissed them goodbye before going off into the house to find her own element of peace. She was troubled, there was no mistake about it but then so was Dad. What a mess life could be, with its twists and turns amidst the secrets we all keep in the guise of protecting one another. Unfortunately, the unexpected release of this particular can of worms was one that I was very reluctant to get involved with for many reasons, but I knew that I had to face it once and for all.

Chapter 18
Making the Call

Once I'd had a fix sat in my special place under the trees watching the boys rolling down the green hill giggling and laughing, I felt refreshed mentally and restored emotionally. I glanced across to the horizon marvelling upon the landscape ahead of me the focal point of Emley Moor mast almost directly opposite. The numerous fields were knitted together like a patchwork quilt with their perfect endings and new beginnings. I mused how life wasn't as clear cut as the puzzle in front of me but a whole lot messier with undefined edges and murkier episodes. However, as the saying goes one chapter does have to end for a new one to begin. I may not have had any control upon what the latest page had revealed but this current situation was the hand I had been dealt, so I needed to decide how I was going to play it.

Despite the historical abuse and the inevitable negative feelings, I had towards *him* I did not have an axe to grind. Therefore, I did not share Ruby's attitude of 'I am going to get the bastard' so I didn't really want to be party to anything that involved putting him away. However, I could not ignore the possibility of his guilt although I also decided it was not my responsibility to cast aspersions or to determine his fate. It was really difficult because I knew I could not have some misplaced family loyalty either so I decided to look at it from the viewpoint of if a friend came to me to ask me for my advice, what would I say? This perspective allowed me to reach the conclusion that I would have to take all emotional elements out of the situation, step back, look at it objectively and make a rational decision. The only viable option to deal with this delicate situation was to just be honest.

So, I decided I needed to give the police my statement, to tell them what I knew regardless of how difficult it may be. That was the only way I would be able to live with myself knowing that I had stepped into the gap for the children.

If it went down the route of going to court, then all the evidence would be presented in front of 12 strangers who would weigh up the information and they would decide without a shadow of a doubt where the truth lay. If he was then found guilty, it was by his own hand and he would have to accept whatever punishment he was given.

Afterall, I had been delivered a lifetime sentence so let's be honest *he* wouldn't get as long a punishment as I'd received. More importantly, if it protected and prevented any subsequent children, he came into contact with from being abused then it was worth it. I argued with myself over and over, back and forth but it always came back to the same conclusion, when I was a child, I had no voice but now I am an adult, so I have no choice.

I called the boys and Poppy and began making my way back to the car which was parked in the little car park adjoining the edge of the field. We sang our obligatory songs on the way home starting with "Lollipop" Mica, "Angels" Robbie Williams and "This Charming Man" The Smiths. Once home the boys wiped Poppy's feet, washed their hands and then Jack put on Joe's favourite film "Flushed Away" whilst I cut up strawberries, grapes, melon and apples before placing them in two bowls. Settled in front of the TV, wrapped in one of their cosy blankets, a snack bowl balanced upon their laps, I decided to bite the bullet and make the call I had been dreading.

I took the business card out of my pocket and made my way out through the back door where I initially sat on the top step however after inputting the number my nerves got the better of me. As I waited for the call to connect my heart racing and my mouth suddenly bone dry, I had to move so began pacing up and down in anticipation but became so agitated I disconnected. I tried to take a few deep breaths but it just created a sense of vertigo, so I walked to the top of the garden where the outdoor furniture sat and plonked myself down heavily on to one of the chairs. The sun was high up above the house, so I sat eyes closed letting its rays bathe me in its warmth for a moment or two asking God to fill me with His peace and to give me the courage to execute the call.

I suddenly became overwhelmed again, what a choice of words I'd used to "execute" the call, oh my goodness my thought process was even negative. I opened my eyes and glanced across to the house next door noticing that Glen was in the upstairs window where he was observing me. He must have thought my behaviour bizarre, so he had stopped to study me, my negative thoughts persisted unhelpfully. I smiled and waved in the hope that he would continue with his daily routines and leave me to my ridiculousness. I knew I had to speak to the police but what if I came across to them in the same way as I must have done to Glen. I rationalised that whatever the situation I could run round like a headless chicken or I could take the bull by the horns. I knew what I wanted to do but did what I knew I had to do and put the call in again only this time allowing it to connect.

'Hello, this is Inspector Daniel Davies; how can I help you?' the voice informed me.

'I am Lois Rodgers, and a card was put through my letterbox asking me to contact you with regards to an investigation concerning Timothy Rodgers,' I said shakily, the mere sound of his name choking in my throat as I tried to extricate it.

'The name of the officer from child protection assigned to the case is Melissa Maya, if you could hold the line whilst I put you through, Lois?' he asked.

'Yes, that is fine,' I responded more firmly feeling anything but fine as I sat twiddling furiously with the strands of my hair twisting it round my finger.

'Good afternoon, Ms Rodgers; this is Melissa Maya, thank you so much for making contact,' she began and when I didn't respond she continued, 'as you know we are investigating allegations made against Timothy and would like to organise a meeting with you,' she said more gently. 'Ms Rodgers are you still there?' she asked.

'Yes,' I managed then closed my eyes and sighed deeply suddenly not feeling very sure of my decision in spite of everything.

'I appreciate this must be quite difficult for you Ms Rodgers, but it is imperative that we speak to you at the very earliest convenience,' she urged gently.

'Yes, I understand,' I said my eyes filling instantaneously at the exposure of my reality not unlike defining the clarity of light density through the aperture of a lens of a camera. My eyes blurred but the focus in my mind's eye clear.

'Is it possible to arrange for you to come into the station this afternoon?' Melissa Maya asked hopefully.

My nerves got the better of me and at the risk of sounding unhelpful I said, 'I am sorry, but my children are off school this week and I am a single parent.'

'Ms Rodgers, we have a short timeframe in which to work, if it would help you, I would be willing to come out to see you at your home,' she queried.

'But what about my children, I really don't want them to become upset having police turn up at their home,' I ventured.

'We do not wear the traditional police uniforms, Ms Rodgers, but if you are concerned maybe a friend could have them for you,' she sounded helpful.

'When do you want to come?' I asked outright.

'Would 10.30 tomorrow morning work for you?' She asked.

'Ok,' I said because there was nothing else I could say; at the end of the day I had been forced in to walking this tightrope so far better for me it took place in the comfort of my home than in another soulless police station.

'Thank you and just so you know I will be accompanied by another officer called Dena Samuels who is also a member of the child protection team,' she informed me.

'Ok,' I said again not able to communicate more than this one-word answer.

'Right, thank you for calling Ms Rodgers and we will see you in the morning at 10.30,' she finished, and the line went dead before I could retract my consent.

I sat there in the garden for a few minutes, the phone in my hand just staring at the screen, numb and then dread filled my every fibre at the thought of speaking candidly about my early childhood. Although Ruby was the last person I wanted to talk to, I concluded that she had dragged me into this and so she could stand in and support me like I had supported her. So, the next call I made was to Ruby, after 3 attempts I finally got through to her and explained the situation and that the officers Maya and Samuels were arriving at 10.30 the next day.

'Do you want me to come over and be there when they arrive?' she unexpectedly offered. I wasn't sure if it was through genuine willingness to support me or just for evidential reasons but either way I didn't care.

'Yes, I do, Ruby, because I want to keep things as open and transparent as possible so we both know where we stand,' I admitted.

'Ok, I will be over to yours around 10 to 10.15, see you tomorrow,' she confirmed, and the phone instantly went dead as though she was in a rush to pass this new nugget of information on…to Sarah maybe?

It made me wonder again about the validity of her evidence and whether all this was some kind of game. What I did know for certain was that I didn't want to find any knives sticking out of my back at the end of this little escapade. I recalled Mum's reflections about why she had felt the need to protect me and her concerns I would be left holding the can and taking the blame. I felt open to the elements right now unsure of what twists and turns this unforgiving rollercoaster was going to take never mind its final destination.

I was aware my call to the police had caused the cogs to shift, the ball was rolling, and that the momentum would propel it forward, but that from now on I would cease to have any control. Tomorrow could be just another day, or it could be the day that would bring with it a revelation of my worst nightmare.

Chapter 19
Maya and Samuels

I had a fitful sleep which consisted of much tossing and turning with my being unable to get comfortable despite whatever position I tried, although luckily my thought pattern was inactive. At one point, I ventured downstairs for a comforting cup of hot chocolate made with warm milk thinking it may soothe me and help me to drift off. When this hadn't worked, I tried a lavender filled aromatherapy air and pillow mist spray it was essentially used to aid sleep, it didn't work.

So, I decided to settle myself on the blanket box in front of the window to gaze out across Netherton towards Horbury and Ossett. In the distance, I could hear the low rumbling of a train running along the tracks at the bottom of Quarry Hill I found it soothing in the regularity of its tone. The night sky seemed patchy in places, but I decided that this was probably due to there being some intermittent low cloud which was difficult for my eyes to differentiate at such an early hour. The house cast deeper shadows across the garden at this time of night and it was easy to make yourself believe you had seen movement despite the improbability.

As I became transfixed with the approximate position of where my parents' house sat, I wondered if Mum was having an equally disturbed sleep or was it a case of now that things were out in the open, she would finally be able to relax. She must have lay awake many, many times over the past 18 months sick with worry about where the investigation would lead. The thought must have plagued her whether she could have done more and if she had acted all those years ago could she have prevented the present abuse.

One thing struck me, I may be her daughter, but *he* was also her son and when she held him in her arms as a baby, she would have had the same depth of love that I had for both Jack and Joe. How distraught she must feel, how helpless and hopeless the situation when she was unable to protect her daughters and now torn between her son and grandchildren and his possible guilt. It didn't bear thinking about to be in a situation where my boys were at loggerheads tearing each other apart and my having to choose a side. My heart went out to her, and I sent feelings of love and positivity across to Ossett for as much use as it was.

I continued to gaze out of that window but no longer saw anything in front of me, my eyes were merely an open door to the darkness what I was really seeing were the images of my mind. I could not be sure how long I sat there transfixed by the memories of my life that replayed like a film in my mind's eye but eventually my eyelids became heavy, so I relocated myself to the comfort of my bed. With the quilt firmly tucked in at my neck and down my back, I thankfully drifted off in to a deep, contented sleep.

The next morning, I was up, showered and had breakfast set out on the table by the time I heard two giggling boys upstairs. I knew their game; they thought I was still asleep so they would be daring each other to sneak in and put their cold hands on me. So, I quietly tiptoed to the bottom of the steps in time to hear them running the cold tap for that extra special effect.

'I will go first, Joe,' whispered Jack.

'Why can't I go first, you went first last time?' Joe asked sulkily.

'Ok, I will open the door because I am quieter than you and we will slowly lift up the quilt together and do it at the same time,' Jack compromised.

'Yes,' Joe sniggered.

As they began to depress the door handle, I sneaked up the stairs 2 at a time as stealthily as possible knowing full well the boys would be focused on their antics so not expecting an entrapment. When the door clicked to signal its freedom from the door jamb, I was ready to spring into action so used the click to deliver my shock element of surprise.

'What are you two doing?' I spoke.

Like burglars in the night caught with their spoils upon them, the little culprits screamed in terror at their unexpected exposure. Jack looked terrified at first shocked to find me behind him rather than asleep in the bedroom in front of him. However, he soon regained his composure and began to exude a nervous laugh. Joe had immediately burst into tears a result of the emotional extremities of a child so young but once Jack had begun laughing, he half-heartedly followed tune. This was perhaps more to console himself than actually having the ability to see the funny side of the situation as Jack did.

A couple of hours later breakfast was eaten, the washing up had been put away and Jenny had collected the boys for a play day at her house. And then the house fell silent. I went through into the kitchen, filled the kettle, switched it on and placed four cups in front of it one each for Ruby, Samuels, Maya and myself. I knew Ruby would want coffee, no sugar and I was having tea, so I popped them in the cups ready before taking the milk out of the fridge. I decided against arranging biscuits on a plate as this was not a social occasion that lent itself to biscuits on a plate. I stepped back and decided I was as prepared as I could be.

I glanced at the clock; it was 09.50, Ruby would be arriving any minute and not long after Maya and Samuels would follow. I was determined to stay focused on the mundane in order to keep the nerves at bay and to not allow my head to take me on yet another journey of self-destruction. I had made my decision; the officers would currently be in transit, so I was refusing to allow myself the guilty pleasure of further critical thinking.

For anyone who has been abused, you will understand the concept of analysing the minutest of details from every conceivable angle. You will be aware that the mind is a very powerful tool but that it can also be used as a systematic battering ram. The dangers are the circles of despair we tie ourselves up in and the spirals to which we can plummet without a person in sight ever even noticing we have mentally left the room. What happens within our own minds or the lengths to which we travel would astound and exhaust the person sat right next to us living in blind ignorance. We are persistently hounded and tormented by the trauma of our past there is no mercy and thus no sustainable peace.

It is calamitous attempting to make decisions where there are options to choose between for fear of it hurling us along the wrong path. We are deep, we are emotional, we may come across as irrational but please just know it is the torture within us it is not the person who we are or were meant to be. Inside we are fighting demons that you do not know exist so please do not judge, do not try to understand us just be there to hold our hand. And that is what I wished for right at that moment that I had someone there to hold my hand as the doorbell rang to alert me to Ruby's arrival.

'It's open,' I shouted as I made my way out of the kitchen, but when she didn't come in, I figured I must have automatically dropped the latch.

'Come in,' I said, expecting Ruby to bound in as I opened the door but then I stopped dead in my tracks there were two ladies both sporting police lanyards around their necks.

'Good morning is it Ms Rodgers?' the lady to my left asked and when I nodded, she continued, 'I am Melissa Maya and this is my colleague Dena Samuels I know we are a little early. I hope that is not an inconvenience.'

Open-mouthed I glared before stuttering, 'no, not at all sorry I was just expecting my sister Ruby to arrive first,' I declared.

'Would you like us to wait in the car for a few minutes until she arrives?' Maya asked.

'No,' I said stepping to the side and widening the door for their entrance, 'that won't be necessary, please come in.'

Maya had thick, tight curly hair slightly greying that hung just below her shoulders. She worn a loose-fitting grey long sleeved ribbed t-shirt with a pair of black baggy trousers, upon her feet were ballet type shoes. She was quite plain but seemed cheery enough. Samuels was a complete contrast she had short neatly cropped hair that was gelled and styled perfectly to a quiff at the front with a grade 2 shaved to the back and sides. She sported round turtle shell glasses, had a white shirt upon her lithe body, figure hugging black Levi jeans with a pair of well-polished black Dr Marten shoes upon her feet. I led Maya and Samuels into the lounge area and invited them to sit before asking if they would like a coffee.

'We had one at the station before we left,' said Maya, Samuels nodding in agreement.

'You don't mind if I finish making myself and Ruby a drink, do you?' I queried.

'No,' they both said in unison with a smile. Samuels looked so much different when she smiled, less harsh and much prettier although I wasn't sure she would see that as a compliment. She was approximately 35 years of age, wore no wedding ring and gave the vibe of being lesbian if my gaydar had anything to do with it. I also noticed that she had a silver plain band ring donned on her thumb, yes, she was definitely my type I caught myself thinking. I walked through into the kitchen glad to have the space to compose myself but was then caught totally off-guard having not heard Maya's ballet shoes behind me.

'How are you feeling this morning, Ms Rodgers, I appreciate this must be a very difficult situation for you?' she asked.

'It's Lois, please call me Lois, Ms Rodgers sounds ever so formal,' I said flicking the switch to re-boil the kettle.

'Sorry, Lois,' she corrected herself.

'To be honest I feel like my world has suddenly been turned upside down,' I admitted. 'Apparently this investigation has been going on for some time, but I only became aware of it a few days ago.'

'Right, I am sorry. I assumed that you had been part of the initial information gathering,' Maya stated.

'No, that was Ruby which is why I wanted her here today because it has been a lot for me to process,' I told her, and she nodded as I poured the hot water into the cup and began mashing the teabag. As an afterthought I decided to also pour Ruby's coffee out to save me having to delay things further when she arrived later, this was excruciating enough.

'Does Ruby have to travel far?' she asked.

'No, it is only about 20 minutes' drive away; she lives in a little village just over the border,' I vaguely explained as there was a knock at the door and Ruby could be heard entering.

'Right on cue,' Maya smiled.

I picked up the cups, took a deep breath in, slowly exhaled and then followed Maya through to the lounge with a more than cheery smile on my face. This did not represent what I was feeling on the inside. Samuels was sat on the two-seater settee positioned in the bay window opposite me which was set to the left of the entrance door, whereas Ruby plonked herself down on the larger 3-seater to the right of the entrance door. Maya hovered in the middle of the room for me to take a seat before she planned where she would sit. I placed Ruby's coffee beside her on the heavy-duty pine sideboard to Ruby's left that stood between the door and the settee then plummeted to hold my cup and sat to Ruby's right. We all looked towards Maya for guidance to proceed; Maya grabbed the pouffe forward and sat directly in front of Ruby and I, a little too close for my comfort.

'Can I just introduce myself? I am Melissa Maya and this is my colleague Dena Samuels,' she said addressing Ruby much to her delight. 'As you know we are collating evidence with regards to some very serious allegations of child abuse concerning Timothy Rodgers. I believe you were interviewed on Monday 30th May, Ruby?'

'Yes, that's right, Melissa,' Ruby said as though they were old friends, 'it was requested that I attend the station in Huddersfield at 20.00 hrs on Monday evening. I gave a full statement to officers Rathbone and Evans; Lois was present to support me and I am here today to return that support.'

'Thank you, Ruby,' Maya said glancing over at Samuels. *When I followed her gaze, I noticed that Samuels had produced a notebook and was scanning its contents, she smiled at Maya, a signal to continue,* I thought.

Turning to face me, Maya declared, 'Ok Lois, we believe that on Monday 30th May you informed the officers that Timothy your brother had sexually abused you as a child,' she said as Ruby glanced at me, unable to mask the surprise upon her face. 'Is that right?' Maya continued.

'Yes,' I began, 'once Ruby had been interviewed, she requested to use the toilet so I took the opportunity to speak to the officers off the record to let them know that I would give them my statement but that I wasn't immediately available,' I explained as much for Ruby's benefit as for Samuels and Maya's.

'I see, in that case I would like to suggest that we do not take down the particulars of your statement today Lois but that we schedule you in for your statement to be recorded,' she spoke.

'Do you mean I will have to come to the station?' I asked.

'Yes Lois,' she said.

'Will I have to go all the way to Huddersfield again or can I go to a station nearer to here?' I asked.

'You will not have to go to Huddersfield, Lois, it will have to be at our suite in Mirfield,' she told me.

'In Mirfield?' I asked befuddled initiating another queried look from Maya to Samuels.

'Hasn't anyone spoken to you about us extracting the statement from you, Lois?' asked Samuels.

'No, as I said I only found out about everything on Monday night when Ruby rang me to accompany her to the police station, I told the officers afterwards that I would give my statement however I was taking my dad to the hospital the next day. An officer rang to speak to me whilst he was in the car but because it was such a sensitive matter, I couldn't speak about it in front of him. You know my dad has cancer, right?' I asked.

'I am so sorry, Lois, no we didn't,' Maya stated.

'I was taking him for his chemotherapy treatment so you see I couldn't possibly make myself available,' I explained beginning to tear acknowledging the words that were coming out of my mouth.

'I am sorry, Lois, that must have been an awful position to be in,' she offered.

'Dad and I always get an ice-cream to sit in the park where he will often talk freely about things that are on his mind,' I paused as I saw Ruby home in on what I was saying. 'Tuesday was no different and due to the content of our conversation I needed a bit of time and space to process everything. When I came home and found your calling card along with a message on the Ansa phone, I wasn't in the right frame of mind to chat which is why I left it until Wednesday,' I explained.

'So, the first police officer you officially spoke to about taking your statement was myself, yesterday,' she clarified.

'Exactly,' I said then asked, 'is there something I am missing?' I looked from Maya to Samuels and back again.

'The thing is, Lois, we haven't come today to take your statement; we were coming to collect you to take you to the suite in Mirfield,' Samuels said.

'I don't understand,' I was puzzled.

'I am sorry Lois but due to the nature of the case we are not looking to take a written statement, what we need is for you to provide is a video interview,' she said gently.

And then the penny dropped along with my mouth so wide it could have hit the floor. The room was silent for a few minutes to give me time to take in the magnitude of what Samuels had just delivered. Once she was sure I had regained some measure of understanding and I was able to proceed without her having to snap her fingers in front of my eyes saying 'back in the room' Maya continued.

'I understand this is quite a shock for you, Lois, but it is imperative that we have your statement on video because it could formulate a key piece of evidence for our investigation,' Maya said.

'Why would hers be a key piece of evidence?' asked Ruby. 'Mine wasn't videoed,' she said almost sounding peeved to have lost the top spot.

'Because he sexually abused me as a child and therefore you want to film my reactions and responses in case you need to show it to the jurors,' I filled in for the two officers.

'Precisely,' Samuels confirmed.

'How do you feel about having your interview filmed, Lois?' Maya asked.

'I cannot think of anything worse; it is bad enough having to voice those details out loud to a stranger never mind having a camera pointing in my face knowing you are going to play it to a room full of people.' I hid my face in my hands the shame too great to bear. I wanted to burst out of the room, jump in the car and get the first plane out of here it was too much for me to comprehend.

I lifted my head as Maya shifted her position to come sit beside me. She took my hand in her right hand and placed her left one between my shoulder blades and rubbed back and forth as if to give me comfort. It did nothing to help.

'I understand this is horrendous news for you, Lois, but if we are going to have any chance of making a prosecution case, we need to ascertain tangible evidence. The two children in question are so young that unless your brother openly confesses to what he has done it will be yet another case that is left on file. So far, we are aware of the potential attempted abuse of Ruby, the actual abuse of yourself and we have one other line of enquiry to pursue as well.'

'Clearly, your brother has been committing acts against children over a lengthy period of time and unless we stop him it could continue. Our job is to make a case to CPS so that we can exhibit official grounds to hold him thus enabling us to delve much deeper into his offending behaviour, but we need your evidence to do this,' she said.

The dimples in my cheeks depressed as I tightly pursed my lips willing the involuntary quiver of my chin to cease, I closed my eyes momentarily trying to compose myself. 'I am sorry, but I just can't do it, that is just too much for me to contend with,' I said keeping my eyes down and feeling the first drip fall on to my lap.

Maya gave me an extra little rub on the back, 'Lois, I do not want to pressure you into doing anything that you are not comfortable with but do you think we could perhaps take a ride to the suite just so you can see for yourself that it isn't as scary as it may seem?' she urged.

'It won't make any difference, I hate being photographed at the best of times but to be on film so you can capture every facial expression, every tear, every sordid detail because of him, I can't,' I said adamantly.

'Lois,' Ruby began, 'if the children are too young to be interviewed, we have to do it for them, we have to protect them we cannot let him get away with this again,' she stated.

'I am sorry I can't,' I said and shrugged them off whilst I made my way out of the room and upstairs to the solitary area of the bathroom. I needed to take a break and obtain some head space from the pressure of the knowledge that everything now suddenly rested upon me. I could hear their muffled voices floating up from downstairs but my interest to home in to gain any clarity was zilch, I had shut down. I had stayed where I was longer than I needed to and perhaps more importantly than I politely should have done but when the officers failed to leave, I knew I had no option but to return to the lounge. A little sheepishly, I retook my seat, thankful that Maya had returned to her spot on the pouffe.

'Officers Maya and Samuels have just been explaining to me that as you had not been informed in advance about the video interview, they could leave it for today and perhaps organise for you to visit next week,' Ruby attempted.

'That's right,' said Samuels, 'we appreciate it has come as a huge shock to you so if you would prefer it, we could schedule a visit for after the weekend.'

'Yes,' Maya began, 'we can leave it for today and give you the weekend to think about it, then see how you feel on Monday.'

'I will feel exactly as I feel right now,' I said 'overwhelmed, pressured and like the weight of the world is on my shoulders,' I told them both.

'Lois don't make any decisions right now please; we may never get another chance like this again; this is your opportunity to set the record straight,' Ruby spoke.

'Set the record straight? I have nothing to prove, Ruby, nor do I need anyone to validate what happened, he abused me and that fact will always remain whether I give a video interview or not,' I stated.

'I think what Ruby is trying to say is that the police are listening and we have a chance to prosecute this offender for the crimes he has committed and as I said before, you are a key witness in that investigation,' Samuels tried.

'Can I at least leave my direct number with you so you can think about it, or should you have any questions you can call, and we can discuss it further? That is all we are asking of you, Lois, please just think about it over the weekend,' Maya said as she proceeded to stand nodding to Samuels who did the same.

As though in a trance I automatically followed suit and pursued them towards the door however it was not through politeness it was to ensure I could firmly lock the door behind them. I felt shattered this particular snowball seemed to be increasing in size as it gathered momentum down the hill of no return. When I returned to the lounge, Ruby had already rinsed her cup out and was ready to leave as though she had got what she had come for and there was no longer any reason for her to hang about.

'You are going already?' I asked unable to keep the surprise out of my voice.

'Yes,' she said matter-of-factly. 'You asked me to come over whilst the police came to interview you but that's not happening now, I need to get back. Oh, by the way, Kelly's fallen off the fence!'

'What?' I was perplexed.

'Kelly rang Tim last night to invite him over to her house on Sunday so they can find a way to get him off, she isn't sitting on the fence anymore, she is actually going against us,' she delivered and with that she promptly made her way into the hall and out through the door.

As I peered out of the window observing her whilst she reversed into the gateway to manoeuvre her car towards the direction she had come, I couldn't help feeling anything but supported. Once the car had disappeared out at the end of the road, I slid down on to the little 2-seater settee Samuels had occupied during their visit to let the details of our conversation wash over me. I was flabbergasted it was one thing for Kelly to sit on the fence but to actively look for ways to get a paedophile off the crimes he was charged with was abhorrent. She knew his guilt which is why she was initially staying out of it maybe her ideas to get him off would include using me as a scapegoat, again!

As I said earlier, Mum knew her children, but would they really stoop to the disreputable depth of dishonesty by committing perjury? It really did not bear thinking about, it was against everything my father was as a businessman, my parents were as people and against everything we had ever been taught. It was one thing to keep out of it but another completely to stand alongside the guilty to further abuse and bully the innocent. For the moment, I decided to push this new nugget of information to one side as it was too much for me to contend with under the present circumstances of making a video statement.

Inevitably I could completely understand why they would want to film my interview as they would be capturing first hand not just the details of the testimony but more importantly my reactions and emotions. The jury would not only see me as a person, but they would be able to feel the weight of the despair first hand that *he* had caused me and so develop empathy. This would give the prosecutor a great advantage point and help to set the scene of an historical abuser who was still acting out his fantasies.

This knowledge did nothing to absolve my discomfort at being filmed whilst giving my testimony. It almost felt like I was being exploited further by having to submit to these conditions although I was inevitably torn because I did not want another child to be subjected to any form of abuse. Did I have a right to refuse when I could potentially put a stop to *his* antics. Would it prevent another child from being violated and having to undergo years of therapy or worse still self-harm.

It was a horrendous position to be in and I felt as manipulated as a contortionist's body. I did not want to waste more time mulling over the issue any further so decided to do what Maya and Samuels had suggested to give it thought over the next couple of days although I did not see anything changing. Little did I know that I was about to come face to face with the monster himself which would change the course of everything.

Chapter 20
Dreams

That night my dream world was chaotic, darting from one extreme to the next with no measure of sense to it other than my being in distress with each scene. During one episode I found myself in a building which seemed to represent the prison in which I worked and seemingly there was a hostile inmate on the loose. At first, I was with a fellow officer exploring corridor after corridor in search of our missing ward systematically unlocking and locking doors. Then my ears were assaulted with the extraordinary piercing sound of an alarm and the officer suddenly represented the charge I was searching for only now he was a flesh-eating zombie.

In terror, I raced down the walkway to be faced with several more zombies making their way up the stairs and along the landing towards me. Their heads lolled to one side, blood dripping from their mouths, their arms hanging out in front of them making grabbing movements with their hands like the pincers of a crab. In terror, I jumped over the balcony to the floor below and scurried to the underbelly of the stairs, trapped in the knowledge it was only a matter of time before I was devoured. I woke distressed with fear at the potential risk to my life and startled at the physicality of Joe clambering over me also seeking comfort having awoken in the middle of the night.

Once he had settled himself down, I tucked the quilt in around him to ensure he was swaddled enhancing his return to sleep. On the other hand, I lay there for some time trying hard not to allow my brain to unpick the dream too deeply as the last thing I wanted was to lay awake for the rest of the night. However, I couldn't help reflecting upon my walking along the landings in safety with my colleague was regular to my everyday life parallel to my enjoying the picnic with friends. Then the sudden threat to my safety and change in the atmosphere was replicated when Ruby rang to inform me of *his* arrest.

Being chased by the zombies felt a lot like the pressure of the police requiring my evidence and the entrapment under the stairs not unlike my experience of being in the interview room with Ruby. Yet the jumping over the balcony in my efforts to break free was a great show of faith and trust that I would land with my feet on the floor and not get hurt. I was delving too deeply and beginning to send myself crazy so decided I needed to make a concerted effort to get myself back to sleep. I was determined to clear my mind and used the method of counting back slowly from 100 using each breath in turn as a number. After several attempts, it finally worked and I was able to swiftly drift off again.

In the next dream, I was basking in the glorious sunshine enjoying the delights of an open-top bus tour. We were passing along a beach that was brightly coloured with overpopulated brollies, deckchairs and people. I felt content, safe and happy until the voice of the guide was starting to slur, then it developed a high-pitched tone before finally resting on the robotic. I turned to gauge the reactions of my fellow tourists to find that they had been replaced by upturned metal garbage bins their heads faceless, shiny silver spheres. When I looked back towards the beach, it was a mass of smouldering compost with hundreds of the same metal bin robots scavenging through it sifting out the rubbish. The bus came to a stop and as if programmed the bins simultaneously stood and lined up to form an orderly queue along the aisle ready to decamp. Instantaneously the bins disappeared and as if by magic they appeared outside the bus upon the pavement. Within only a few seconds, my dream had shifted from viewing the beach scene to my being completely alone on the upper deck of the bus.

Before I had any chance to react, the bell on the bus suddenly started to ring. I tried to stand in order to get off, but the bus suddenly shot forward hurling me back into my seat. We were moving again only this time the speed started to increase at an alarming rate and the top deck began to sway dangerously from side to side. I clambered upwards grasping the handrails, pulling with all my might against some invisible power trying to pin me back into the seat. When I finally got to my feet and into the aisle, I began driving each leg forward despite a gravitational pull backwards. It was like trying to infiltrate an impenetrable forcefield. I dragged myself to the opening where the steps should have been only to find that a slide was in its place. With every ounce of strength and valour, I had left in my body I willed my legs to buckle until the weight of my body hauled me downwards.

But this was a dream and they do not have the rationality of every day normal circumstances so instead of sliding down towards the door the swift movement directed me straight into the driver's seat. The wipers of the bus were furiously sweeping back and forth their rubber strips grinding on the exsiccated windshield. I needed to make it stop but as I tried to click the lever adjacent to the steering wheel several more stalks sprang up, so it was impossible to ascertain which was the correct one. I tried to stamp on the brake pedal yet despite several firm pumps with both of my feet there was no response so I grabbed what appeared to be the handbrake but that snapped clean off in my hand. The wire cord it was connected to springing into action to weave itself around my body like a boa constrictor.

I tried in vain to navigate the bus with the steering wheel, but it spun incessantly without any purposeful affect. I may have been sat in the driver's seat, but I had absolutely no control of the direction we were taking, the speed we were travelling nor the ability of stopping the vehicle. Exactly as in the first dream overwhelming fear flooded through me to an intense level until finally panic obliterated my dreamworld demanding my immediate return to consciousness.

My eyes scanned the dark shadows within the bedroom the large six drawer chest with the TV set upon it, the double barley twist wardrobe and the corner posts at the edge of the bed. I breathed in through my nose slowly and deliberately then blew out through my mouth to try and get the rapid race of my heart under control. I contemplated the field day an oneirocritic would have interpreting my dreams and concluded that the most obvious analysis was the clear portrayal of the absence of any control in my life at the present.

I was inevitably stressing about the impending interview with the police regarding an investigation that I'd had no previous knowledge of and that I would have no control in the direction in which it would take me. Not unlike the bus being unable to navigate it despite using every measure at my apparent disposal. Perhaps these elements were also reflective of Ruby's stance and my uncertainty regarding her honesty and my subsequent question whether I could trust her. Then there was Mum who I'd thought was implicitly trustworthy but whom I had consequently felt betrayed by and subsequently questioned her ability to protect me. This was not unlike the colleague in the first dream who had walked alongside me before suddenly metamorphosising into a zombie on an opposing side precipitously in pursuit of me.

Then there were the group of zombies hunting me down from all directions and my jumping over the balcony. Perhaps this was indicative of Kelly up there on the fence and my trying to get out of her way upon sensing the danger. I guess it also bore similarities to my suspecting that once I spoke up everyone might be pointing their finger at me and I would be standing out from the crowd. Not only due to being the one abused but that if I was unsupported, I would be standing alone and as Mum had warned blamed for the bullets Ruby had given me to fire.

Perhaps the robots were my subconscious analogy of how Ruby was appearing to me in how she had delivered her evidence so matter of fact without emotion and the bins picking through the rubbish my mind trying to sift what was true. When they simultaneously stood and lined up together, I was not compelled to do the same but then suddenly they disappeared. I knew I was worried about the side of the fence my other two siblings would sit but surely, they wouldn't abandon me when they knew he was guilty of other such acts. The truth was Nick had witnessed him albeit as an adolescent, but I had also heard his statement in the pub regarding his opinion 'that *he* would get himself in to trouble with the police for fettling school kids.'

Then there was Kelly who had made the comments regarding Elena's mouth and her suspicions of what he may be doing to her, yet she had done nothing to help. Surely, they would not be so cowardly to negate all knowledge and as the robots had done on the bus jump ship to get him out of his sordid predicament. No that did not bear thinking about even they could not be that cold blooded I was their younger sister whom they should have protected surely, they would step up to the plate and at least be honest. I felt like the person in my dream who had been basking in the sun one minute and was now being catapulted into my worst nightmare.

Then a chill went right through me; maybe the unseen force at work against me was a premonition of how Nick and Kelly were going to play their part and the facelessness of the robots a semblance of not being able to see who friend or foe was. Mum had stated the reason she hadn't told me about the investigation was because she was trying to protect me so maybe she was predicting the outcome based on her knowledge of her children as people. Inevitably I did not want to be left to stand alone in the firing line but equally I wanted a choice as to whether I got off the bus or not. I knew without a shadow of a doubt that once I had given my statement I would unwittingly be placed in the driver's seat. Here,

I would have no control upon anyone else's viewpoint whichever way they chose to examine the evidence it was there's alone to determine.

However, once given the facts I just hoped they realised the gravity that certain actions would instigate as the last thing I wanted was for my family to be split down the middle due to the depravity of one person. Ultimately, if they decided to lie when given informed choices then their decisions would have far reached, consequences and life would never be the same for any of us again. One thing I did know for sure was that once Dad found out about this whole sordid mess he would be unreservedly at my side because he was no fool and saw through each and every one of them.

I felt some comfort in knowing Dad's resolute position he was a man of honour; he would not lie to get *him* off he would tell the truth to protect the integrity of his young daughter and to ensure the family name was not dragged through the courts. Dad had seen his behaviour in the nightclub, heard his demeaning comments regarding women, experienced his violent and controlling behaviour first hand and been embarrassed by him both at home, work and socially. He also knew me because we were very much alike, we gave, we put others first and we did our very best in every situation for the greater good of those around us. I felt rest assured that even if I only had Dad as my ally, it would be like having 10 men behind me so it replenished my soul to know that I could take control back of my life.

I may have dreamt of being rooted to my seat on the bus and having to fight my way to the exit, but it was time for little Lois to stop being scared and to get up and fight her way through. I had to do the right thing even though I had been desperately attempting to grasp at the stalks to find the right controls I had to stop mulling it over and over like the wipers back and forth. The cord from the handbrake could be perceived as the enemy trying to restrict me further or I could depict it as a lifeline to finally bring a stop to the situation.

I couldn't deny that I had grave concerns about every single detail of the picture in front of me not to mention the anxiety of talking openly about such intimate details to the police. I knew it would be embarrassing and humiliating but my other concern was whether I could trust in the judicial system. What if the details of the abuse were recorded and left on file to be used at a later date for training purposes? Could I actually trust that the police would handle the case sensitively and what if more people came forward how big could this potentially become? Worse still what if I went through being interviewed and then the case was dropped, it would have all been for nothing. Then again what if it went to court and I had to give evidence and tell a whole court room what had happened. Would I then feel I was being judged depending on how I coped on the day. It really was a mine field and then I was back at the start wondering if I had done the right thing contacting Melissa Maya at all.

I was beginning to convince myself that I should telephone Maya in the morning to call the whole thing off until the soft whimper of Joe next to me alerted me to his forgotten presence. As I gazed at his angelic little face, safely tucked up in bed next to me, the blond curly locks of his hair hanging loosely about his face a fact penetrated my head like a piercing spike. This beautiful, innocent pure little child was more or less the same age as myself when that monster defiled me. I swallowed hard but not quick enough to stop a stream of tears from surging down my face. How on earth could anyone look at a child of his age and seek to sully them for their own self-centred gratification and in that moment, I knew without a shadow of a doubt I had to press forward. I may feel the personal shame when talking to the police and I may have carried *his* guilt all these years but there was only one person to blame and that was *him*, Timothy Rodgers!

And then I saw it! All those years before how I had been enjoying the sunshine when we first arrived at Grey Gables until I had roughly been pushed to the ground. He had targeted me, isolated me, rigid with fear against an invisible force that became my daily prison but as a child I was too weak to fight against *him*. All through my life I'd lived as faceless as the bins in my dream, a disposable nothingness equivalent to their taunts of the bins they had found me behind. The child growing up without a voice sifting through the rubbish of everyday situations being forced to deal with the uncompromising ridicule of *him*. I had not been able to make it stop so I had tried hard to grapple with anything around me to get a footing, to try to ground myself in order to cope.

However, this had caused an inward panic my default response to the outward circumstances causing me to freeze and fragment. I had to break free once and for all even if that meant I had to fight my way through little Lois's terror in order to protect us both. I had to secure some semblance of a life, and this was my chance, I had got a second bite at the cherry and I was taking it.

As far as I was concerned, from that moment on, my decision was final and I would march forward unswervingly in my pursuit for justice as no child deserved to be used and abused with the abysmal disrespect of a rag doll.

Chapter 21
The Monster

Surprisingly, the next morning I arose feeling quite refreshed, perhaps the turbulence of the dreams and the restless thought process had put to rest the ghosts that had been wreaking havoc. Either way I welcomed the restoration of my new inner found peace regardless of how long it would last. Joe continued to sleep as I surreptitiously slid out of my side of the bed and quietly collected my things together for the shower. I paused briefly as he began to stir, changing the position of his head so he was now facing me. The blond lock of hair that had been gently resting upon his cheek fell forward causing his little nose to wrinkle in mild agitation. So sweet, I smiled to myself and sneaked out of the room to get ready for the day ahead.

I had just finished brushing my teeth when I heard the dulcet tones of my mobile rising up from the table in the hallway where it was plugged in to the socket, charging. As I raced down the stairs to retrieve it, hoping not to disturb the boys, I noticed the screen displayed Mum's number.

'Hiya,' I said cheerily.

'I need your help, love,' Mum said worriedly.

'What's wrong?' I asked gravely nervous that Dad might be unwell again.

'I had Tim on the phone last night, he was in such a state, I have been worried sick all night,' she said. Clearly, the positive vibes I had sent her in the middle of the night had been useless then.

'I don't know what you expect me to do, Mum,' I was frank.

'I have just spoken to him now and I am really worried he might do something to harm himself, Lois,' she said sounding quite frantic.

'But Mum, with the risk of sounding harsh, he is in his current predicament by his own hand; why should I care if he is having a pity party for one after all he has done to me?' I fumed.

'I know, but I cannot sit back and do nothing,' she said.

'I appreciate he is your son, but he is nothing to me and I cannot afford to get involved,' I insisted.

'But Lois, I don't know what else to do, I wouldn't be able to forgive myself if he took his own life,' she began to get upset.

'I don't know what you expect me to do about it, Mum, or why you think I should even give a damn. Besides, he is too much of a coward to harm himself; he would rather hurt little children,' I delivered quite a heartless punch.

'Despite what he is accused of, Lois, as you have just said he is my son and I know you are angry, but I know you do give a damn because you are you,' she said.

'Please don't try to manipulate me, Mum, that is not fair why can't you ring one of the others let them show how much they care,' I said flippantly.

'Please Lois just go and check on him, for me,' she said stressing the last two words.

'You have got to be joking; why on earth would I want to go see him? I cannot believe you of all people are asking that of me!' I told her. I then caught some movement at the top of the stairs, so much for my not waking the boys.

'Please Lois, I am begging you, go see him and make sure he is ok. Do it for me,' she implored.

'I am really cross that you are putting me in this position; it is unfair of you, and I am not happy about it,' I stipulated.

'But will you, do it?' she urged.

'Give me his number,' I demanded quite offhand and wrote it down as she recited it on the pad that had been next to where my phone was charging. I did not even say goodbye; I just ended the call to show my annoyance and protest at her unreasonable request.

Jack appeared out of the bathroom and sauntered back towards his bedroom where I had laid out his clothes the night before.

'When you have had your shower, Jack can you get Joe up and assist him, please I have an important phone call to make,' I told him.

'An important call, Mummy, who to?' he asked.

'Just someone Grandma needs me to ring on her behalf,' I told him.

'Why can't Grandma do it; she has a phone of her own?' he said innocently.

'I know love, but she needs me to do it, just help Joe please,' I said turning away to mark the end of the conversation.

There is no doubt about it I was fuming why on earth would Mum put me in such a predicament by requesting my help she had three other children she could have asked. Maybe because she knew damn well no one would give a toss but then why would she think I should when it came to *him*. This was one of those moments in life where people could exploit your good nature and subsequently use it against you with guilt trips and emotional blackmail.

Mum knew full well that I would be compelled to do the right thing so of course I was her number one choice, but it didn't make it appropriate. She was not considering the impact it might have on me even though it was a huge burden and at a great cost to my own well-being. I decided I did not want to waste any time other than what was absolutely necessary by giving it valuable space in my thoughts mulling it over and doing my own head in. So, I decided to just bite the bullet and get it over and done with so I could move on and then drop it in the folder with everything else regarding *him* labelled "behind me".

'It's me,' I said, 'I think you and I need to talk, don't we?'

'Err yes, I think we probably do yes,' he said.

'Mum has just been on the phone worried sick about you and she wanted me to check in with you,' I explained making it plain I wasn't willingly initiating contact for any other reason.

'Right,' he said as though resigned to the fact he understood perfectly well why.

'Can we meet?' I asked, then feeling nauseous at the thought of being alone with *him* I continued, 'Perhaps at Green Park?' My rationale told me that meeting in a public place would be safer and also that I could comfortably walk away at any sign of trouble.

'Yes, that is fine,' he said, 'about 11.30, is that ok?'

I glanced at my watch, it was 10 am so it gave me one and a half hours to sort the boys out, drop them with Mum and get there on time. '11.30 is fine, there is a little bench along the path between the gates. I will meet you there,' I confirmed and disconnected the call.

Once the boys were safely with Mum, I reluctantly made my way towards Green Park which was only a couple of minutes' drive from Grey Gables. As I pulled into the narrow entrance flagged by two huge stone pillars one at either side, I followed the tarmacked path as it swept round to the right to the gravel laid car park. There were only two other cars a silver Toyota Yaris that had its boot up where a lady was depositing her dog and a red Nissan Micra. I chose the space nearest to the exit and reversed my car into it so that I could make a quick getaway should I need to do so. I got out of the car and made my way towards the little bench that I had described, thankfully it was not occupied and then I sat down to wait.

I momentarily closed my eyes to absorb the warmth of the sun upon my face the colour orange emblazoned behind my eyelids. I asked for God's peace, His grace and strength then I sought His wisdom to deal with the conflicting feelings that were swarming within me. However, I was determined to keep Little Lois at bay because if she came to the forefront I would be consumed with panic, fear and dread. Right now, to successfully exhibit an attitude of great strength and calmness along with confidence I needed a whole measure of self-control.

I was beginning to enjoy the serenity of being present in the moment when I sensed that *he* was near. I opened my eyes but there were no new vehicles in the little car park so absentmindedly I scanned the area and that is when I saw *him* walking from the opposite direction towards me. My stomach churned and I immediately felt uncomfortable fighting the impulse to jump in my car and speed off before he got any closer. It was like looking through a distorted lens that was obscuring my sight everything in my peripheral vision was being completely blurred out and with every step he took there appeared to be a glitch where he would jump at least another ten paces forward.

I could feel my heart thumping with each beat of his steps like a sonic boom sending waves bellowing outward shaking the blurred peripheral vision further. I was rooted to the spot unable to move paralysed by engrained fears trapped by the newly surface buried memories of the past. I had to fight through it, I could not allow him to continue controlling my whole being in this way. I knew I had to flip the coin and quieten Little Lois's panic to overcome the escalating anxiety. I had to be present and drag the self-assured, confident prison officer persona side of me to the fore. I pictured myself at the prison going into a cell removal with my team to take control of a violent inmate. I was kitted up, I was the one carrying the shield, an officer at either side we were a team, powerful and strong, *he* stood no chance against our training, our manoeuvres, our skills. *He* was getting closer but equally so was I.

I reminded myself that *he* had no control over me that I was able to walk away at any point, I was not trapped and I was not alone. Today I had a voice and if this was my one and only chance to challenge the beast to address his offending behaviour against me then it was going to happen. I was the person in control here I was the one who had the power because *he* had finally been exposed no longer having the luxury of hiding amongst the shadows.

'Hey up,' he said the silence broken and *he* was there. *He* took a seat on the opposite end of the bench to my left I resisted the urge to recoil not wanting him to know that his very presence sickened me. I was fine there was enough space between us.

'Mum rang this morning and said you were in a bit of a bad state, mentally and emotionally,' I told him.

'I would say that it's hardly surprising given the circumstances, wouldn't you?' he sounded cocky but looked dishevelled, unshaven and panicked. This gave me deep comfort and a further boost of strength.

'I guess not, so what happened?' I asked calmly cutting to the chase.

'I was away last weekend at a vintage vehicle show and when I returned, there were police at the garage waiting to arrest me on my return,' he stated.

'I will let you know before you go any further that I was dragged into this by Ruby after she was summoned to the police station to give a statement. Up until then I knew nothing about any investigation, so I have got to admit it has been quite a shocking week for me too,' I told him.

'Not as much of a shock as it has been for me,' he retorted.

'I guess not but there again whatever you are going through right now is a result of the poor choices and decisions that you have made. Not just once but over and over again, so please don't start with a pity party because I have run out of any fucks to give,' I declared.

'Fair enough,' he shrugged resigning himself to the fact that this was not going to be as easy as he thought, and I was no longer a push over that he could manipulate.

'So, I ended up having to accompany Ruby to the police station on Monday night and heard what she had to say. I guess there are always two sides to a story so what's yours?' I asked.

'Like I said I decided to go away for the weekend, but it was last minute and I couldn't really afford to stay in a guesthouse so I threw a mattress in the back of the van. I came home on Monday and the police arrested me,' he admitted.

'So, when the police arrested you, you had a mattress in the back of your van?' I asked speechless.

'Yes, I know it doesn't look good, but I just wanted to get away,' he told me.

'Under the circumstances I wouldn't say it didn't look good I would say it is quite a damning piece of evidence. For goodness' sake, have you not read how many paedophiles use this mode of operation before they abduct, rape and kill children?' I said in disbelief.

'I know, but I can't do anything about it now, can I?' he said almost defeatedly.

'So, what is this shit about what went on with Ruby when she was young?' I asked without giving too much information.

'I was only mucking about, just having a laugh,' he tried to brush off.

'It didn't sound anything like mucking about to me, in fact it sounded quite predatorial,' I stated.

'She is just blowing it all out of proportion,' he said.

'So, you have already been interviewed with regards to her statement then?' I asked.

'Yes, on Tuesday,' he told me.

'Inevitably I cannot repeat what she said specifically but why would she say those things if they were untrue?' I asked.

'She is just being a bitch,' he dismissed.

'Why would your sister make such a detailed complaint out of the blue unless something else has happened for her to turn against you?' I queried.

'No,' he shrugged, 'she is just being a bitch.'

'So where are the allegations coming from with regards to Danny and Elena?' I asked.

'Come on, you know that Ruby and Sarah are best mates it is something that they are concocting between themselves,' he stated.

'So why would Elena react in such a distressed state when a social worker attended the house?' I asked, 'distraught that they were coming to take her daddy away if it wasn't something that you had put in her head to stop her from talking?'

'I don't know, I wasn't there when it was supposed to have happened,' he said.

'Supposed to have happened? Does that mean you don't think it did happen or that they made that up too?' I queried.

'Yeah, more than likely they did make it up. Who is to say that they haven't been putting shit in her head,' he feebly retorted.

'The police said there is another line of enquiry they were following do you know what that is?' I asked.

'Yes, it is Sophie,' he replied.

'Sophie? What the heck?' I freaked out a little, 'what has Sophie got to do with this case, surely there are no allegations being made regarding her?' I felt so upset and sickened.

'Oh, it was one of the times she came out in the wagon with me,' he dismissed. When I remained silent, he continued 'it was the week before Sarah and I got married and I had to do an overnight delivery, Sophie wanted to come with me. She loved it when it was just me and her, so she came with me. We had been and had something to eat, got parked up and she was asleep,' he told me.

'What so she was in the bunk behind the seats in the cab?' I clarified.

'Yes, and she was fast asleep,' he affirmed.

'So, what happened for it to be another line of enquiry?' I asked.

'I hadn't been to the loo and was busting for a pee before I settled down, so I climbed out over her side of the truck and she woke up,' he said.

'I don't get it, why would that raise a red flag,' I was baffled.

'I had already unzipped my fly,' he attempted to minimalize the scene, 'so when I leant over her, I was hanging out.'

'There is no way you could have exposed yourself even if your fly was open, not unless your boxers were down,' I reasoned.

'Well, the thing is I was missing Sarah,' he began, 'so yes I had my boxers down and was having a wank.'

'Sophie, an 8-year-old child, was in the cab with you and you were pleasuring yourself; no wonder it's another line of enquiry,' I was flabbergasted.

'You don't understand. Sarah and I hadn't been getting on and we were only a week away from getting married I just wanted to be at home with her,' he argued.

'But you were not at home with your adult partner you were in a confined space with a little girl!' I stressed.

'I know, I know that, but there was so much stress going on with the wedding and I didn't even know if Sophies mum was going to let her and Cerys come to the wedding,' he whined.

'So, you're telling me that because you were missing your partner you think it is a perfectly reasonable excuse for not only exposing yourself in the presence of a child but to have a wank?' I could not comprehend the tripe I was hearing.

'Well, no, obviously not when you put it like that,' he answered.

'When I put it like what?' I began, 'when I break it down into an easy-to-understand statement of what is totally unacceptable behaviour in front of a child?'

'I didn't mean it like that,' he squirmed.

'Just hold on a minute, why would you need to get out of her side, why not get out of the cab at your side?' I asked.

'Well yeah I suppose I could have,' he stammered.

'Not been funny but this does not ring true at all and besides you said she was asleep in the back of the cab so you wouldn't have come in to contact with her at all,' I jumped in.

'Yeah, she was asleep, but she woke up,' he tried.

'Or you deliberately woke her up because you were aroused and as you say you were missing the partner who was not there,' I ventured.

'No, she had rolled over, but I didn't realise that she was awake at first because she was just laid there,' he said.

'So, your 8-year-old child is watching you pleasuring yourself and you don't realise. So, it has absolutely nothing to do with busting for a pee and having to get out of her side of the cab at all then?' I said shaking my head in disbelief.

'She was watching me,' he stated.

'So, what? Did that excite you further because she had suddenly become part of the act of pleasuring yourself,' I pushed.

'She asked me what sex was and asked me to show her,' he lied.

'Ok, I need to stop you right there,' I said trying my hardest to keep my emotions under check given the similarities to the statement that Ruby had delivered when she was 14 and he had questioned her if she knew what it felt like and he would show her. I swallowed, breathed and caught my breath again before continuing 'there is no way an 8-year-old child would instigate such a question without already being sexualised. I will tell you right now that story is a crock of shit and I will say it to your face you're a liar,' I delivered pulling no punches at all.

'That's fair enough,' was his pathetic response.

'The prison officer side of me says, you have the chance here to do the right thing so be a man, grow a pair and take responsibility for your actions,' I told him.

'That is easier said than done,' he responded.

'You can run around like a headless chicken in all different directions whining to Mum making her feel sorry for you, lying to the police or trying to get people on your side to back those lies. But that is all they are in the end, lies,' I was pulling no punches.

'Well yeah, I know what you are saying,' he bleated but still taking no responsibility.

'You obviously need help, but the first step has to come from you and that is the admission of your own wrongdoing. Without that the cycle will continue and with it an increased danger to any subsequent children you come into contact within the future,' I pointed out.

When he just sat there, I continued, 'There is no use thinking that this is something that Nick and Kelly can get you out of with some farcical rubbish, it isn't, this is serious,' I spoke wanting to make sure that whatever went down on Sunday at Kelly's he knew that it was not the right approach.

'I hear what you are saying and yes, I have felt out of my depth and like a headless chicken not knowing which way to go. That's why I rang Mum last night because I honestly thought everyone was better off without me being here, he admitted.'

'This is not the time for a self-adulating pity party you have orchestrated situations to take advantage of children for your own indulgence time and time again. You need help, you have been caught and it is time for you to hold your hands up and take back the blame, shame and guilt that is yours and yours alone to carry,' I told him.

I needed to end this but first of all I had to address what he had done to me so that I could attempt to loosen the chains that had ensnared me my whole life. 'You do know that the police will want my statement, don't you?'

'Yes, I know,' was his only reply.

'Again, I will tell you to your face just so you know I will be giving them a full account of everything,' I pressed. 'And I mean everything.'

'Yeah, well that is something I am not looking forward to and I don't know what to say about it,' he replied honestly.

'I would suggest the truth! The last thing Dad would want is for you to drag our family name through the courts, the shame alone would kill him, he would never be able to show his face again,' I enforced.

'No well hopefully it won't come to that,' he said.

'You do realise the gravity of things, don't you?' I asked.

'Yes of course I do it was me in the cells this week getting asked all the questions,' he muttered.

'All I am trying to say is please do not put any of us through anymore, Mum does not need to be dragged to court to give evidence and neither do I! Don't put your kids through the indignity of having to voice what you have done to them, that would be inexcusable. Do the right thing and set them free to get the support they need now rather than compounding it with the years and years of counselling and torment you have put me through,' I urged him.

'Yes, I will,' he said not too convincingly.

I stood to mark the end of the conversation and he did too, but before walking away I turned to say, 'Depending on the informed choices and decisions that you make now will determine whether this is the last conversation we ever have.'

'I see, right yes, I understand that' he stammered.

'I do hope you will honour Mum, Dad and the children by accepting responsibility but if not, just know that your decision will inevitably split our family apart and then things will never be the same again,' I said honestly.

'I hear what you're saying and your right I wouldn't want that to happen, so I am fully prepared to accept the consequences,' he stated.

I took one last look at the person who had stolen my innocence, the one who had manipulated, groomed and incited my compliance and the loathing that I had harboured for years evaporated. He was not so powerful anymore I just hoped that like every perpetrator he didn't start playing the victim as that was the path, I could see him taking. Don't all paedophiles blame their victim, "they came on to me"; "they enjoyed it"; "they participated"; "they wanted it". It was no different with *him* "she asked me about sex" so she was willing, and he was only showing her. Why do they always see themselves as innocent bystanders and not the monsters that they actually are?

They never seem to understand the concept that a child has no idea about sex until they are introduced to it whether that is through porn, demonstration or inciting them to participate. He had really made my blood boil but as I made my way back to Mums for the children, I was certain my words had fallen on deaf ears. The only reason he had turned up was for the purpose of wanting to moan about his self-made predicament but thankfully I had cut him to the quip and not given him the opportunity.

I had no faith that he would grow a backbone anytime soon and knew that whatever scheme Kelly came up with to try and get him off he would buy into it. Neither one of them had integrity, they were both born liars and worse for him Kelly actually thought she was clever enough get him off despite the compelling evidence against him. I just hoped she did not lead him down a path of false pretences because I knew that this would be his downfall. Or worse still when she failed then I would still get the blame for his demise.

Unfortunately, there was one thing for sure it was a very dangerous game. To not own up would result in it going to court and then life as we knew it would change dramatically, he would end up in prison and she would have split the family down the middle. Maybe it would have been safer for all of us if she had remained on the fence. One thing was certain I knew that I was going to have several more battles to fight but like Harry Potter in his final clash with Voldemort, I had defeated the power of my nemesis. However, the war would still continue to rage.

Chapter 22
Cliffe House

Over the course of the day, I battled to keep my conversation with *him* at bay and whenever elements began to invade my thoughts, I made a focused and determined effort to kick them to the kerb, *he* was not welcome. The boys and I decided to burn off some energy at Cliffe House in Shelly which has an outdoor climbing frame to explore and wooded area making it a child's paradise. It is a venue that we had visited many times during school holidays as they ran different activities and there were always new friends to meet.

I decided to buy us all meal deals enroute so that we could make the most of our day and to ensure the boys did not become grouchy due to their rumbling tummies. From the roadside, all that was visible of Cliffe House was an unassuming stone wall wrapping itself around the perimeter of the property. The entrance was accessed off a busy main road opposite some residential dwellings and guided you through a woodland area to an imposing Edwardian mansion. From this viewpoint, it looked a little dilapidated however from the front it was palatial.

As we pulled alongside the large newly sand-blasted building, I could feel the boy's excitement rising at their impending freedom. I left our lunches in the boot of the car so that we could explore uninhibitedly and once we had crossed the car park and accessed the play area the boys were unleashed like my childhood Evil Knievel toy. They scampered to the foot of the slide ascending the steps in quick succession before careering down feet first hands held sitting side by side. That's what I loved about my boys there was no competition they lived for the thrill of experiencing everything jointly. They even had a signature pose which was for them to stand or sit back-to-back hands folded across their chests, faces beaming with a little nod of the head.

Partners in crime was probably the best way to describe them although they never got up to any mischief it was always just good fun, wanting the best for each other. We laughed and giggled as they tried to scour the spiders web an entanglement of intertwined ropes. They walked the high bridge and navigated the boards before hurtling down the zip wires. It was an uninterrupted, family fun filled day which was exactly what we all required before they were due to return to school a couple of days later.

When we had finally dispensed our pent-up energy, the boys located a picnic bench whilst I collected the food from the car so we could take a timely break. It was awe-inspiring being in the presence of those two amazing little boys and an absolute pleasure to absorb the simplicity that enveloped their worlds. I often mused over them and secretly envied the blind trust they were able to bestow upon me as their care provider, their safety net and protector. How I still yearned for Little Lois to have had that too, wishing that she had received it as naturally, willingly and lovingly. It still remained as sharp as a double-edged sword brimming with pure regret for neither being able to comfort nor protect myself. Although the truth remains, a child is not emotionally mature enough to manage adult related themes nor sufficiently experienced to be able to console themselves.

It didn't stop me marvelling over the way both Jack and Joe were able to exude an uninhibited reserve of pure love, empathy, compassion and loyalty for each other. Their individual needs were met because they trusted one another implicitly and gave without measure openly and transparently the personification of a true sibling partnership without the destruction of rivalry.

As the boys chatted, I glanced around to observe the way other families interacted there was the odd child who was not listening, misbehaving or screaming because the inevitable "No" word had been used. Or maybe they were just tired, hungry or anxious. I was then drawn to a father with his two little girls and specifically the way he tended to their needs. One of the little girls was trying to tear something out of the other girls' hands and rather than be angry he walked around the table to her, knelt down before her and spoke quietly and softly. She was listening and clearly understood what he was explaining to her, she then handed the item back to her sister without quibbling before returning to her side of the bench. There was no fear, no coercion with promises of sweets if she did as she was told, he guided her into what was an acceptable solution to the situation.

That's a great advantage children possess the power to resolve things and move on quickly despite the high levels of emotions they can sometimes convey. I liked the fact he had gone down to her level, made eye contact, not raised his voice, he had encouraged her to be reasonable and then given her the opportunity to make the right decision for herself. I couldn't help feeling that those little girls were very lucky to have such a positive role model and that inadvertently he was also demonstrating their base level for a future life partner.

I sat musing over the difference between my experiences of isolation, of being spoken at rather than to and of being viewed as an irritant rather valued like those two little girls who were being guided and supported to regulate their emotions. Then there were my own boys who were treasured equally seen as individual people with their own thoughts, feelings and supported to develop a strong knowledge of self-worth. I couldn't distract myself from wandering down the cul-de-sac contrast that Danny, Elena and Sophies life had taken them and a new lesion across my heart was sliced open so raw. It was no good I had to act and fast as I knew I couldn't comfortably live with the knowledge that those children had been open fodder to that monster. I collated our rubbish together in the shop bought carrier bag our food had come in and picked up a few discarded items that other people had left behind then placed it in the waste bin. Once the boys were off for round two, I took a moment to return to the car to make the call.

'Hello, is either Melissa Maya or Dena Samuels available please?' I asked.

'Hello, this is Melissa Maya, can I help you?' she said rather cheerfully.

'It's Lois, Lois Rodgers,' I said.

There was a sharp intake of breath and almost as if she was holding it daring not to part with it in case, I floated away she waited with bated breath for me to continue. 'I am willing to go with you to observe the suite that you were talking about,' I stated.

I got a mental picture of Maya punching the air as she dared to release her breath, 'That's great Lois, thank you so much for agreeing to take a look is it possible to book that in with you now for Monday, say 11 am?' She enquired.

'Yes, do you want me to meet you there?' I offered.

'If it is ok with you, Lois, we would prefer to pick you up and escort you there,' she said.

A shiver went down my back at the word "escort"; it sounded very official, and it generated an image of being trapped in the back of a police car and having no form of escape. As if to read my mind, Maya suddenly interjected, 'It is just standard procedure, Lois, and don't worry; we will not turn up at your house in a police car we use an unmarked pool car.'

'Ah, alright that is fair enough, I will see you at 11 on Monday then,' I confirmed.

'Yes, see you then and Lois, thank you for agreeing to check it out I know it cannot have been an easy decision. I appreciate it must have taken immense courage on your behalf,' she said.

'I have had to dig deep for this, Melissa, so it isn't me confirming I can go through with it but I am prepared to take a look which will still be difficult enough,' I told her not wanting her to think that anything was set in stone yet.

'I understand Lois, see you Monday.' And she ended the call.

They say everything happens for a reason, but I think that is only a true statement in part as there are no reasons children are abused, people are killed, disasters occur or why we go through life enduring pain and suffering. However, there are interlocking parts that feed off one other and if you look close enough you can often see connections with perhaps revelations confirming valid patterns. For instance, I could not for the life in me fathom why Mum had pressed me to talk to *him* especially knowing the circumstances. I mean I could see no viable benefit at all for myself only an endurance, however by responding in good faith it had allowed me to assert some form of control back over my life.

Also, by going for a blow-out with the boys I was able to analyse the core relationships around me which had given me a clearer view and led me to summon the courage to hopefully have made the right decision, time will tell.

Chapter 23
Visiting the Suite

Once I had dropped the boys off at school early on Monday morning, I retraced my route straight back home. I could have dropped in to see Mum and Dad at Grey Gables, but I really didn't want to fend off any awkward questions as a result of the tension I exuded. The last thing I needed was a conversation having to explain where I was going, why and what we may be discussing. Equally I was nervous enough without Mum's pleas to save *his* sorry ass or worse still a poor attempt at emotional blackmail hoping to prevent me from giving a statement to the police. Therefore, I returned home and firmly locked the door behind me.

Maybe I just required a few uninterrupted moments to realign myself and regulate my emotions to enable me to complete the mission ahead. Situations that push you out of your comfort zone are often very difficult to approach let alone accomplish but once overcome they can be exceptionally edifying. These are the moments that stretch our capacity, but they also help us to reach our full potential and demonstrate how strong we really are.

I have always strived to push myself to be the best that I can be whether academically, personally, socially or workwise. I have a thirst for knowledge and pursue a continual growth pattern that also creates an independence in all aspects therefore I am happy in my own company. Perhaps this has sustained me when relationships end as they inevitably do as I am unable to tolerate others who do not match my high standards. Therefore, I have never needed anyone to make things right for me, or to try and save me and I would hate for anyone to view me as a problem they needed to solve. I am not looking for an answer to any unasked questions, but equally I don't require anyone to show me a different way or to berate my efforts.

If I ever feel I am backed into a corner or that life is tearing me in a million different directions, I am prone to explode. Others may think that this is an extreme reaction to a current situation it isn't, it is a product of having my early emotional development disrupted through trauma. I do not mean to take it out on others and nor is it personal I just allow things to bubble under the surface rather than face it and then I erupt. I don't ask people to understand as half the time I do not understand myself which is why I may cry because I have been squeezed too tightly into a small space and are trying to break free. It is merely due to the fact that I am not always able to regulate what other people may define as a "normal" response.

To explain this better is that when I am dealing with my two boys, I view their behaviour as separate to them as a person. Their behaviour is something they react emotionally towards which can have many underlying symptoms like being hungry, in pain, under pressure, stressed or tiredness. Therefore, by managing these elements along with installing appropriate guidelines with regards to acceptable behaviour and discipline we have created a happy equilibrium. I am still working on myself in these areas as I often forget to eat, I don't get enough rest or sleep and I am always on the go putting everyone else's needs first because I have the abuse mentality of wanting to please.

If people opened their eyes, they would see I have come a very long way since we first met because I am exorcising those demons little by little each day. I know some do not understand why I react or behave in a certain way but know that I will never use my past as a get out clause to substantiate or excuse my behaviour. I will always own who I am, I will confess my wrongdoings, I will try to rectify my failings because I will always be on the road to new growth. If we fall out or simply go our separate ways please do it with dignity, I will have no bad words to say regarding you so please honour me in the same way. Just remember, whatever negative utterings you may voice will have little to no effect on me because it will simply fall upon deaf ears. You see you cannot hurt me as no one is capable of being more critical of me than I am of myself, so please don't waste your breath.

With this strength and positivity in mind, I decided to approach today's outing in the same way I do when I go to the dentist and that is to not create negativity through worry but to wait until I was sat in the chair with nowhere else to go.

I stood outside my front door teetering on the top step like a victim of the hangman's noose waiting for the board beneath my feet to drop. To say I was nervous was a gross understatement. My mouth was so dry that it felt like a thousand shards of glass had splintered in my throat with every attempt to swallow. My head was throbbing to the reckless beat of an unrestrained heavy metal gang whilst my ears counteracted to the buzzing of an overactive wasp's nest.

I was just contemplating running in for a cool glass of water or of filling a bottle to take with me when the familiar face of Melissa Maya pulled up in a car outside the house. She could see I was not in a good place so attempted to bridge the gap between us by getting out of the car. It was unnecessary as the instinct of fight or flight had abandoned me the moment panic had taken root and then my psyche had crumbled to freeze and fragment. Gone were my instincts to run and escape the arrangement with Maya and diminished along with it was my zealous spirit for justice. In its place was the overwhelming physical anguish cascading into every particle of my body to render me incapacitated. I wasn't just reacting through my emotions anymore my body was actually shutting itself down to protect me, but I knew I had to prevent it before I detached mentally completely. I gazed through glass eyes in Maya's direction though saw nothing and gradually everything else around her was beginning to fade until it went black.

'Lois, can you hear me?' Maya's voice vaguely penetrating some atom of my brain.

'Lois,' I heard it again a little louder although it appeared garbled like I was under water.

I tried to move but felt as though my leg was caught in some kind of fisherman's netting. It was coarse and it hurt. I knew I had to find that fighting spirit not the one where I felt trapped or cornered and it instigated the self-protective measure to come out fighting. No this was the courageous variety where I had become accustomed to fighting to save myself by finding the way out. It's a similar panic of needing to get out like being stuck in a maze at night with no sense of direction. I knew I had to concentrate on the pain in my leg as this was my major link to reality with Maya's voice the secondary back up.

I focused all my energy into the pain in my leg willing it to move so that I could at least feel rather than just sensing discomfort. Again, the sharpness as though the skin was being cut but no sound would escape my mouth. I was locked somewhere deep my body having submitted to the soporific trance like state of a hypnotist. There was a comforting essence of gentle movement as though I was laid in a boat that sat upon still water. I soaked in the peace like a sponge absorbing water and again heard a far-off cry.

'Lois, come on open your eyes,' said a familiar voice, was that Mum?

An involuntary smile must have slightly made its imprint on my face as the voice became more urgent. 'Lois, I want you to open your eyes, come on Lois come back to us,' it commanded more audibly and clearer.

I felt something soft yet moist run across my face, it was a strange mixture of pleasant and yet not very nice too and then I got a whiff of something putrid not unlike fish. Was I really in boat or caught in the fisherman's net? It was confusing but that was the perfect imperfection of thoughts because it signified a reconnection with consciousness. I counted the anchor points: my leg hurt; the familiar voice; the softness to my face and the pungent fish like odour to create a path to follow the footprints out. My hand was being held, no it was being rubbed and my fingers moved. The moistness again followed by the fishy stench and that's when I actually felt my face scowl in protest, it was a reaction thus pointing me in the right direction. I wasn't fond of the feeling or the smell but it was the most prominent, so I focused upon it breathing deeply now and sensing my chest rising and falling rhythmically.

'Lois, can you hear me?' Maya tried.

'Lois, open your eyes,' Mum said again only this time with a slight flickering of my eyes I obeyed. 'What on earth happened?' she addressed the stranger in front of her.

'I honestly don't know. I had only just pulled up, when I saw Lois stood by the door,' Maya began, 'I realised something was wrong because she didn't look well so I got out of my car. Before I could get to her, she had hit the floor.' Maya explained.

'Lois, what on earth is going on? You haven't had this type of episode for years, is it because you are letting his arrest overwhelm you?' Mum asked.

I stared, exhausted, my energies spent and with nothing of significance to offer. Maya assisted me to a sitting position whilst Mum went into the house to get a dining chair for me to utilise. I saw the trickle of blood at the lower part of my leg along with the chicken wire edging that was now flattened. I felt nauseous and not just because I realised the soft moisture across my face and the fishy smell were Poppy's kisses and breath. Urrgh, there is a reason I don't let dogs kiss me!

'It's a good job I came to check on you,' she said returning with the chair, 'I had thought you would call after the school run and when you didn't arrive, I got a bad feeling so I decided to take a drive over,' she explained.

'I am ok now,' I said trying unsuccessfully to minimise the situation and to stop Mum from fretting. It didn't work. I felt decidedly embarrassed in front of Maya but not as much as if the curtain warriors along the street had been monitoring the scene. I wouldn't hear the last of it if those gossipmongers had witnessed everything.

'Quite clearly, you're not, Lois, why on earth haven't you managed your mental health better? You know what happens if you let yourself slip down this far?' Mum chastised more out of worry than her actually berating me.

'Oh, let me see, perhaps learning that you and Ruby have been in cahoots regarding your son's offending behaviour and then, oh I don't know maybe forcing me to meet with *him* tipped me over the edge!' I stated none too kindly.

'Lois, under the circumstances, I don't think it's feasible to do the visit today, shall we leave it for later in the week? Say Thursday to give you ample time to rest?' Maya asked.

'Visit, where are you going, Lois?' Mum jumped straight in. 'And, sorry I don't think we have met before who are you?'

Maya looked at me for some kind of confirmation that it was alright to disclose information. I gave her a reluctant nod, so she gave Mum a brief introduction outlining her role, the planned visit and the dreaded video interview. Mum was silent as she listened and seemed on edge once she had finished.

'You see, this is why my trauma responses have been ignited and reduced me to near complete shutdown,' I told her.

'If the thought of attending this place has triggered such a negative mental impact, Lois perhaps you need to completely abort the idea.' Mum stated.

'The point is Mrs Rodgers a video accounting Lois's early childhood is a much clearer and more defined representation of those events for the jury,' Maya tried.

'Is it more important to obtain one than to protect Lois's state of mind?' Mum implied.

'That is not what Melissa is saying, Mum, I have agreed to visit the suite providing I can make a decision about the statement depending on how it goes.

I know *he* is your son, but this needs to end before any more children are added to the list,' I said steadfastly.

'Obviously, we do not want to cause Lois any further distress and I can assure you it will be dealt with sensitively and that you will be in full control, Lois,' she reassured both of us.

'Would you mind getting me a drink of water, Mum?' I asked her directly just to change the subject.

Once Mum had ventured inside, I answered the queried look upon Maya's face, 'Right, I am feeling much better now, and I am not prepared to leave this to fester for another three days so are we going to do this visit or what?' I delivered.

'That is your call, Lois, if you feel up to it then I will be guided by you,' she responded quite taken aback by the sudden turn of events.

'I need to do this today if you are going to have any chance of getting me there, so let's get sorted and I will tell Mum,' I commanded.

'Here you are, love,' Mum said handing over a glass of water and then noticing Maya had returned to her car, 'is she leaving then?' Mum presumed sounding pleased.

'We all are, Mum,' I said gently, 'I have told Melissa that I need to do the trip today as I cannot worry all week anticipating a repeat performance of today on Thursday morning.'

'Oh,' was her only reply a subtle indication that she wasn't that happy now.

'I will take the chair in and lock up,' a signal it was time for her to leave 'afterwards I will come over to Grey Gables,' I told her.

'Ok Lois, I hope you know what you're doing,' she retorted.

'I wouldn't say I know what I am doing however I do intend to see what I am up against at least then I can decide on the best avenue going forward,' I told her.

Once in the car with Maya a sense of great relief seemed to clothe me, I wasn't sure whether it had something to do with my returning energy, being glad to be getting on with it or Mum's lack of resistance. Either way I no longer feared the journey nor succumbed to the impending doom of a claustrophobic soulless interview room. Maya attempted to install an appropriate level of light-hearted chat whilst overtly skirting around the elephant in the car and before I knew it, we had shifted through the country lanes and popped out at the far end of Ravensthorpe. The next village on was Mirfield. Surprisingly we pulled into an interconnecting residential street with rows of red bricked terraced houses facing the full length of them. Amongst them was a low-level single-storey building that stood out like a copper on a drugs bust in a crack house. It appeared so rundown that it was easy to believe the houses had been built around it, like the house in the film *Up*.

The building had a side entrance with possibly just enough room to fit the car although I wasn't holding my breath and thought Maya would definitely park on the road. She didn't, she expertly swung the car in to demonstrate she had clearly manoeuvred this space many times. At that moment, my brain decided to revisit the reason we were there, and I suddenly did not feel as self-assured as I had done. That is the problem when you give yourself a false sense of security a little tremble and the rocky ground shakes like an earthquake.

'How are you doing Lois?' Maya enquired sensing my unease.

'A bit nervous but the worst thing for me is to hesitate so our best approach is to face it head on and get straight in otherwise I will talk myself out of it.' And with that I was quickly out of the car followed by Maya and entering the building before I could bat an eyelid.

The small untidy entrance had a dank smell of damp and the windows looked like they hadn't been touched in years. Maya led me through into a small office like area that she explained would be occupied by herself and one other person from their technology department. At the risk of seeming sexist or stereotypical, I gathered that this would be a man, specifically because she had omitted that detail. The shock of horror on my face signalled Maya that a tad of reassurance was immediately required so she explained he was there to monitor the systems to extract a court room quality sample. This explanation did little to allay my fears it just resulted in my feeling like some kind of experimental lab rat.

On the desk were two monitors, a keyboard, twin plastic in/out trays aligned on top of one another and some discarded notepapers all of which wreaked of age. This was not the hi-tec state of the art equipment I had expected it was literally bog basic and looked like a clip from some seedy motel. The two vacant murky grey office chairs were stained and had tears exposing their foam innards, this was not going well.

Maya then led me to another office sized room situated at the back but adjacent to the first. There was a soft blue armless chair sat in the far-right corner opposite me with its back set square against the corner of both walls. To its right was a low-level circular table with a box of tissues on top, it made me feel exceptionally uneasy to think of the number of victims who had probably paced these floors. There was a second chair slightly to the left of the first sat more centrally in the room and little else. I walked further into the room and then I saw it and stopped rigid in my tracks. Having probably witnessed this numerous times before Maya hesitated to give me a chance to catch my breath, she was scrutinising my reaction.

'It's ok, Lois, the camera is not recording, it is inactive at the moment, but this is where you will be during the interview,' she said, 'how does it feel?'

'It isn't anything remotely like how I pictured it would be, I imagined it would be more hi-tec and that it would be housed somewhere in the bowels of the police station. I also thought there would be a two-way mirror or something but maybe I have just watched too much TV,' I said honestly.

'We like to do it here away from the station as it is more private, less formal and hopefully less threatening, that's why we do a visit first,' she told me.

'Feel free to take a seat,' she offered extending her arm to the one in the spotlight.

'I am not sure I feel comfortable sitting there,' I said glancing up at the camera.

'I know it feels strange and disconcerting right now Lois but please have a wander round to familiarise yourself as it will help to acclimatise yourself with the surroundings,' Maya suggested.

I gladly backed myself out of the room and retraced my steps through to the exit to get as much of a fresh breath of air that the town allowed. Anything was better than being cooped up in that claustrophobic dank smelling building. I wanted to cry, an outward emotion of the inner torment raising its ugly head yet again but instead I gritted my teeth and remained resolute. I battled to overcome the impending stress actively reminding myself of what Maya had said, my statement was a key part of the evidence. I allowed the picture of *him* sat on the bench next to me lying through his teeth to filter through my memory banks and regained the importance of my compliance. It was for the greater good of my nieces and nephews and the unknown future child victims whom he would come into contact with if I pulled out.

In my mind's eye, I began symbolically cutting and pasting a picture of my boy's face upon the face of each of the known victims. Once I was done, I was then able to march right back into that run down building with a new fervour and enhanced vision. I made a bee line for the room with the camera and without any hesitation sat straight down in the seat opposite the camera.

As President Franklin D Roosevelt said: 'The only thing to fear is fear itself.'

Chapter 24
Making a Statement

When Maya had dropped me off after arranging to take the statement the following Thursday, I had silently congratulated myself for taking charge and for overcoming this personal difficulty. I felt relieved that it was over with but also elated that I had conquered my fear and achieved the goal. For the next couple of days, I eased back in to doing the school run with the boys, the monotony of cleaning the house, doing the shopping and of course visiting my elderly parents.

Mum never asked about the visit nor the outcome of my decision regarding the statement, so I didn't mention it either. I figured that as *he* was her son, she simply did not want to discuss the subject and bearing in mind the secrecy she'd had to uphold for Ruby I wasn't comfortable putting her in a similar position. Besides if Dad was right and she did have the early onset of dementia the last thing I wanted to do was to do was put her in a predicament to cause further stress or upset. However, I did desperately yearn to talk it through with Dad who would always apply his words of wisdom and gentle guidance especially in times of confusion.

Unfortunately, although Dad had been privy to his son's antics over the years, he had apparently been kept completely in the dark regarding the subject of child abuse. Therefore, I had absolutely no one apart from Ruby to discuss matters with and there was no way I was going to offer any information her way just in case it was used against me at a later date, which was her usual style of operation. There again I also knew that when Ruby didn't have the correct information, she was prone to make up some random crap or fill in gaps as though what she was saying was the gospel truth. I knew that I would have to play this by ear and tread very carefully indeed.

When Thursday arrived, I was surprisingly calm and accomplished my morning routine with thorough and organised precision. Having the ability to extract the emotions from a difficult situation allows one to exercise great self-control and to detach completely. This is a great benefit but as with any strength there is also an alternative flip side in that a strength can also be a weakness. For me, the detachment meant that in any form of relationships where boundaries were being damagingly overstepped, I could cut them out without a sideways glance.

Unfortunately, this was also true in cases where I had allowed someone to get too close then a perceived threat had caused my barriers to fly up in exactly the same way. In the past, I have been guilty of not taking the time to step back to give myself the opportunity to assess a situation with clarity, especially in heated situations although I am getting much better. Nowadays I will ask the person to leave if we are at my home or just walk away myself in order to give ourselves the time to assess a situation to allow matters to calm down. My worst-case scenario is of dealing with a person who is exceptionally needy as they tend to receive this as the misconception of being rejected. It isn't, it is about exercising respect for one another and of demonstrating the protection for the relationship and the people you value. As I said I am a working progress who strives to gain a better understanding of myself for the greater good of those around me.

This was probably why I gave myself such a hard time with regards to making a statement inevitably I wanted to do the right thing and protect the children but equally I needed to look after myself too. Having agreed with Maya to go in on the Thursday morning meant that a decision had been made and therefore I could detach myself until the day. And here I was, waiting for Maya to arrive. When the same graphite grey Ford Focus pulled up outside the gate, I still wasn't nervous I simply went through the motions of locking my front door and getting into the car beside her.

'Hey Lois, how are you?' Melissa asked casually.

'Fine thanks,' I said as breezily as I could like we were on our way to do a bit of shopping.

I could tell it confused Melissa because her brow furrowed obviously, she had expected me to be a bag of nerves but seemingly I was as bright as a button. She didn't speak for a few moments, maybe she had rehearsed some words of encouragement but was now having to process this unexpected impassive calmness.

'The technical guy is called Don if you prefer not to see him that is fine, we can go straight into the suite although it may help you to know who is at the other end of the camera. The lady interviewing you is called Sharon Stanley she is very experienced and will guide you along so you don't need to worry,' she explained.

'Ok,' I said, I mean there was little else I could say, to me in this detached state it was just information and it had no connection to the real me.

'Have you been up to much this week?' Melissa changed tact, maybe to encourage me to engage but also to maybe talk about myself so that I was less impartial.

'Not really, just humdrum of everyday stuff,' I responded without feeling.

'Did your mum ask you about the visit on Monday?' she enquired.

'No, she hasn't mentioned it all week so I decided not to either as I didn't want to give her a platform to be able to talk me out of it,' I said blasé.

'So haven't you shared with her that you are making your statement today?' she asked unable to keep the surprise from out of her voice.

'I thought it best to wait until afterwards otherwise I would have had her emotions to deal with on top of my own and that would have been far too much of a weight to bear,' I said logically.

'I understand' she told me though I am not quite sure whether she did or not.

When we arrived at the suite, Melissa was going to perform her previous trick of swinging her car into the tiny space alongside the small building only to find it already occupied. She halted midway threw it into reverse and parked halfway up on to the kerb to leave enough room for passing vehicles. She looked more nervous than I felt. We disembarked and were making our way in through the entrance when she suddenly hesitated and turned to me.

'Are you ready for this Lois,' she asked apparently seeking some form of confirmation.

'I am OK at the moment Melissa because I have already been here so I know what to expect of the environment although I have not accepted yet what is taking place which is why you may feel I am a tad detached,' I tried to explain to her.

'Is it alright to introduce you to Don or would you rather I didn't?' She enquired.

'I think I would prefer to know who is in the building then there are no unexpected surprises,' I said sensibly.

She led the way into the little waiting area with the dirty windows, the smell was just as hard hitting as on my first visit. She then took me to the office with the monitors where a balding chap with headphones tightly clamped over his ears occupied one of the stained grey chairs. It was at that point when my anxiety started to rumble under the surface and I realised my mouth was dry.

'Would you like a drink before we begin?' Melissa asked evidently noticing my discomfort.

'Could I have some water please?'

'I thought that is what you might need,' she said producing two bottles of spring water from her bag. 'I got these for you on my way this morning.'

I took one from her thankful for her kindness but also glad to have something to do with my hands as the nervous energy was increasing. I unscrewed the top and drank greedily from the bottle grateful it was still water rather than the fizzy spring type. She tapped the guy on the shoulder to alert him to our presence he flinched slightly evidently not having realised we were there too engrossed in the task ahead no doubt waiting for the next lab rat, me. He spun around using the castors of his chair to propel himself until he was fully facing us both, he did not get up. I wondered if this was because he did not want me to feel overpowered either due to his height or his gender.

'Lois, this is Don Blackstone; he will be our technical specialist for today who will ensure everything runs smoothly, he has already performed all the necessary tests,' she informed me.

I didn't know where to look so kept my eyes focused on the plastic disc casing that was labelled as subject L015 case TR1-09.06.11. I wondered if it was a coincidence that L, zero, one, five spelt Lois or whether Sophie's would also be 50PH135. I shrugged this line of thought away it was most unhelpful sometimes how my brain worked to distract me in times of stressful situations.

'Are we ready, Don?' she asked, and he merely gave a nod, replaced his headphones and spun back round.

I wasn't sure if he was being Mr Minimal on purpose or whether it was due to the circumstances and it was usual procedure not to engage. Given my reluctance to take part in a video interview it was quite possible he had been briefed that I was delicate and so thoughtful attention had been given to curtail potential stress factors. The other consideration was this could simply be his genuine, scintillating personality. When Melissa turned to leave the room, I took a step back for her to go first I may have been here before, but I was not comfortable assuming the lead. Surprisingly, she led me back through to the small entrance area where a buxom woman of around 55 years old now stood. This took me a little off guard so much for keeping the stress to a minimum.

'Lois, can I introduce you to Sharon Stanley; as I said on the way here, she will be the lady conducting the interview,' Melissa said in a much softer voice than she usually used. I attempted a smile, but it was weak.

'Hello Lois,' Sharon offered. It was a kind voice and I noticed she had a motherly look about her, there was a warmth, and I could picture her elbow deep in flour kneading dough to bake bread. As an artist this happened a lot, I got an almost instant picture of people in my head which helped me to make connections depending on the image. She had mousey coloured tonged hair that fell just below the nape of her neck and in her ears small, looped gold earrings were just visible. She wore a loose-fitting flowered blouse beneath a baggy grey cardigan with a long plain darker grey skirt that flowed to her mid-calf around her neck was the customary police lanyard bearing her identity.

'Hello,' I managed.

Melissa explained that only Sharon and I would enter the suite, and that we would take our seats so that Don could make any adjustments to the equipment with regards to focus and depth of field. I took this to mean how far Mr Minimal would want to zoom in and I guessed it would be far too close for comfort but as long as a camera wasn't right in my face, I reasoned with myself it didn't matter. She told me that at any time I wanted to stop or if I needed a toilet break then I just had to raise my hand to signal to that effect.

It was all becoming a bit too real I was actually being prepared to sit in a room with a stranger who was going to ask me probing questions about my worst nightmare. I don't know what I communicated at that moment but both Melissa and Sharon quickly glanced at each other and that was enough to send my paranoia smashing right through those dirty windows. I turned on my heel and fled out through the door succumbing to my sudden desire to escape. I felt lost, alone and overcome as an impending sensation blasted up to be released through the primal burst of a grief-stricken little girl overwhelmed in an adult world.

Sharon and Maya handled the situation perfectly by simply allowing me to cleanse my soul of the surge of emotions without pressure by simply affording me the time and space. I was then able to return on my own terms in the knowledge that they did understand and with a renewed confidence that I was safe.

'Thank you,' I said, 'I am ready now.'

Both Melissa and Sharon gave me what could only be described as their winning smiles and led me towards the office door. Melissa gave my arm a little squeeze to show her support and wished me luck then disappeared through the door without another word. Sharon gave her a nod as she went and then proceeded towards the dreaded suite door. I tried in vain to push aside thoughts of my being a naughty schoolgirl following the teacher to the headmaster's office.

As I entered the room, I immediately recoiled at the addition of a second camera which sat upon a tripod to the left of the room pointing directly at the chair I was set to occupy. It disturbed me greatly, so too did the rearrangement of the room. My chair was still intact, but the little table would now be in front of me with the obligatory tissues remaining on top. Sharon's seat had been placed about 6 feet away at the other side of the table directly opposite me with the camera on its tripod located over her left shoulder. I would be lying if I didn't say I was exceptionally uneasy about this new arrangement, but I had come this far and there was no way I was backing out now.

'Lois, would you mind taking the seat over in the corner please?' Sharon Stanley asked whilst holding the door with her right hand and gesticulating with an open hand towards the specific chair.

I glanced at her then edge my way around the table and uncomfortably took the offending position she had directed me towards. When she closed the door, I had all on not to run screaming and kicking back through it I felt trapped and hemmed in. She became immediately aware of my discomfort and took the seat opposite me, so she was not stood in front of the door barring my exit. I breathed, closed my eyes and imagined my go-to song: Wake Up Boo! By the Boo Radleys playing in my head. In times of extreme stress, the opening made me smile and helped me to drift from rising panic into my own world and with the constant beat I could ground myself by nodding along. Ready to face the circumstances of the environment I was currently in; I opened my eyes to find a startled Sharon Stanley who probably wondered what basket case she was working with today. It was my time to smile to assure her.

'I am ready Sharon I just needed to reduce my stress levels so that I can focus on the reason we are here and be able to answer your questions rather than having a panic attack due to the impending fear.' I smiled again.

'I appreciate this is a very difficult situation Lois so whatever measures you need to take to protect yourself is absolutely fine by me,' she said kindly.

'I just become unsettled if I am not the one closest to the door and feel hemmed in and the room has changed since I came for my visit. It's quite disconcerting and I wasn't aware that there would be a second camera or that it would be directly over your shoulder pointing at my face,' I tried to explain further.

'The camera behind me at the corner of the room is one that is usually used but Don likes to ensure that we have a backup copy just in case anything happens like we have a power cut or there is a technical fault. The last thing we want to do is to have to interrupt the interview or worse still abandon it and have to redo it another day,' she told me.

'No, it would be impossible to mentally go through this again!' I stated, 'Let's do this.'

'Right Lois, if you're ready, I will ask you to make yourself as comfortable in your seat as possible and to then look straight up at the camera above. If you can count out loud slowly to ten and then look straight at the camera at my shoulder again for a count of ten and then towards me and do the same. I will then leave the room to check with Don and Melissa that the sound level and picture quality are set and then we will begin, ok?' she asked.

I took a slow intake of breath and said, 'as ready as I can be.'

'Right then, if you would like to proceed with the first camera,' she guided me.

I lifted my head and counted slowly as instructed then to the second and lastly towards Sharon each time her voicing the instructions, I guessed for the recordings too. As stipulated, she left the room and I was alone briefly wondering what the hell I had got myself into or more specifically what had Ruby got me in to. And then the door opened and Sharon returned to her seat. She started by stating her name, badge number, job title and why the interview was being conducted presumably so it was on record, possibly in case she had to give evidence and also for future viewers. Then it began.

'Lois, can you tell me your full name?' Stanley asked.

'Yes, it is Lois Rodgers,' I stated.

'Can you give me your full address including your postcode,' she asked which I did.

'As you know Lois, we are conducting an investigation with regards to complaints made against Timothy Rodgers, what is your relationship to Timothy,' she asked.

'We have the same parents,' I said, not to be clever but because to me I had no relationship with that person at all.

'So, is he your full brother?' she asked.

'Biologically he is but I do not class him as being related to me,' I told her.

'On Monday 30 May 2011, you attended the police station in Huddersfield with your sister Ruby, is that correct,' she asked. I nodded. 'For the purpose of the recording, Lois, I will need you to verbalise each answer,' she smiled as if to say you know how it is.

'I did, my sister Ruby had been called to give a statement at Huddersfield police station regarding the case but had rung me beforehand in a hysterical state. I subsequently offered to drive her as I didn't feel she should be behind the wheel or it was wise for her to go alone,' I informed her.

'At the time, were you aware of the reason she had been asked to make a statement?' Stanley enquired.

'No, I had absolutely no idea anything was wrong before I received her phone call,' I stated.

'So, when did you become aware that Timothy had been arrested and the reason of that arrest?' she asked.

'She told me on the phone of his arrest, but I couldn't make out what she was saying I just figured something had happened and he had rung her from the police station. I guess I just presumed that he didn't want Mum or Dad getting involved and therefore wanted to keep it quiet, but she was hysterical, so I went over to assist. When I arrived, she got in the car and then the story unfolded on the way to the station,' I spoke.

'When you say the story unfolded, what do you mean?' she asked.

'Sorry, she told me that there had been an investigation taking place for about 18 months and that it was suspected that Timothy had sexually abused his children,' I relayed.

'How did that make you, feel Lois?' Stanley asked.

'I was absolutely sickened, then hurt, angry and upset all in quick succession,' I informed her.

'What were your thoughts towards the information?' She asked.

'I was annoyed that she had kept me in the dark about it especially considering my background and more so that she had insisted Mum keep her confidence. I did not know where Ruby's loyalty lay so I specifically asked Ruby if she was standing in the gap for the children or for him,' I informed her.

'What was Ruby's response,' she asked.

'She told me that she was "going to get the bastard",' I informed her.

'How did she plan to do that,' she asked.

'I presumed by giving you all the information she had,' I told her.

'In your opinion, did she provide the police all the information she had,' Stanley pushed.

'I could not answer that specifically as it would just be speculating however Ruby said a lot of things about her childhood that again I was completely unaware of,' I stated.

'What things in Ruby's childhood were you not aware of, Lois?' she asked directly.

'I was not aware he used to watch her through the downstairs bathroom window or that he had tried it on with her when she was at school or later when they were out drinking. I was completely unaware of this happening but there again she was unaware of what had happened to me!' I told her.

'At the end of Ruby's interview, she left the room to use the toilet I believe, and you then told the interviewing officers something, is that right?' she enquired.

'Yes, having heard the evidence I felt it my duty to come clean and inform the officers that Timothy had sexually abused me as a child,' I revealed, the very words ejecting my mouth were like darts that once released had turned like missiles in mid-air to hit their target and spiked my eyes. I could feel the tears pricking but I managed to stop the sensation in its tracks.

'I know this is hard, Lois, but I will now have to ask you some very personal questions,' she informed me. 'When you say the word abuse, can you define what you mean exactly?'

'Timothy forced me to touch him on his private parts and he groped me inappropriately,' I said.

'I am sorry Lois, but I need you to name the exact area of the body,' she told me.

'He forced my hand on to his penis and he touched my vagina,' I said recoiling at having to say those words.

'Approximately how old were you when this happened and how old would Timothy have been?' she enquired.

'I was perhaps 4 or 5 years of age and that would make *him* about 12 or 13,' I informed her.

'In your own words, can you describe what you remember,' she prompted and then left me to talk.

'I remember having a bed in my parents' room when we first moved to Grey Gables and then it was moved into the boy's room whilst a bedroom was being prepared for Ruby and I to share. I know I wet the bed a lot and I had a rubber sheet on my bed. It was the middle of the night, and I must have got up because I was in the bathroom. I don't know if I had awoken Timothy, or he had woken me, but he was in the bathroom too. I remember him encouraging me to get into his bed rather than wake my parents where I must have fallen asleep. I then recall him being rough with me where he grabbed my hand and forced it down his pyjama bottoms.

'Obviously, I know now that it would have been his erect penis only at the time, I had no idea other than it was clammy, hot and hard. It didn't feel nice and I tried to remove my hand but he would not allow me to. He grabbed it hard and prised my hand around it moving my hand up and down. I know now that he was forcing me to give him a wank though I do not believe he ejaculated however I have no way of knowing.'

'Can you recall how many times this occurred, Lois?' she asked.

'No, I just know it happened whilst ever I was in that bedroom, but I have no way of recalling how long I was in that room,' I told her.

'So, you couldn't say if it was say between 1–5 times, less than 10 or more than 10?' She asked.

'I honestly could not give a number because after the second time I blanked it out,' I said truthfully.

'When you say blanked it out Lois, what do you mean exactly?' Stanley asked.

'The violation was perpetrated by someone who was much stronger and older than myself, so I had no ability to fight it or to make it stop. I could not flee physically so mentally was my only means of escape. I do not know how I managed to do this but somehow, my only coping mechanism was the ability to detach myself from my physical form. The only way I can explain it is to say that my brain took me somewhere else like it protected me somehow,' I explained.

'Did you tell anyone else what was happening Lois, like your mum, dad or other brother or sisters?' she asked.

'No, as a child I never felt as though anyone cared,' As I began to share this the emotional horror of what I had endured as a child threw itself up like a binge drinkers party. It took several seconds to get myself under control before I could continue. 'There may have been other people in the house, but I was very much alone and besides I had trusted him why would I trust any of them if this is what he had done to me?'

'How did it make you feel, Lois?' she asked.

'I hated being there and I wished my real mum would come back for me because I knew she would not have left me there if she had known they would treat me the way they did. I would fantasise about being a princess in a high tower and she would find me and rescue me, I longed for the day,' I said sadly.

'Your real mum, Lois?' She asked puzzled.

'Yes, because Ruby and Kelly convinced me that I had been found behind the bins and that even my real mother hadn't wanted me. I didn't feel that I belonged there, I knew I wasn't wanted and even felt that Mum was talking about me behind my back. I hated being there with those people so no I didn't tell anyone because until my mum came back, I had no one I could trust.'

By this point, I was sobbing. I am not sure if it was due to the realisation that Little Lois had technically been abused by them all or if it was because I felt stupid for not realising it had all been lies. Either way the only thread I had been able to hold on to was the hope my real mum would come back and take me away. The pain within me was yearning to break free like the walls of a damn so I felt really vulnerable and anxious that I would be exploited further without the ability to protect myself. I was technically sat in a room in the middle of a street with three strangers who were filming me and no one knew where I was. I was beginning to conjure up the scene in Ghosts where the underworld slithers from the shadows to take the character Willy Lopez to hell when Stanley's voice broke through.

'That must have been very upsetting for you Lois, I am sorry that these were your early experiences,' she said kindly but she couldn't possibly understand.

Hell, I know I hadn't ever been able to understand, so how could anyone else fathom the cruelty that one person bestowed on another? As the phrase goes it said more about the inadequacies of them as people than it did about me, the target. It may have affected me deeply as a child but when I became an adult, I worked hard to not allow it to define me as person in fact I used to the contrary to make me a much better person.

'Do you know how old you were when the abuse stopped?' she asked.

'I have no way of knowing as I blanked it out but I do remember another incident when Nick actually caught him in the act but failed to do anything about it,' I then told her the full story about when I was ill on the settee and Mum had been out. 'So, you see again it solidified the ingrained belief that I had no one, I could trust no one and that I did not matter,' I finished.

'Was there ever a time that you were able to disclose the abuse?' she asked.

'Mum challenged me about it when I was about 8, had she approached it in a different manner who's to say I may have been able to disclose it,' I said frankly.

'Was there ever any other time,' she pressed.

'Yes, but it did not come until I was about 26, I disclosed it to Ruby and Mum,' I told her.

'Ahh right, thank you Lois,' she seemed satisfied that there was an historical trail that could be investigated.

'You said earlier that you weren't aware of the incidents that had occurred with Ruby and Timothy, is that right?' Stanley changed direction.

'That's correct. When I heard the information about him looking at Ruby through the window watching her after the shower, I realised that this would have been at the same time Mum had challenged me,' I said then clarified, 'our ages would have coincided, she was about 12 and I was 8 so putting two and two together I realised it had been the catalyst to incite Mum's action. Besides they were constantly whispering at the time amongst themselves and if I entered the room, they quickly changed the subject. At the time I thought they were talking about me behind my back which activated the paranoia and further induced the belief that I couldn't trust anyone,' I told her.

'Are there any other episodes that come to mind Lois, or events that may need investigating?' she enquired.

'Yes,' I said, but this was the hardest to confess as I still felt Mum should not have forced me into the vulnerable position of having to stay at his house overnight or more importantly maybe I should have refused more vehemently. I then let the details of that night unfold, before stating, 'again the significance in our age is interesting as this incident coincides with when he grabbed her hand to touch his erect penis and tried to force her into sex behind the mill,' I finished.

'And just to verify that before the interview took place on Monday 30 May 2011, you had no knowledge of those incidents?' she asked.

'No, I knew nothing about it until she made the statement,' I confirmed, then at once wondered if Stone was trying to establish whether the events could be collaborated or ascertain if they were true.

'Earlier you said that there was an incident that took place when you were around 26 years old where you were able to disclose to someone that Timothy had abused you,' she stated. 'Could you please tell me the circumstances that led up to that disclosure please, Lois?'

I took a deep breath to brace myself then made the mistake of glancing upwards and was immediately aware of a red flashing light on the camera to indicate it was recording. Of course, I was already aware of the fact, but I had successfully managed to put it out of my mind whilst I was discussing events with Sharon Stanley. Then it hit me like an express train and I clammed up, my thoughts as blocked as a drain.

'Lois,' Sharon began, 'Lois, are you OK?' She shuffled in her seat in an attempt to get my attention and I peeled my eyes away from the red flashing light.

When I glanced back towards Sharon, I was alarmed to see the concerned look on her face and found the words, 'Sorry I mentally stepped out for a moment.'

'Is that how it happens, Lois?' Sharon enquired.

'What?' I asked a bit perplexed.

'When you were sexually abused, is that what you meant before about your brain mentally detaching to allow you to escape,' she asked wisely.

'I guess so,' I said vaguely.

'I would like to take a moment to try and understand what happened, Lois, if that is, ok?' She asked.

'Yes, that is ok,' I said, in fact I welcomed her assistance as I actually hoped it would help me, as I said earlier, I am always looking for areas to better myself and embraced opportunities for further personal growth.

'So, I will just explain what I witnessed a minute ago when we were talking Lois,' she told me and then continued, 'One minute we were chatting then you looked up and instantaneously it was like a switch had been flipped and you had mentally disappeared. I said your name over and over again but there was no response from you. You were intently staring at me, but it was quite clear that you were not seeing me. It was as though I was no longer in the room or perhaps you had gone elsewhere.'

'When I experience high levels of stress, it affects me like an Alexia that has lost its internet connection and "I have trouble understanding at that moment," I explained.'

'I appreciate that a video interview would put you under enormous stress Lois, but I am interested to know if there was anything in particular that triggered this episode,' she queried.

'The discussion I had with Ruby and Mum regarding the disclosure came out of the blue and inevitably caused me extreme distress especially as it was never mentioned again. To talk about it again indicates their lack of support and my isolation so regurgitating those feelings on top of the childhood suffering could have tipped me over the edge,' I admitted.

'At the point you seemed to "lose connection", you were staring up at the camera above our heads in the top corner of the room,' she informed me gently.

Like a driver late at night you cannot help but look at a car's headlight even when you don't want to my eyes were instantly drawn back to the camera for me to zone out again.

'There it was again,' Sharon said, 'but it was more of a flicker this time, yet it was definitely there.'

'It was the red light,' I identified 'I shut down because I knew that someone else was watching.'

'Earlier you told me that Nick caught Timothy in the act of sexually abusing you when you were ill on the settee. You said that it resulted in your belief you could no longer trust him or anyone else. Could this have also affected you and your trust with people in general?' She wondered.

'I hadn't really made a link before, but I do know that the abuse in his bed caused such deep-rooted damage that it still affects me today. In times of stress, my brains default mode is to protect me so like the old-fashioned method of editing film my brain cuts unwanted segments out.' I was beginning to feel drained.

'Thank you, Lois it is very helpful, to understand the impact that the abuse not only had on you as a child but has continued to have throughout your life,' she said.

'It continually affects me in my responses to everyday things and in my relationships,' I told her.

'In what way does it affect your relationships, Lois?' Sharon asked.

'Throughout my life I have never felt comfortable being with a man and in my early adult life I actually only engaged in same sex relationships because I felt safer and less vulnerable. However, during the 1980s, I found a lot of the females, (not all) that I came in to contact with had also experienced the degradation of childhood sexual abuse. It was not a lifestyle that I wanted to pursue given that it could have been born out of my early experiences as I viewed it as *his* potential continued control over my life,' I admitted.

'So can I just clarify are you saying that you sought the comfort of a female as opposed to a man because it made you feel safer rather than a natural genuine sexual orientation?' she enquired.

'I think at the time it was just a direction my life went in not only due to my environment, the people I liaised with but that it was a choice because I could not be with a man. I was safe, happy, loved and was in love especially when I was in college so yes it became natural and genuine. Would I have taken this path had I not been abused, I cannot say though there is an argument to suggest that I wouldn't because I would have felt safe with a man,' I reasoned for the first time admitting it to myself too.

'So, can we just go back to when you were around 26? You said earlier that you had spoken to your mum and Ruby with regards to the abuse, how did that come about?' Sharon back tracked.

'It came out of blue one night when I had been out,' I began. Then I let the details of the night unfold with Ruby on the Lane, my feelings her reactions, my being forced to tell Mum and the bizarre aftermath of silence the following day.

'So, it wasn't mentioned at all the next day?' she asked incredulously.

'No, in fact it wasn't mentioned ever again. As I said earlier, I was always alone with my thoughts, isolated mentally, physically and emotionally to deal with my own personal nightmare,' I stipulated.

'Wasn't there ever anyone else who you could talk to Ruby? Even outside the family,' she enquired.

'Yes, I spoke to one friend a girl I had known since school, Leanne I only spoke to her because I knew I could rely on her to keep my confidence,' I said.

'We will need the details of your friend Leanne so that we can include her in the investigation Lois. Was there anyone else that you discussed your experiences with, say professionally,' she prompted.

'Yes, I have had years of therapy with a number of professionals, in fact I am undergoing psychological support at the moment,' I informed her.

'Again, we will need a list of the professionals with whom you have seen over the years along with your present therapist if that is ok Lois,' she stated.

'I have no issue granting you consent to my medical records,' I said easily.

There was the smidgen of a smile upon her face, 'Thank you Lois,' she said then continued, 'I will just need to confirm with Don and Melissa that I have covered all the areas that were requested in the briefing.' I nodded, 'I will be just a moment,' she said and left the room.

I sat for what seemed like an eternity before Sharon returned and concluded the video interview. To say I was relieved was a gross understatement and then the flood gates opened and the damn well and truly crashed the scene. I drew my knees up towards my chest, rested my feet upon the edge of the chair and wrapped my arms around my legs then wept openly and unashamedly. I had done it I had stood in the gap for my nieces and nephews and answered all the previously unasked questions. Today I had pushed myself not just out of my comfort zone but beyond all surpassable expectations. I was in no doubt that I had excelled myself but equally I also knew that I would need the time to heal as these scars would require a little more than a band aid. I didn't even care what Maya, Stanley or Blackstone thought about me as I wanted no one else's validation other than my own. Today I had accomplished my greatest goal, I had spoken out despite the skeletons in the closet, or the threat of it splitting my family in two, or the fear of upsetting Mum and despite what anyone else thought I had exposed *him*.

I was now a survivor of child abuse, not a victim anymore, I had overcome what I had always viewed as the impossible and I was no longer the misfit. I was free and more importantly Little Lois no longer had to drown in the blame, shame or guilt that was never hers to carry in the first place. Together we had just demonstrated how strong we really were.

Chapter 25
Dad's Birthday

Over the next couple of months, I put the experiences of taking Ruby to the police station, my visiting the suite and the making of the statement behind me choosing to live each day instead of being chained to the past. The boys and I looked forward to the summer holidays and began making plans of how we would spend them. I collected information leaflets from various different sources and before we knew it, we had almost planned our full summer.

There were activities with the local swimming baths who were doing a weekly canoe course that Jack was particularly interested in and archery that Joe wanted to do. The Wakefield countryside services were doing many workshops, the ones that we chose were build a birdbox, bug hunt and butterfly safari. We planned days out to Bridlington, Blackpool Pleasure Beach and The Forbidden Corner in Middleton near Leyburn. To say we were all excited when the school term came to a close was an understatement.

The day the boys broke up from school our car was packed, and we were merrily on our way to Grassington with an old school friend of mine. We had recently become friends again and he loved to go camping with his partner, their family members and friends. The boys and I really enjoyed their company and were thankful to be included as it is often very difficult as a single parent and with Gary we always felt supported. Joe was really funny, no sooner had he met someone, but they were instantly his best friend, he also had a habit of slightly changing their name. For instance, Gary was soon fondly known of as Barry and Russ was known as Wuss, which Joe said in an exaggerated wwwuuusss like woof. The funny part was that our entire group of school friends also started calling them Wuss and Barry.

We had a wonderful weekend away to celebrate the start of our summer having breakfast in the market town café, sitting around a campfire drinking and telling stories and walking along the countryside trails. I loved the boys being off school as it gave us all a sense of freedom not being tied to school runs or the monotony of everyday life. The summer had begun, it was ours for the taking and we were ready to explore all it had to offer. We still saw Mum and Dad on a daily basis either calling in before the day's activities or afterwards to share a meal with them where the excited chatter of the boys' experiences would be unveiled. It was carefree, happy and relaxed.

Halfway through the holidays was Dad's birthday so we arrived with numerous presents for him to open and then to take him out for a meal. Joe scooted up beside him at one side with Jack stood at the other whilst he went through his bag full of goodies. I always put two extra chocolate treats in his gift bag so that Dad could give them to the boys, this way they felt included whereas Dad didn't have to share his own. We then had the mandatory photographs taken and once everyone was ready, we set off for Toby Carvery at Calder Island for our celebration.

It was a firm favourite with the boys as they were in full control upon what was placed on their plates. Jack, an old pro was able to source his own food whilst I assisted Joe before helping Mum and Dad. Afterwards we went for a short drive to Newmillerdam where we parked up, got ice-creams and fed the ducks. It was a lovely, sunny afternoon and life felt good, we were all happy, safe and content in the security of our family bubble. After a wonderful afternoon together, Dad was tiring so we took them to Grey Gables, settled them in and made our way home too feeling fulfilled and a family film on the agenda.

As we arrived home, we busied ourselves the boys selecting a DVD each whilst I collected popcorn, a quilt to snuggle in and their chocolate from Dad. As the film began to start the three of us huddled on the settee Joe with my arm wrapped around him at one side and Jack at the other, I couldn't help but feel so blessed. I loved those two little boys so much; they were my world, and I couldn't imagine ever not putting their needs first. It gave you a sense of well-being like no other to see their happy little faces grateful for all we did no matter how small. As I gave them a little squeeze, I felt my phone begin to vibrate. I was going to ignore it but whoever was trying to contact me was not giving up.

'Just answer it, Mum,' Jack said finally unable to ignore it any longer.

'Ok,' I said, 'sorry I won't be a minute.' As I struggled to retrieve it from my jeans pocket, I knew I would have no alternative but to remove myself from the warmth of the duvet and give whoever it was the attention they were seeking.

'Aww that's cold,' Joe said shifting closer to Jack who helpfully tucked the quilt back in around his brother.

'Hello?' I said vaguely the caller ID stating "private number".

'Hi, Lois, sorry to bother you on a weekend, it's Melissa Maya,' she introduced herself.

'Oh, hello Melissa,' my heart doing a complete plummet to the floor, 'how can I help you?' I said not wanting to help her with anything if truth be known.

'I just wanted to let you know that we have had Timothy in this morning for questioning,' she began, 'and one of the matters was regarding the crimes he has committed against you.'

I instantly felt sick and took myself in to the boy's playroom so they wouldn't overhear any bits of the conversation. 'And?' was all I could say.

'He has denied everything,' she delivered. I slumped down on to the little blue two-seater settee and waited with bated breath. 'In fact, he has said that you came on to him and that you voluntarily put your hand down his pants and began wanking him off.'

'He said what?' I asked in utter disbelief so much for him taking responsibility and getting the help that he needed to avoid splitting the family up and forcing everyone to testify in court.

'He was really cocky and actually stated that he doesn't remember any of the incidents that you described happening when you were a child and the one when you were older was instigated by yourself.'

'I am sorry, Melissa, I really do not know what to say. I knew he didn't have a backbone, but this has knocked me for six,' I said honestly.

'To be honest, Lois, I would have been more surprised if he had confessed; the majority are not going to go down without a fight,' she told me.

'So, what was your gut instinct,' I asked, 'when he was sat in front of you and you were questioning him?'

'Well, put it this way; the officer who sat in the interview with me has just come back off holiday she hasn't been present during briefings, not been privy to any of the information nor has she met him before,' she laid out, 'her immediate comment afterwards was "what a crock of shit."'

'So, she got a good impression of him then?' I spoke.

'We all did Lois, it was more than clear that everything he said was utter bollocks, sorry for being so frank,' she said.

'No, thank you for being so honest it gives me reassurance that you can see through him, he has always been a poor liar so hopefully if it goes to court, they will too,' I said.

'Lois if it goes to court, they will make mincemeat of him especially if he continues down this route,' she said.

'So where do we go from here?' I queried feeling utterly dejected.

'Don't worry Lois he isn't going to get away with it that easily, basically we will continue to collate information. He may think that denying it will result in it being your word against his, but we have a long line of enquiries still to follow. Firstly, we will start by collaborating the allegations by interviewing your parents for starters, your ex-husband and Leanne. It does not end with his denial it actually opens up an investigation. I will be in touch if anything new comes up, OK?' she asked.

'I am not ok. I am absolutely devastated because now my dad will need to know everything about what his son has been up to. If only the slimy piece of shit had done as he had promised and confessed to his debauchery instead of dragging us all further down with him,' I declared.

'So, your dad has no knowledge at all, Lois?' she asked.

'No, we have tried to protect him from the shame and embarrassment whilst he has been going through his chemotherapy treatment,' I informed her.

'To be honest I would urge you to inform him sooner rather than later as things will start to gather momentum soon,' she said.

'I will ring Ruby and Mum to see if we can meet in the morning and tell him together,' I said resigning myself to another shameful confession in front of the people I loved.

'I know it is easy for me to say Lois but try not to worry this is where the fun starts, the next time he comes in we make him squirm and tie him up with his own lies,' she disclosed. We then proceeded to say 'good-bye' and ended our call.

I took a moment to sit and absorb the conversation completely perplexed from the information I had received. So, Kelly hadn't just fallen off the fence she had actively jumped straight off it and gone out of her way to give support to the person who had abused me. That was not just about taking a side she was effectively cutting me off and stabbing me in the back to boot. What a vile piece of work she really was and to cook up some bullshit to get him off at my expense was beyond contemplatable.

I could not imagine for a second those beautiful boys in the other room behaving so detestably towards each other. How devastating for my parents to face the public shame of going to court because their daughter was scheming so Timothy could avoid the consequences of his paedophilia crimes. I could scarce believe that she could hate me so much to not only cause me such extreme distress but to stand in the gap for him and actually blame me was simply outrageous. As far as I was concerned, she had no shame and she was as guilty as him, although on a flip side it was nice to see who my enemies were.

Chapter 26
My Worst Nightmare

Before going back to resume my home cinema afternoon with the boys, I took the opportunity to contact Ruby as I didn't want these matters intruding any further in our time together.

'Hiya, I have just had Melissa Maya on the phone she has informed me that they interviewed Timothy earlier and he has denied the charges regarding me,' I informed her.

'What the heck, really? So, what has he said?' she asked surprised.

'Just that he cannot remember the earlier incidents feigning he was a kid himself no doubt,' I said.

'Well, you were a kid and 8 years younger than him so how the hell can you remember but he cannot recall it. Utter bullshit,' she said.

'Funny, that is more or less what one of the other officers said when they heard his explanation,' I joked.

'Really, she said that to his face?' she said laughing.

'No, after the interview Melissa asked the officer what she thought of his account and she stated it was a "crock of shit,"' I relayed.

'Ah well they have the right impression about him them,' she said light-heartedly.

'They saw straight through him however as the investigation is now going to dig deeper, she has said that they will need to speak to Mum,' I hesitated, 'and Dad.'

'Right, so I guess it is time we come clean then and inform him his son is a lying paedophile then!' She said matter of fact.

'Unfortunately, I do not think we have any other alternative and if I were in his shoes, I would be more pissed off that this has been going on for years behind my back just to protect that piece of shit,' I declared, 'I for one do not know why he hasn't been told before now but that has been Mum's call.'

'So, how are we going to do this?' she asked.

'I personally think that the three of us should sit down together so we can give him a full picture from all angles that way if there are any questions one of us can answer them. Besides, I do not want to have to deliver what happened to me to my dad on my own, I couldn't bear his reaction,' I spoke, 'it will kill him.'

'So, when do you want to do it,' she asked.

'Let him enjoy the rest of his birthday and meet there tomorrow about 10.30, if that is ok?' I queried.

'Yes, that's fine,' she said and hung up.

I returned to the lounge to find Joe keeled over his head on a cushion fast asleep and Jack barely able to keep his eyes open. No doubt the big meal they'd eaten along with the excitement of Dad's birthday and the fresh air had knocked them out. I pulled the quilt up and secured it around them before taking myself upstairs to ring Mum. I relayed the conversations I'd had with both Melissa and Ruby then told her the arrangements we had made for the following morning.

'But Lois, he will be devastated,' she responded.

'Yes, I know, in more ways than one. Firstly, in having no knowledge of what happened to us as children, then the secrecy of the last 18 months, his arrest and now his intention to plead not guilty. To be honest he should have been told from the beginning not kept in the dark,' I stated.

'I thought I was doing what was best for everyone,' she said timidly.

'No, you weren't you were protecting *him,* so Dad didn't give him the leathering that he deserved,' I said coldly.

'I was trying to keep your dad out of it he had enough in working all the hours God sent to keep a roof over our heads,' she said.

'I understand that but if I was with someone, I would expect them to be honest with me no matter how hard it may be to tell the truth. At least then you have a choice in the matter of how to deal with the things within your family rather than being excluded. I dread to think how he will feel that you did not honour him with the truth,' I told her.

'You know how things were Lois your dad would have killed him,' she said quietly.

'And now having to find out after decades it will probably kill Dad!' I stated unrelenting. My father meant everything to me I had given my heart and soul to him over the years and in return he had given his to me too. I was sickened by the circumstances: of Dad being excluded, *his* arrest, Ruby's statement, the length of time Ruby and Mum were discussing it in secrecy, *his* denial, Kelly's betrayal and now having to inform Dad. It made me wonder if there was anyone in this family with a backbone.

'Anyway,' I paused, 'Ruby and I will be over in the morning at 10.30 so the four of us can sit down together and air our dirty laundry.'

'Lois, I just need to let you know that after you left earlier Kelly called with your dad's birthday gifts,' she said.

'And?' I asked bracing myself for the finale.

'She stated that if anything happens to him or he ends up going to prison because of this she will never forgive the three of us and will cut us all off,' she told me.

'So, there is a silver lining after all?' I sighed, could this day get any better.

'I am sorry. Sorry for all that you have gone through and the mistakes that I have made along the way, but I promise you this if they are going to continue lying then it will be woe betide them!' she said with passion.

When I went back downstairs, the boys were well and truly in slumberland, so I followed Poppy out into the garden and sat on the decking for a while just to piece together the story so far. It felt like a huge jigsaw puzzle where you build the outer frame before searching the inner parts to build a bigger picture. Each selected piece didn't seem to fit with the next and there were plenty of jagged outlines yet without the box depicting the full picture it was hard to follow let alone see it in its entirety. I was utterly soul destroyed not only due to the consequences of his denials, but my sister was actually working against me to try and get him off. She had jumped off that damn fence so quickly I really did hope that time would ensure she got the biggest splinters in her butt.

I could understand not getting involved if she did not want to incriminate him or carry any sense of responsibility for his incarceration but to lie and in return dishonour me. It amazed me that she was so blind to the fact that I was the innocent party having no choice in the degrading acts he had committed against me. How could my own sister choose to have no compassion and show no mercy towards me or the abuse I had sustained. In retrospect, she was actually condoning his behaviour by actively supporting him and encouraging him to further mistreat me only this time it was not behind closed doors they were trying to publicly humiliate me.

As much as I was dreading the conversation with my dad there was one thing I knew and that was I could get through anything with him by my side. My dad wouldn't allow anyone or anything to harm me and he would also make sure Timothy and Kelly were held accountable for their actions.

Chapter 27
"We've Got You, Grandad"

Needless to say, that night I had a very restless sleep where nothing in my dreams was within my control whether it was my teeth falling out or I was behind the wheel of some vehicle that was falling to pieces as I drove it. The next morning, I felt dizzy, disorientated and my eyes were all puffy like I had gone ten rounds with Muhammad Ali. I dragged myself to the shower and stood for ages under the warm flow to soothe myself. Then, once out I splashed huggins of cold water upon my face to stimulate my mind to wake up I tore myself away feeling a little more refreshed but not any lighter about the task ahead. The boys obviously picked up on the strain I was feeling because breakfast was conducted through the silence of my trauma response. I was somewhere deep within myself so unfortunately there was not the usual chatty excited buzz of the morning. Even on the way to Grey Gables the car was quiet like we were on our way to a funeral which in retrospect I felt like we were, mine.

On arrival, the boys quickly jumped out of the car to race in to see their grandparents but stopped dead as grandma appeared at the door with a grave look upon her face. Moments later Ruby arrived so now they knew something was wrong and gazed at me worriedly expecting bad news. I knelt down to their level a hand around each waist explaining, 'I have to talk to Grandma, Grandad and Auntie Ruby about something very important boys, so I want you to play out in the garden, is that ok?'

'Is Grandad alright, Mummy?' Jack asked grabbing Joe's hand as his lip began to quiver, he searched for reassurance between his grandma and myself.

'He is fine, love, we all have something we need to chat about that's all,' I said trying to comfort them but not feeling particularly strong myself.

'Is that why you were quiet this morning?' Jack enquired.

'It is love, but everything will be ok,' I told him though I do not know if I was trying to convince him or myself.

'Are you sad, Mummy?' Asked Joe placing his tiny little hand upon my cheek.

I nestled into it, smiled and honestly said, 'I am a little, love, but as you need to come to me when you are sad, I need to see my mum and dad.'

'Ok Mummy,' my beautiful sensitive boys replied, so caring, understanding and empathetically in tune with each other and with me.

Ruby got out of her car and walked into the house whilst I hushed the boys out into the vast expanse of the garden to play and explore. Oh, how I wished right now that I had the abandonment of childhood upon me with their ability to allow the stresses of life to wash so easily and quickly away. I watched them disappear around the corner of the house and began to see myself in my mind's eye as a child. The figure of eights that I had endlessly performed on the top of the drive not just on my three-wheeler bike with its white plastic seat and the elephant sticker on top. I had also perfected it on my first 2-wheeler bike, a red Raleigh that I got for one of my birthdays. Then there was a green racer bike, a blue and red mountain bike whose handlebars I ended up going over having had a puncture and not tightening the bolts enough, so the wheel had come off.

Lastly a blue Hobson Jawa motorbike, yes, I wish I had that kind of abandonment again to escape the inner torment but today I had to face the past and share those secrets with Dad. That ever-ticking clock had brought us all to this moment and now it couldn't be put off any longer, whether I wanted to do this or not it was time my father knew the whole truth.

I turned and walked through the kitchen into the lounge where Dad was seated as usual in his favourite chair in the bay window opposite me. To his left, my right on the settee were Ruby and Mum, I smiled weakly.

'Where are those little rascals?' Dad asked in his usual cheery tone and then he saw the look on my face. 'What is it, love?' fear in his voice, 'where are they, are they ok?'

Before I could speak, two little faces appeared at the window and gently tapping it, they said, 'Grandad.' There was a look of confusion on his face inevitably he must have thought something bad had happened to his two favourite little people but when they appeared behind him, he was out of sorts. He waved an "Hello" then as they scampered off, he glanced firstly back towards me then to Ruby and Mum a query of "what's going on" upon his face.

'Is everything OK, love?' he faltered.

'No Dad it's not. I have to tell you something, but it is so hard to find the words for me to say it to you,' I confessed walking into the middle of the room and kneeling down in front of him.

'You can tell me anything, love, you know that, come on, you're frightening me, what is it,' he enquired.

'First of all, I need to tell you that Timothy has been arrested and due to his arrest, I have also had to give a statement along with Ruby,' I informed him.

'Been arrested? For what?' he asked incredulously.

'I think maybe it would be better for Ruby to tell you this bit because I wasn't part of this process,' I said.

'About 18 months ago Sarah and I suspected he had been interfering with his children,' she began.

'What? Whose children?' he asked alarmed.

'His own,' Mum said in a quiet voice.

'Which one?' Dad wanted to know.

'Elena and Danny,' Mum stated.

'But we also think it could be Sophie too,' Ruby said.

Dad bowed his head in his hands and rubbed his hair furiously back and forth, as though he was trying to force the words to sink into his head.

'When he was here one time with Sophie, she told me something that sent shivers down my spine that "her and her daddy had a secret",' Mum interjected, 'I have never been able to forget it.'

'Is that why you insisted on bathing them when they were here and you didn't like him having the children in bed with him rather than using their own rooms?' Dad asked.

'It is,' she said simply.

'So why didn't you tell me this at the time?' Dad queried.

'Because I knew you would go mad and if you threw him out, I wouldn't be able to keep an eye on him.' She told him but this wasn't only information for Dad's ears, it was also news to me too!

'So, when was he arrested?' Dad enquired.

'He was arrested on the bank holiday Monday at the end of May,' Ruby stated.

'Hold on a minute; that was nearly three months ago!' he spoke.

'The thing is Dad we did not want you to get stressed about it, so we have tried to keep it under wraps,' I told him.

'So, why are you telling me now?' he was beginning to sound annoyed.

'Yesterday whilst we were out having the meal for your birthday Timothy was being questioned again by the police,' I told him.

'Again? Why, has someone else come forward?' he began, 'I hope this is not going to be another Jimmy Savile case?'

'He was being questioned about me,' I said with tears beginning to stream down my face the emotion completely irrepressible.

'No,' he bellowed looking directly at me his eyes fixed upon mine contorted in pain his also beginning to tear and then freely falling upon his face.

For a few painful moments, we were locked into the pain of each other's grief, a parent unable to console himself at the horror his child has been abused, the child revealing her worst nightmare not wanting to disappoint her hero. I felt a cavity like a sink hole swallow me from the outside in and knew from this moment on there was no way back. My heart ached for this ill elderly gentleman but due to the betrayal of Kelly and Timothy they had set these wheels in motion, and I was helpless to stop them. Kelly had openly and willingly decided to try to get Timothy off the charges that she knew he was guilty of at the expense of everything and everyone else.

Dad was just another by-product of her collateral damage along with Mum, Sophie, Elena, Danny, Ruby, me and anyone else that would now be called to testify. Lies are always damaging regardless of how they are presented and can have such a devastating affect especially when they are used to save your own skin at the expense of those around you. Lies turn into more lies and more as the bearer has to invent reasons for the lies in the first place. For instance, if Kelly was telling her family Timothy was innocent to excuse her involvement, then she would have to tell lies as to why the allegations were being made. This would then create a divide so she would then have to substantiate it with more lies, if it went to court then she was putting herself in the position of committing perjury. She would then have to create more lies if he got sentenced or to explain why she was cutting us all off and then everyone's relationships would be ruined.

All because the guilty party had lied to the people, they purportedly loved to cover their own wrongdoing instead of owning what they had done, accepting who they were or acknowledging the mistakes they had made. The result would be an irreconcilable family blown apart by Timothy and Kelly's lies.

In a shaky quivering voice, I let the whole story unfold about my early childhood memories and the later ones, all the time Dad locked in eye-to-eye contact. He did not interrupt, he did not waiver his eye contact he just listened. At any other time, I may have found this an intimidating stance, but I didn't this was my father allowing me the space to divulge the underbelly of my childhood and to cleanse myself of the closeted raw emotions. I spoke openly and transparently all the time my father receptive and attentive to each word no stern facial expression nor accusations like Mum had done, he just listened. Once everything had been exposed there was silence and I sat there like a lamb to the slaughter, waiting.

Dad turned to Mum and asked, 'Did you know about this?'

'Not at the time, I only found out when Lois was in her mid-20s,' she said.

'So why am I only finding out when she is in her mid-40s?' Dad asked angrily.

He was sickened not just about the news but the fact that no one had told him, and rightly so. When Mum failed to answer, he looked back at me.

'The thing is there is more,' I began, 'he also used to watch Ruby getting dressed through the window when she was in the shower room,' I looked towards Ruby and waited for her to continue, when she did Dad turned back towards her.

'There were other incidents like when I was 14 and again when I was 21 that he grabbed my hand to touch him and he tried to have sex with me,' Ruby said succinctly.

'Did he rape either of you?' Dad asked directly.

'No,' I said seeing his relief flood through him, 'but he did try when I was made to stay over at his house,' I explained.

'Let that bastard come here if he dares and I will knock him through to next week,' Dad roared unable to control his impending rage. 'The filthy beggar! So why am I only being told this now,' he went on.

'When I got home yesterday, the police officer dealing with the case rang me to tell me they had just interviewed him with regards to the crimes he had committed against me,' I told him.

'Yes,' said Ruby, 'he has told the police that he cannot remember the incidents from when they were younger and he has blamed Lois for the incident at his house.'

'The little weasel,' Dad said, 'what's the saying "if you cannot do the time don't commit the crime?"'

'The thing is, Mum will need to be interviewed and perhaps you will too, Dad,' Ruby said.

'So that is why you are telling me now, because you have no option?' he said irritably, 'I have got to say I am really angry that you have kept this to yourselves all this time. Don't you think I had a right to know, Emmeline, I am their dad!' he chastised Mum.

'I thought I was doing the right thing; you brought the wage in, and I dealt with the family,' she said lamely.

Dad dismissed her poor excuse. 'So where do we go from here?' he asked Ruby and I.

'He is also denying having any inappropriate contact with regards to his children,' Ruby said, 'so they now have to build a case to see if they can find sufficient evidence to charge him.'

'So, what you are saying is the police are having to waste their resources because he isn't owning up to what he has done?' he queried.

'Yes, that is exactly what will happen. I met him just after his arrest to beg him not to put the children, mum or our family through any further torment as I have had to have years of therapy.' He glared at me at this disclosure and as if I hadn't noticed I continued, 'he said he would do the right thing and acknowledged it wouldn't be fair to drag it through the courts and force us all to testify against him.'

'So, what has changed?' he asked alarmed at the prospect of it going that far and I could inevitably see it turning over in his mind the disgrace it would bring to the family name.

'Kelly is what changed!' Ruby interjected.

'Oh, my goodness don't tell me he has done something to her too?' he asked deflated.

'No, quite the contrary maybe if it had happened to her too, she wouldn't be so quick to jump off the fence,' Ruby blurted out, 'she is assisting him to see if she can help him get out of it!'

'What, he abuses you two and his own children and she is looking at how SHE can get him off?' he asked disbelievingly.

'Apparently so,' Mum said, 'and she has stated that if anything happens to him or if he goes to prison because of this then she will never forgive Ruby, Lois or myself and will cut us all off,' Mum stated.

'Oh, will she now, maybe she needs to take off her rose-tinted glasses and wake up this is not some soap opera she has been cast in,' Dad said. 'As far as I am concerned if he doesn't own up and get what he deserves he is not welcome here again. And if Kelly or anyone else lies for him then they aren't welcome here either. Just imagine if it was her children, she would be screaming it from the rooftops playing Holy Hell and expecting us all to rally around her and rightly so. Well, these are my children and grandchildren so if she isn't with me then she is against me and she needn't bother coming here either,' Dad stated adamantly.

'To be honest they are our thoughts too,' Mum said, Ruby and I nodding in agreement. 'And to think she trained as a nursery worker, and this is her view towards child abuse.'

'Apparently Kelly has told Ruby that I had better not tell her what she should or shouldn't do or feel about it and if I say or do anything I am cut off for that too,' I told him.

'Right then, is that everything?' he enquired.

'Yes, I think so,' I said as two little faces appeared at the window again Joe bringing his hand up on to the glass and cupping it around his eyes to peer through.

'I am sorry, but I cannot help thinking that this should have been done years ago so I could have dealt with it then,' he pointed out.

'I am sorry love, but I did think I was doing the right thing at the time,' Mum admitted.

'I will tell you this, when Timothy turns up, he will get the shock of his life because I will be ready for him and likewise when Kelly comes there will be one hell of a show down. These enquiries need to stop now, he needs to take responsibility whether she likes it or not I will not have my name dragged through the mud and that's an end to it!' he raged.

And then the patter of little feet could be heard entering the kitchen and through into the lounge where we were sat. Their faces bright, alert and red with the chill of the day they looked from person to person as though wondering if it was ok to interrupt our grown-up chat. Dad opened his loving arms towards them and as they ran to him, he wept openly for the lost innocence of the children he had not been able to protect. The children held on to him as dearly and robustly as he held on to them and beneath the sobs, we heard a comforting voice.

'It's ok, Grandad, we've got you.'

Chapter 28
And I Smiled

Over the following week, I tried to put everything to one side for the sake of my beautiful boys but none of us had felt much like doing anything or going anywhere. Neither Kelly nor Timothy made contact or called to see Mum and Dad from the day we had spoken to my parents on Sunday the 7th of August to Monday 15th the day Dad had his last appointment at the hospital. I had asked Ruby to take him to this one on my behalf so that the boys and I could regain our spark and summer holiday plans to enjoy a day at the beach together. She had agreed. I spoke to Dad wishing him well and then the boys and I set off for Bridlington. It was an approximate 1 1/2-hour journey so we set off nice and early with everything, but the kitchen sink packed into the car.

'So, what do you most want to do when we arrive?' I asked the boys.

'I want to go on the land train,' said Joe.

'I want to go on the spaceship simulator,' said Jack.

'Oh yes I would like to do that too,' said Joe.

'And of course, we have to get doughnuts,' Jack laughed.

'Maybe we need to do all those things,' I suggested.

'Can we really, Mummy?' The boys asked.

'Well, it is the summer holidays, and we don't know the next time we will have the opportunity to come back so perhaps we will,' I told them playfully.

Once we had arrived in Bridlington, we followed the one-way system through the town and found a parking space alongside an amusement arcade. I ensured I had the most important items my phone, bank card/cash and the boys. We decided to have a walk along the promenade its stretch of neatly positioned paved blocks creating a zigzagging pattern. The boys jumped in and out stepping on different coloured bricks whilst trying to miss other ones out. I popped on my sunglasses to filter the glare of the sun and stopped by the newly painted blue railings to gaze out to sea. The seagulls above me squawked loudly as they darted back and forth seeking the remnants of holidaymakers' castoff food.

The unmistakeable tang of salt and seaweed hung in the air along with the distinct aroma of doughnuts wafting from somewhere close by. Amazingly the walkway was pretty quiet for mid-August although there was the odd elderly couple sat along the benches enjoying the warm sea breeze. My attention was soon taken by the yap of a little dog heard beneath me on the beach its owner too slow in picking up its ball for it to retrieve. I smiled, I loved to see animals included and enjoying all that life had to offer. My personal bugbear was owners who kept their dogs on leads instead of letting them have fun. After all, when on a walk it was their time to run free so like children if trained, they will behave and so enjoy life. I pondered the idea of a dog never being allowed off the lead due to the owner's misgivings which would be like bringing my children to the beach and not letting them out of the car. Or taking them to see Blackpool illuminations but putting a blindfold on them so they couldn't enjoy them.

'Mummy, can we go down on to the beach?' asked Jack.

'Yes love, let's take the next steps we find and walk back towards the town,' I suggested.

The boys ran ahead but waited at the top of the steps for me to catch up and once on the beach we took off our shoes and socks to feel the warm fine sand between our toes.

'Can we go for a paddle?' asked Joe.

'You can love but remember we haven't got the towel with us and you might get wet sand stuck between your toes,' I reminded them.

'We don't mind, do we, Joe?' Jack said.

'No, we don't mind,' said Joe parroting Jack.

The boys carefully removed their shoes and stuck their tiny socks snug into the toe areas of each shoe and then as usual passed them to me to carry. I smiled, sometimes I think children believe this is what their parents are there for to carry their belongings for them. As we neared the water's edge I decided to sit for a while to give them the space and time to enjoy each other's company. The squeals of delight as they first entered the water mixed with the horror at its coldness sent me belly achingly laughing. They jumped and pranced around sparkles of water droplets tumbling around them, not a care in the world just giggling and enjoying the pleasures of just being.

And I smiled. The sun beat down, the waves gently flowed in their hypnotic movement back and forth upon the beach leaving a wet patch each time it retreated. I picked up a handful of dry sand removing tiny shards of wood and then allowed it to seep through my fingertips, the sensation felt comforting, so I repeated it over and over again.

I thought about the verse in Psalms 139: 17–18 which says, 'How precious are your thoughts about me, O God. They cannot be numbered! I cannot even count them; **they outnumber the grains of sand!** And when I wake up, you are still with me!'

For a moment or too, I became lost in my own thoughts thinking about my life and the many sleepless nights I had endured recently. It was comforting to know that no matter how difficult my life had become God held precious thoughts about me and they were as numerous as these grains of sand. I cast my eyes down each length of the beach and tried to fathom the magnitude of those precious thoughts and settled for them being too many to count. I felt assured that no matter what happened God was with me and despite the numerous sleepless nights He was still with me at the start of each day. I felt as though this was something I needed to keep at the forefront of my mind in the days, weeks and months to come. And I smiled and gave thanks.

'Come on then, you two; who is ready for lunch?' I asked.

The boys looked at each other and then in unison said, 'we are!'

We had a walk back towards the car where a lovely little bakery sat nestled between a charity shop and a clothes shop to buy sandwiches and a drink. We then found a seat on a lovely little square close to the fairground rides right next to the simulator I knew Jack wanted to go in. Once we had eaten and the boys were raring to go, we walked down a steep cobbled street to the harbour where lots of tiny shops sold a variety of the fisherman's catch. There were cockles, muscles, crabs and all kinds of fishy smells perfectly displayed to entice people passing by to sample their delights.

The ice-cream parlour was next to our favourite do-nut cabin so whilst the boys decided on what flavour ice-cream, they would like I got the do-nuts. We sat beside the harbour watching the boats bobbing gently upon the water's surface ensuring we held tight to our spoils, so the seagulls didn't steal them from us. There seemed to be a lot more people at this end of town meandering in and out of the little shops and a queue was forming about 20 yards from us. So, once we had finished our desserts, we had a stroll over to take a look as a pirate ship swung around the harbour wall towards us. The people were queuing up to take a ride and at less than £2 per person, I nudged the boys to join them.

'Can we really, Mummy?' Joe shrieked with delight.

'I think it would be rude not to,' I joked.

Jack began doing his little excited dance where he would bring his fists up like a boxer and then rotate them round in circles, beaming and jiggling on the spot.

'I take it you would like to enjoy a ride too, Jack?' I said chuckling.

They were so excited as we stumbled aboard and were delighted to be handed a pirate flag each to flap in the wind as we rushed by. It was only a short ride which was fair enough considering the price, but we thoroughly enjoyed it especially the spray of water as the boat dipped after riding each wave. The next stop was the simulator. On the outside were various experiences to try like the big dipper, the cascading raft riding, a bird's-eye view, etc. The boys made their choice and were safely strapped inside before the door of the capsule firmly closed with them inside. The purpose of the ride is that it gives the user an impression of being on a big dipper as it twists, turns and takes the highs, lows and fast turns whilst you sit and watch it on a virtual reality screen. When the boys came out, they were wobbling from side to side as though they were totally disorientated making fun that it wasn't really that bad at all.

We then decided to go on the dodgems where I was amazed at how Jack so expertly drove in and out swerving any collision but managing to hit whomever he chose, Joe holding on for dear life. It reminded me of the last time we had been here where Dad had ridden with Jack the first time driving himself and the second giving Jack the wheel. I could see him in his light blue shirt, navy jacket and flat cap careering around the course Jack oblivious to the fear on his face whilst Mum and I literally wet ourselves. It made me check the time and wonder how he was getting on at the hospital then a tinge of sadness and guilt consumed me because I had missed his last one having taken him to every other for the past 15 months. I wished he and Mum were with us right now having the time of their lives like we had done the year before, so I made a mental note to make sure we came back again before the end of the summer.

As the afternoon wore on the boys enjoyed more rides although the cyclone was maybe the wrong choice as it was a little too fast and poor Jack got squashed every time, they were catapulted outwards. When they got off, he was in tears which resulted in Joe also crying because he felt responsible for his brother's pain.

'I am really sorry, Jack,' Joe wailed, 'I couldn't help it.'

'It's ok, I know you couldn't,' Jack said trying to pull himself together to ease Joe's upset and then he tugged Joe towards him and kissed his head.

I could have wept; my two beautiful little boys were the epitome of what siblings should be. Maybe I had not received the care, love, empathy and understanding that I had required as a child but thankfully somehow, I had managed to install it for my children. I felt touched and so proud to be able to witness their love for one another and knelt before them to give them the comfort they both required whilst also allowing Little Lois the pleasure of their healing power. And I smiled from somewhere deep within.

Our next stop was to the penny arcades where armed with their bags of 2p's the boys eagerly rolled them down the slots to win the little prizes balancing on the edges. There was lots of noise surrounding us with machines whirring, coins dropping and the bingo caller competing with the man on the horse racing machine. It was a hive of activity with people huddled around each machine in the anticipation of a win even if it was only a 2 pence piece all of us surrounded by multicoloured flashing lights.

Again, I thought back to the previous year when Mum, Dad, Jack, Joe and I had sat side by side competing against each other to win the derby on the horse racing machine. We had 3 balls each which we had to roll up a shoot to try and get them into holes that would then propel our horses along the course. Each time the balls shot back out we had to quickly fling them back towards the holes as fast as we could competing against each other to be the winner, the man commentating throughout. It induced an excited rush of adrenalin throughout until finally a winner was announced. No matter how many times we tried to win, my dad always came first much to Jack's annoyance until Joe realised his grandad had been cheating all along because he had 6 balls! That is what Dad always did he found a way to cheat in a harmless fashion to make people laugh, always the joker and such a joy to be around. I thought about him and I smiled again.

As we left the arcade, I noticed Joe looking towards the little land train as it circled around the edge of the promenade to reach the kerb to allow the passengers to disembark. Jack noticed what we were both looking at and then suddenly seemed sad.

'I know you wanted to go on the little land train, Joe, but I don't think we will be able to do that today; Mummy has already spent a lot of money, maybe we can do that first the next time we come,' Jack said.

My heart burst for this little boy so mature for his age thankful for what they had enjoyed and also considerate for the costs imposed.

'But I really wanted to go on the land train, Jack,' Joe said looking upset.

'I know you did but we have been able to enjoy many things and we cannot always do everything,' Jack explained.

'Can we do it first next time though, do you promise?' Joe asked.

'Yes, I promise we will do this first if that is ok with you, Mummy?' Jack said.

'I have a better idea,' I teased.

'What's that, Mummy?' asked Joe.

'Why don't we pretend we have just arrived?' I spoke.

'But we haven't, Mummy,' Joe said earnestly.

Jack immediately understood and excitedly grabbed Joe's arm and started jumping up and down. 'Mummy means that if we are going to do the land train first and we have only just arrived; you can go on it now, Joe.'

It took a moment for this to sink in but when it did, they were both soon jumping for joy because Joe hadn't missed out after all. The train set off from outside the swimming baths in Bridlington and drove along the promenade all the way up to Sewerby Hall and gardens. We bought a return ticket which took about an hour in total. Of course, along the way we waved at anyone passing by, we sang we chatted we pointed out landmarks and we enjoyed the fullness of the journey.

I thought about the simple pleasures that we sometimes take for granted along with the relationships we don't always protect or invest in, and I felt so grateful and blessed to be relishing in our day together. When we returned to the car, neither the children nor I wanted the day to end so we drove a little further up the coast to a fish and chip shop where we sat on the beach whilst the boys shared a bag of chips. It was almost 18.30 hours, yet the sun had not lost any of its heat and although we had experienced an amazing day, I was reluctant to return to the normality of my absurd life.

I sat on the soft fine sand whilst the boys searched for pebbles to take home and glanced out towards the sea wishing we were still in Tunisia before Dad had become ill and before *he* had got arrested. I suddenly felt a tinge of sadness at how our lives had changed overnight from the dreams and hopes of a better future to being shackled and chained to an investigation. Life could be so cruel sometimes, I wanted more of today's experiences with Joe and Jack not the intrusion of the degenerate reprobates within my so-called family. To me Jack and Joe's childhood was merely a blink of an eye in comparison to the whole of their lives and I wanted to fill it with love, laughter, kindness and good morals. The last thing I wanted was for it to be tainted in any way by the self-indulgent transgressions of these sinful individuals. So, I made the difficult decision that if the guilty were prepared to lie to force the innocent to be scrutinised then I would have to start cutting the bacteria out before the rot started spreading. We may all have had the same parents but since I had been a small child, they had never been my family and the only people that mattered to me were my children, mum and dad.

When the children had totally tired themselves out, we returned to our car for the long journey home. I finally reached the M62 at south cave around 19.30 hours and glancing into the rear-view mirror I observed the restful sight of two deeply asleep little boys. I thought about each of the day's experiences and reflected on the way they interacted with each other, their gratitude, their love and our relationship and I smiled for the umpteenth time today. God had truly blessed me with these two boys and at that moment I felt content and happy. I rang Dad to see how he had got on at the hospital.

'Hiya just thought I would ring to see how you got on today,' I said.

'Hiya love, everything went well, and I got the all clear,' he said cheerily.

'Oh, that is wonderful,' I told him feeling this day couldn't get any better.

'It is love but whatever you do don't ever ask Ruby to take me to the hospital again,' he said.

'Why, what was wrong?' I queried.

'First of all, she turned up late, then when I went to get in the car, she had brought her daughter Aleigha with her, and the bloody dog was in the back too. So, when we got to the hospital, she wheeled me in, just left me there and then they went for a walk with the dog. I was waiting ages for them to come back having to just sit there feeling like discarded rubbish with everyone staring at me. So please don't ever ask her again, love; if you cannot make it then I will get the hospital transport,' he said really upset.

'I am so sorry Dad if I had known she wasn't going to care for you I wouldn't have dreamt of letting her take you. I feel absolutely dreadful now that you have been treated like that,' I told him feeling guilty after having such a good day with the boys.

'It's not your fault love,' he said.

'I know but I would have thought she could have put your needs first and done a simple hospital appointment without causing you further distress. I feel awful now, but I just wanted to get the boys out to spend the day with them,' I admitted.

'I know you did love, how are they, I've been hoping you would call on your way home,' he said.

'We are still on our way home now,' I begun, 'I was going to call to find out how you had got on as the boys will want to tell you all about their day, but they are fast asleep.'

'Oh, don't worry about it then love you get them home and I will see you tomorrow,' he sounded sluffened.

'It is ok by the time we get to you they will have had a good hour's sleep so we can swing by I am sure they would hate to miss out,' I told him honestly.

'No love it's getting late; take them lads' home to bed and I will see you tomorrow,' he said adamantly.

'Ok if you're sure you don't mind?' I checked.

'No, it's fine; I will see you tomorrow,' he told me and we said our goodbyes.

When we arrived home, the children dragged themselves upstairs only having enough energy to have a quick wash, brush their teeth and then fell into bed.

The next morning, they arose with the same vigour they had displayed the day before and to my surprise enquiring on what today's outing would be. Initially I had intended to have a lazy morning and was then going to pop over to Grey Gables to see my parents. However, the boys had other plans, so we ended up in the Calypso Cove at Barnsley Metrodome and it was packed. Nevertheless, we raced into a vacant cubicle, got changed and placed our belongings in one of the lockers provided. The boys ran to be the first into the water where we had a fantastic couple of hours jumping off the diving boards, playing tag, hurtling down the various slides and swimming.

In the middle of all the fun, a sudden blackness fell over me which seemed to appear from nowhere. I felt a crushing sickness along with a dizzy disorientation followed by a claustrophobic sense and a need to get out of there. It affected every part of me completely and I could feel myself shaking from within to the point I think it scared the boys. We quickly made our way towards the changing rooms and then to the car where I knew I had to get the boys home otherwise we would be stuck.

All the way back I felt this strange illness enveloping me so much so I went home to lay down on the settee rather than going to see Dad as promised. It worried me but then I just put it down to my blood sugar being low. At home, I did not see the answer machine flashing as I had moved it further behind the curtain nor did I see the missed calls as my mobile battery had died whilst we were swimming. So, I took rest to allow myself the time to repair.

Around a half hour later the house telephone was ringing so I reluctantly answered it as I made my way up the stairs towards the toilet.

'Lois, where the hell have you been?' Ruby shrieked, 'we have been trying to get hold of you.'

'We have been in the swimming baths, so I didn't have my mobile with me and then it was dead when I got out,' I explained. 'I didn't feel well so came straight home.'

'Lois, Mum has frantically been trying to get hold of you and when she couldn't get you, she rang me to come over,' Ruby continued.

'Why, Ruby, what's wrong?' I asked worried sick.

'It's Dad, Lois, he's had a massive heart attack and they couldn't save him,' she announced.

'What do you mean, Ruby?' I asked in shock.

'He has gone, Lois, he has died,' she said.

The deep grief-stricken howl that escaped my lungs was not of this world and without hesitation I flung the offending telephone at the wall screaming, 'Noooooooooooooo!' I collapsed onto the floor sobbing and screaming unable to suppress the outpour like a volcanic eruption full of desperate emotion to bring my father back. The onslaught of, if only we hadn't gone to the swimming baths or if only, we had gone to Dewsbury baths instead. I momentarily felt angry at the boys for steering me from my chosen path because otherwise I would have been there, I would have been able to help him and maybe I could have saved him.

Though I knew this was unfair, I was simply in shock and there was probably nothing at all I could have done; it was his time and God had called him home. I sat at the top of the stairs evaluating the last conversation I'd had with him and wondered if I'd told him I loved him when I'd wished him goodbye? I couldn't remember but I was sure I must have, I always did, why didn't I insist on calling last night? Why didn't I just go there this morning? Why was my phone dead when I needed it the most?

My head was swarming with so many questions that I couldn't think straight. Had I really heard what Ruby had said correctly? That my beloved father whom I cherished with all my heart had passed away, how could this be, he had got the all clear yesterday although that was for cancer. How ironic, he has 15 months of treatment, gets the all clear for a massive heart attack to take him. And then I saw it; his heart, his broken heart oh how it must have ached finding out about what Timothy had done. Then there was the fear of people finding out and his name being dragged through the mud because the "weasel" was refusing to take responsibility. Then there was Kelly's interference in the investigation which had absolutely nothing to do with her as her life hadn't been affected nor had her children's.

Dad had been so upset and angry at the way both of them had conducted themselves and no doubt had been stewing over it waiting for one or both of them to turn up. He would have been beside himself stressing about all of it until his heart had literally broken in two. He had died being ashamed of his two eldest children and now nothing would heal his heart nor mine. I also knew that now my father had gone, I was well and truly on my own open to the elements and I would no longer smile again.

Chapter 29
On Autopilot

I did what I always do in a crisis, I quickly assessed the situation and formulated a strategy that would protect the boys as much as possible. Mick and Michelle, their godparents, lived just around the corner from Mum so if I took them there, I could drop them enroute and get to Mum as soon as possible. I made the call.

'Hey Lois,' Michelle greeted me cheerily.

'Hiya Michelle, I have just had news that Dad has passed away,' I started.

'Oh no Lois I am so sorry, what do you need?' she asked immediately.

'Can I drop the boys off with you whilst I go see Mum and find out the details, just so you know I am not going to say anything to them yet,' I told her.

'Yes, yes of course you can, how long will you be?' she asked.

'I am going to put them in the car now if that's ok?' I spoke.

'Yes of course I will be watching for you,' she told me.

'Ok, and thank you,' I muttered, I was now running on autopilot.

I ended the call and shouted the boys out of their playroom to put their shoes and coats on.

'But where are we going, Mummy?' Joe asked.

'Yes, we have only just come home,' stated Jack.

'I know love, but I have to go over and help Grandma with something,' I told him.

'But Joe and I were building some Lego, weren't we, Joe?' Jack said looking for some support from his brother.

'Yes, we were building Lego,' Joe repeated.

'And I thought you didn't feel well,' Jack added sharply.

'Why don't we take the box with us and then you can build it with Mick and Michelle whilst I go and see Grandma that way you can have a fun time whilst I am busy,' I tried.

'We can go see Mick and Michelle and build some Lego with them?' Jack asked and they both looked at each other then, nodded frantically.

They quickly retrieved the precious tub of Lego then had their shoes and coats on in record time. When we arrived at their house, Michelle was at the gate waiting to scoop the boys in whilst Mick was stood by their open door both wore sympathetic expressions. Only when the boys had reached Mick and were out of earshot did I explain.

'Apparently Dad had a massive heart attack this lunchtime and Mum was frantically trying to reach me, but we were at the swimming baths and then my battery was dead,' I told her.

'I am so sorry, Lois,' she said comfortingly, 'if there is anything we can do just say and you know we will be here for you. For you all,' she offered kindly.

'You are doing it right now just know I appreciate you watching the boys so I can gather the information, I will ring you as soon as I can,' I told her.

'Don't worry, take your time we have nothing planned I will sort them a snack out,' she said.

'I haven't said anything to them yet but will probably tell them when I return if that's ok. They will want to see Grandma, but it will be far better them knowing before they do,' I spoke.

'That is fine, I will see you when you get back,' I turned to go when she touched my arm and I turned back to face her, 'I am really sorry for your loss,' she said.

I swallowed down the tears that were trying to force their way out as right now I had to be strong for my mum and couldn't turn up crying otherwise she would go to pieces. 'Thank you,' I muttered and left.

I arrived at Grey Gables within a couple of minutes Mum was in the lounge with Ruby in the kitchen making her a drink. I nodded solemnly at Ruby and asked how she was before venturing through to see her. Mum was in shock. I walked over to her and knelt before her taking her in my arms and she wept openly and unashamedly.

'I couldn't do anything, Lois,' she said, and I let her cry until she was ready to talk.

'What happened?' I asked when she was a little more composed.

'I had just gone into the kitchen, and he was asking me about when his next hospital appointment was. I told him I didn't know. He then wanted me to go upstairs to look in his red folder to check for him. I told him I would look later but he was adamant I should go and look at that moment. Begrudgingly I did, but when I came back downstairs, he was laid out,' she informed me.

'Was he still alert and conscious?' I enquired.

'No, he was motionless,' she said.

'So, what did you do, call an ambulance?' I asked.

'I couldn't think straight, I called you first,' she said, 'the decorator was here, and he knew what to do so started CPR and told me to ring an ambulance, which I did. When they arrived, they tried to save him, but they couldn't, Lois. It was awful. I just wanted you here, you would have done it,' she sobbed.

'I couldn't have done anything, Mum; if it was his time to go, there was nothing anyone could have done,' I said gently.

'Where were you, Lois?' she asked so I told her and of coming over really ill at 12.50.

She stared at me. '12.50; that was when he sent me back upstairs, I remember looking at the clock and being irritated because I was waiting for the Meals on Wheels people to arrive. It was 12.50,' she began to sob again. 'Do you think he knew what was going to happen to him and that is why he sent me out of the way?' she queried.

'Who can say, people who have had a near death experience say they have seen loved ones coming to guide them, so I guess it is possible,' I said comforting her.

Ruby entered the room with our drinks, 'the next-door neighbours were at the gate waiting, expecting you to arrive at any minute ready to take Joe and Jack to their house,' she said.

I felt dreadful at the time my parents needed me the most I wasn't there all because the boys had wanted to go swimming and my bloody mobile was dead! As much as I berated myself, I also knew that everything happened for a reason and maybe I just wasn't supposed to be here at that time. Perhaps the images I needed to hold in my mind were of our talks in the park, our trips to the seaside and Dad having fun on the dodgems.

'Have you told the others?' I asked referring to Kelly, Timothy and Nick.

'No,' she said, 'not yet. I wanted to speak to you first.'

'You need to ring them, Mum, and tell them,' I told her.

'I can't, I can't face them it's been a horrendous day and I have had people in and out all afternoon with the ambulance, police and undertakers. No, I can't. Will you tell them for me?' she asked.

'It wouldn't be right, Mum; they need to hear it from you besides I do not think they would take kindly if it came from me,' I said gently.

'I can't, it will have to wait until tomorrow I have had enough for today,' she said desperately.

'I can understand that' I told her 'But he is their father as much as he is ours and they need to know besides I would be devastated if you did that to me.'

'Lois is right, Mum, you need to tell them, and you need to do it as soon as possible,' Ruby ventured.

'Maybe have your cup of tea first and then make the calls,' I said.

We sat in quiet contemplation as we sipped our drinks each of us weighing the magnitude of the situation and albeit what that would mean to each of our lives. And once Mum was ready, I took out her phonebook and rang each number passing the phone to her before it connected. The third call was to Kelly and feeling Mum was coping extremely well I took the cups into the kitchen to wash them whilst she broke the devastating news.

'Lois,' she called me, 'Lois.' I was just about to go into her when she stomped through the kitchen door frantic, 'go and tell her I don't want her here.'

'What? What's wrong?' I asked not wanting Mum to have any other stress at this time.

'Tell her, I don't want her to come over here tonight. I have had enough of people being here today, I want to rest not go over it again. I am fine with you two being here,' she screeched.

When I picked up the phone, it was the usual sanctimonious attitude dictating and not listening. 'I have just been telling Mum that I will come straight over,' she said.

'Thing is, Kelly, Mum is not in the right frame of mind at the moment she is in shock, and she doesn't want to have to go through it again,' I tried to reason with her.

'Well, you two are there,' she spit out.

'That is as may be, but it is not a competition, and we were only asked to get here because we live the closest. She is exhausted and mentally drained so does not feel she can cope with anymore tonight she just needs a good night's sleep. Come over first thing in the morning,' I suggested.

'Ok, if you think that would be better, tell her I will see her in the morning,' she said reluctantly.

I rung off to find Mum had come back into the lounge and sat down. 'So, what did she say?' Mum asked.

'She will come in the morning,' I started, 'but she was clearly unhappy for me to relay that information as I told you she would be.'

'You will not believe what she has just said to Mum,' Ruby said.

I looked quizzically at Mum and she explained the reason for her stress, 'the first thing she said when I told her dad had passed away was, "well, I would like to sing at the funeral,"' she said as I gazed in absolute disbelief. 'Just imagine, what does she think it is, a bloody karaoke bar!'

'She said what?' I queried absolutely astounded at the insensitivity and ridiculousness of the statement not to mention the self-centredness.

'Exactly and she wonders why I don't want her here,' Mum said.

'By the way Lois,' Ruby cut in, 'I told the undertaker that you would want to see Dad straight away,' Ruby informed me.

'Thank you, I would,' I said surprised at her straightforwardness with them and assessing the situation correctly. 'Where is he?'

'He is at the Chapel of Rest on the Green,' Mum said.

'Can we go straight away?' I enquired thankful that I could see him one last time to help me process things and then move forward in helping Mum sort things out.

'Yes, they are expecting us although he did say to be aware that they would not have had time to do anything yet,' she said to prepare me.

'Will you be alright if Ruby comes with me, Mum?' I asked sensitively. She nodded.

It only took us 5 minutes to get to the chapel of rest, so the journey was very quiet whilst I steeled myself to observe my father in death. I parked on the street as we arrived needing those few seconds to clear my thoughts and to prepare myself. The notice on the door requested that we ring the bell only once, I complied and waited patiently my heart in my throat, my hands clammy and my heart racing to the point it felt like it would burst through my chest. The door was opened by a tall elderly gentleman in the obligatory black pin striped suit, he nodded in recognition towards Ruby then held the door wide.

We stepped into a small entrance that was only a couple of metres wide and maybe 4 metres in length. There were two doors one directly opposite us and another to our right that displayed a plaque stating "reception". He stepped back to allow our entrance and then on closing the door he held out his hand to demonstrate the direction we should take. That was when I noticed the gurney at the other end of the entrance and upon it was a body bag apparently containing the body of my beloved father. Tears escaped my eyes at the reality of the situation. I was rooted to the spot unable to go either forwards or backwards in this tiny space, the outside door now closed. I looked towards the kind elderly gentleman for guidance and from his years of experience he understood and quietly walked over to the gurney.

'I apologise that we have not had time to prepare your father, but your sister said that you would want to see him immediately. May I offer my deepest condolences,' he said whilst beginning to open the zip. 'Please take all the time you need.'

I kept my eyes on him for a few moments unable to remove them as I did not want reality to smack me in the face anytime soon. Again, another one of those moments in time where everything has stopped still and seems to be teetering on the edge waiting to fall like a spinning coin. Then within seconds its axis changes and it stops flat a bit like my world that was spinning right now and as soon as I looked, I knew it would never be the same again. So many of these life changing moments had occurred recently but this was by far the most heartbreaking. And then it happened my eyes fell upon his grey ashen face so still and expressionless peeping out of a body bag. As I stepped forward, Ruby thankfully took one of the 4 seats that lay in a row and gave me the space to pay my respects to my father.

'Oh Dad,' I wept, 'I am so sorry I wasn't there to comfort you in your last moments. I am so sorry.' I stood a few minutes as though he was somehow telepathically speaking to me to recall the thoughts, he had shared with me during our times alone at the hospital. And I remembered. 'I promised you I would look after "the love of your life" and I will keep that promise come what may, so don't worry I will step in the gap for her. I will protect her, support her and ensure your final wish is carried out and she kisses your coffin.'

I placed my right hand where I gauged his chest would be and felt the stillness. 'I will always love you and continue to live as you instructed for your blood runs through my veins.' I bent down and kissed his cold forehead, 'Love you, big man,' I finished and turned around to find Ruby sat in tears absorbing my love for this amazing man whom only 9 days earlier we'd had to inform him of Timothy and Kelly's behaviour. We hugged briefly and I actually think it may have been the first and only moment that Ruby felt something for me or maybe it was just because she was experiencing grief for her father.

On our way back to Grey Gables, I informed Ruby that I had to call to see one of Dad's cousins to inform her of his death, another promise I had made. I wanted her to hear it from me and then we went to Mick and Michelle's where the boys were nestled together cuddling Molly and Betty, their cherished pooches.

'Mummy,' they greeted me.

'Look at the trick I have been showing Betty,' said Jack.

'And I have been teaching Molly it too,' Joe said not wanting to be outdone.

'Boys, there is something I need to tell you both,' I said, and here it was again that moment teetering in the balance waiting to plummet and take the hearts of my two little boys with it.

'What is it, Mummy?' they asked clutching each other as they suddenly felt the insecurity oozing out of me.

'I have to tell you something really upsetting and there is no easy way to say this, darling,' I began their big green eyes widening at the prospect of what terrifying news I was about to deliver. 'Grandad passed away this afternoon.'

The horror at receiving this information reverberated like a thousand tennis balls from the walls of the room their anguish escaping their tiny bodies through an animalistic howl. It ricocheted through my body tearing my heart to shreds I felt powerless to protect them from the horrors of the cycle of life. I held them and they grasped on to me with all their might no doubt the bedrock of their existence now obliterated and replaced with the fear of the unknown.

Mick and Michelle looked on quietly observing the decimation of their godchildren's life and their hearts ached too. When we were finally able to stand, I could see the depth of the love they held for the three of us etched in each of the tears that now stained their faces. They hugged us individually holding on to each one of us that little bit longer than normal and assisted the children on with their coats whilst they continued to sob their little shoulders rising and dropping. I thanked Mick and Michelle and made our way to the car. Once the boys were safely clipped in, I kissed them both and relayed my gratitude then we set off for Grey Gables.

'I know this is very hard, boys, and that Grandad is your hero, but we have to be really strong for Grandma right now,' I told them.

'Will Grandad be coming back?' asked Joe.

'No darling, he has gone to heaven to be with his mum and dad,' I said as kindly as I could to help him grasp the situation.

'So, I won't see him ever again?' Joe asked.

'No Joe, we won't be able to see him ever again,' Jack advised him, and they both began to wail again.

As we arrived at Grey Gables, I encouraged Ruby to go in ahead of us to let Mum know the children were here but as soon as we stopped the car, they released their belts and tore in to get to her first. When I caught up with them, they were at either side of Mum holding on to her so tight that I stepped out to give them privacy, they needed each other right now. I decided to go back into the kitchen to organise drinks with Ruby. On my return, it was shocking to see the irreparable damage that was etched on each of their faces, and I knew I would have to put my feelings aside to help them navigate their grief. And then Ruby entered the room.

'You are not going to believe this, but Kelly has just pulled up outside,' she delivered.

'You are joking,' Mum said furiously, 'why won't she ever listen to what people want instead of bulldozing in where she isn't wanted, trampling all over everyone's feelings.'

'It is never about anyone else, Mum, there is only her in Kelly's world,' said Ruby.

'I will put the kettle back on and make her a drink, play nice,' I said trying to lighten the mood.

When she burst through the door, she was in actress mode, 'Oh my beautiful father, I couldn't stay away. I had to come,' she declared.

'I told you not to, Kelly. I have had to deal with enough today,' Mum told her.

'But I should be here; he would have wanted me to be,' she said. 'When I got off the phone to you, Haley asked what was wrong, so I told her. She ran off out of the house and we have no idea where she is,' she stated.

'And you're over here?' I said doubtfully.

'So, what happened to him?' she asked ignoring my retort.

Mum just shook her head not wanting to repeat herself again so I asked Ruby to explain as she had been the one there and knowing full well, Kelly wouldn't want to hear it from me. Though quite frankly I do not know what reception she thought she would get when essentially, she was coercing Timothy to lie and being prepared to go against us all. Once Ruby had finished, I told Mum that I would get off as I wanted to settle the boys and get them ready for bed. The reality was I didn't want them surrounded by the drama that was Kelly, so Mum followed me into the kitchen.

'Please don't go love I really don't want to be on my own tonight. Could you and the boys stay here with me?' she asked.

Inevitably I could not deny her request, so I agreed whilst also taking the opportunity to leave to go and get an overnight bag for the boys and me. When I got back, Mum and Ruby were up in arms at the visit paid by Kelly.

'Why doesn't she ever listen?' Mum was saying.

'What has she done now?' I asked carrying our overnight bag in through the door.

'Just after you left, she mentioned about wanting to sing at the funeral again,' Ruby said shaking her head.

'So, the first thing a person says when hearing of their father's passing is "I want to sing at his funeral"?' I pondered; it was incredible.

'He is barely cold, but she doesn't ask how I am; she just declares that she wants to sing at his funeral. She may as well be dancing on his grave, the selfish bitch!' Mum stated.

'When you rang me, Ruby the grief hit me instantaneously that I could barely speak never mind being compos mentis enough to think so far ahead to want to sing at his funeral. I mean when the time comes, I will be broken I don't know how anyone could hold it together enough to sing, it is beyond me,' I said.

'He has only just passed away for goodness' sake I think we are a long way off from making plans about a funeral,' Mum said. 'I haven't even come to terms that he has gone yet!'

'Another case of all the world's a stage for Kelly to use it as a performance even at her own Dad's funeral,' Ruby said bitterly. 'When she didn't get the favourable response, she was clearly expecting she tried to make out that Haley had put the suggestion forward.'

'You mean Haley who immediately ran out of the house and was still missing, according to Kelly who had still come over here,' I said.

'Exactly, it was obviously Kelly's idea all along not only had she said it to me straight away on the phone but then she back peddled throwing her own daughter under the bus to try and make it sound kosher,' Mum stated.

'Her story doesn't add up at all like you say, IF Haley ran off, she couldn't have said it, it's a load of rubbish like everything else that comes out of her mouth.'

'I am not being funny, Mum, and obviously it is entirely your call but if she gets up to sing, I will be walking out, it would be so disrespectful to Dad and he wouldn't have wanted that at all,' I stated.

'I couldn't agree more, and I can tell you this it will be happening over my dead body,' Mum said, a poor choice of words under the circumstances.

Chapter 30
Singing Lessons

The following morning, I awoke to the telephone ringing, so I jumped up and ran down the stairs as Mum picked it up, so I retreated back to the small bedroom from which I had come. Somehow the inducement of sleep had anaesthetised me to the knowledge that Dad had passed away until I saw the boys red eyes and then it hit me like a baseball bat. I felt numb, the denial of grief overwhelming but the reality of the despair through their eyes was palpable. I pulled the cover back for them to seek the comfort they were so desperately searching for and in truth that I also needed too, and we wept. I could hear Mum's voice getting more agitated and louder as it carried its way upstairs and wondered who on earth was upsetting her given the circumstances. The boys were tired and obviously hadn't been able to get sufficient rest so once their sobs had subsided, I cuddled them up and went downstairs to check on Mum. She was in the kitchen the call having now been concluded.

'I cannot bloody believe it,' she said irately.

'What's wrong?' I asked trying to search her face for some answer.

'That was Peter on the phone,' Mum said.

'Peter, as in Kelly's husband, Peter?' I asked. 'What did he want so early in the morning?' Then I thought no doubt it would have been to give his condolences to Mum.

'He rang to tell me about how upset Kelly is,' she said.

'Does he think she is the only one?' I asked.

'Apparently so, he didn't even ask how I was or to give me his condolences it was just about how upset Kelly was,' she said fuming.

'We have lost our father too and what about you who has lost her husband after 50 odd years? Does that not count for anything?' I was also becoming equally annoyed, why did she always have to be the centre of attention.

'Oh, that isn't the half of it; he then went on about how your dad would have wanted her to sing at the funeral as it was something they had in common and it was her way of demonstrating her respect,' she said irritated.

'Respect? How is it respectful to want to make someone's funeral about yourself?' I queried.

'Exactly have you ever seen a real star actually sing at their parents' funeral or would they show decorum and seek to honour them in dignity, yet they can sing and actually make a living from it. Just because she was in a band donkey's years ago for two minutes does she think it qualifies her as a singer? She really does get my blood boiling!' Mum shrieked.

'Don't let it get to you so much; it isn't worth it,' I said trying to appease her.

'No, she is not the star of the show, and I will not have your father's funeral made a mockery, he was well respected and we have a responsibility to give him the send-off he deserves. I am not going to be bullied by her or Peter!' She said and she was right, how could anyone sit during a funeral and be comfortable listening to that?

'Look I hope I haven't influenced you on this because of what I said last night?' I queried.

'What you said last night?' she asked.

'Yes, my first reaction was that I would have to get up and walk out if she was singing but that wasn't fair. He was your husband and it is entirely your decision, so just to reiterate if you did decide she would sing out of respect for Dad I wouldn't leave.' I tried to ensure she had my support either way as things were difficult enough without our relationships disintegrating.

'No, do not think that had any bearing on my decision it's a ridiculous proposal that she needs to get out of her head and as I said I will not be bullied by any of them, it is not happening and that is final,' she said vehemently.

I decided that the best thing to do was to try and distract her, so I organised breakfast for us all and once we had eaten, we sat down to make a list of what needed to be done. Mum had been made aware that an autopsy was being performed on Dad today as his death had been sudden and unexpected. So, we needed to keep busy to take our minds off the fact.

Mum knew immediately whom she wanted to conduct the service it was a man from her local church, we then had to consider the people we needed to tell like the members of our extended family and friends. We made a list and as Mum was clearly not up to it Ruby and I said we would tell the main people in person and then we would put an advert in the obituary of our local papers. Then there were people like Dad's solicitor, the banks, pensions, benefits or insurance policies. We were well underway with things when the telephone call came mid-afternoon from the coroner's office. It was confirmed that Dad had suffered a massive heart attack which as soon as it had hit him, he would have apparently died instantly before even hitting the ground. I relayed the information to Ruby and Mum who wept at the thought.

'And one of the people responsible for his broken heart has the audacity to want to sing at his funeral?' she shuddered. 'What an absolute joke!'

Ruby and I did our best to comfort her both knowing full well that had *he* owned up to *his* disgusting behaviour as encouraged to do so and if Kelly had stayed on the fence instead of interfering through some misplaced family loyalty to *him* Dad would probably still have been here. At that moment as the three of us drank in the facts, I was certain we were now on our own as they had literally ripped this family apart with their lies. And Dad had paid for it with his life.

The next day I had to get out of the house, so I went down to Wakefield to lay flowers as I did every year on a dear friend's grave who had passed away aged 16. On the way home, lines of a poem started to formulate within my mind, so I kept having to stop to write them down. I hadn't been thinking of it in particular, but Mum had asked me to write something to say at Dad's funeral and it appeared it was coming thick and fast. Inevitably when I got back to Grey Gables, I decided on the solitude of Mum's room to let it flow as what I had got so far was pretty good. After about 20 minutes, Mum knocked on the door and came in.

'I am sorry to bother you love but will you come downstairs?' she asked.

'What, right now, I am just in the middle of writing this for you?' I said pointing to the papers in front of me.

'I know love, but Kelly has just turned up with Peter and she has brought Charlotte, Graham and Haley too. I really cannot do with this right now,' Mum said getting upset.

'You will be fine; it was inevitable the children would want to come and see you he was their grandad, and they will seek comfort being here. Besides no offence to them but right now I cannot be around Kelly, so no I won't come down if you don't mind,' I spoke.

She clearly did mind but imposed no further pressure respecting the fact of why I could not abide to be in Kelly's company right now and went back downstairs. I was so focused on the piece I was creating I didn't hear Mum coming back upstairs.

'Please will you come down here right now and tell her I don't want her to sing at the bloody funeral,' she said tormentedly.

'Why what's wrong, she is surely not going on about it again?' I uttered.

'I have told her over and over again, but she is not listening, it is wearing me down, but I will not be bullied, I do not want her singing and that is that,' she said getting really distressed.

'Isn't Ruby there can't she say something because you know what Kelly is like she won't want me telling her,' I tried hoping to not have to get involved.

'She is but I want you to tell her and then she will get the message once and for all,' she shrieked.

Reluctantly I got up and went down the stairs to the middle room where Kelly and her family were sat knowing full well, they must have heard Mum's distress and why she had asked me to step in. I went to the far wall and sat at the small telephone table with its burgundy brushed velvet cushion, Mum followed and sat to my left in Dad's chair in the bay window. On the settee opposite me were Haley, Graham and Charlotte Kelly's children, she was sat to my right in the armchair behind the kitchen door and Peter was stood mooching about. I may have been wrong, but I can usually accurately assess a situation and I felt like I had just walked into the lion's den. They had come prepared and were spoiling for a fight, so I walked into it tentatively.

'Hiya how are you all doing?'

'Alright under the circumstances,' they all agreed in one format or another.

'Mum has asked me to come down and join you as she was feeling uncomfortably outnumbered,' I said clearly.

'Really, why should she?' Kelly retorted offhand.

'She just felt she was being put under pressure for some reason,' I said very carefully.

'No, not at all,' Kelly started in her usual aloof manner.

'Kelly was just telling your mum that she would like to sing at Jeff's funeral to pay tribute to him and his singing days,' Peter jumped in.

'And I was telling them that it wasn't something I was looking to encourage,' Mum counteracted as both Peter and Kelly scowled at her.

'It is just that Dad was a singer and it was something that he and I had in common, it was our little thing,' she gave as a weak pretend giggle.

'Ordinarily I would say that's a great idea if it was for any other occasion other than a funeral,' I tried sensitively.

'What is that supposed to mean?' Kelly snapped.

'If it had been their anniversary, his birthday, Father's Day then yes I would have to agree with you that would have been a nice tribute and he could have got up and sang with you, if there was a karaoke.' I paused to let that sink in. 'However, this is a funeral in a church where we show our mark of respect with dignity and quiet contemplation.'

'Why would being in the church make any difference; they sing in church, don't they?' she snapped.

'Mum has tried to make it abundantly clear that she does not think it is appropriate for you to sing at his funeral and quite frankly neither do I,' I stipulated.

'We have known lots of people sing at funerals, haven't we, Peter?' she argued.

'But didn't you say that it was Haley's suggestion that you sang at Dad's funeral?' I threw in without warning and glanced towards Haley to see her reaction inevitably she appeared surprised like it was the first time she had heard about it being her idea. 'Obviously it wasn't your suggestion then Haley,' I smiled satisfactorily unveiling the lie.

'Yes, there are lots of people from the operatic society who have sung at funerals,' Peter said trying to ignore me whilst wanting to back Kelly up unrelenting on the fact the answer was still a no.

'That may have been the case, but Dad wasn't a part of an operatic society and what Mum is clearly telling you is she doesn't want it for Dad's funeral,' I reiterated.

'It is about time you realised that you and your mother are two different people Lois and that you are not joined at the hip,' Peter roared as Kelly realised, she wasn't getting anywhere and did her fake tears routine and ran out of the house.

What Peter had said did not sink in until way after they had left. At the time I had mistakenly thought he had used the words "your mother" in error, I assumed because his children were sat there. I thought he had meant to say 'you and Kelly are two different people' suggesting that she was a different person to me and that she had her own way of doing things. Quite clearly, I had been right they were spoiling for a fight and I could only imagine the coercion and preparation beforehand. The journey over in the car must have been quite tense with a lot of very unkind words and accusations thrown for Peter to act so hostile and aggressively towards me. I had never heard him lose his temper before never mind being so argumentative and confrontational but there again, we also did not know what lies she was saying with regards to Timothy. I had never had a crossed word with Peter in the 25 years that I had known him so realised he was merely spouting Kelly's words at me.

I thought about the train of events, on hearing of Dad's death Kelly had immediately stated she had wanted to sing at the funeral, she then bethought herself and on arriving at Mum's changed it to being Haley's idea despite stating Haley had instantly run off on hearing the news of her grandad's passing. She had then got Peter to contact Mum to push the point further and when that had not worked, she had turned up with her entire family to bully the poor woman. Mum who had witnessed her husband's death, the paramedics unsuccessful attempts, endured the police's presence and then the undertakers taking him away in a body bag. That morning had been the first day of Dad's "all-clear" future before it had been so cruelly snatched away from him. This poor woman who had endured all this was now being bullied not only by her daughter but her son-in-law as well with the children brought along for back-up. This disgusting behaviour was incomprehensible and everything my father could not abide. He would have expected the "love of his life" to have been supported, cared for and cherished through sympathy, understanding and most of all clothed in love.

I found it wholly inconceivable they had come heavy mobbed to push this poor defenceless woman into getting their own way even when she had stipulated over and over again her wishes. It reminded me of the reactions of child having been told "NO" they were throwing a tantrum just to get their own way. The low blow accusing me of controlling Mum when their tactics hadn't worked as though I were the puppet master. If truth be known, Mum had always pulled my strings like she had done just now but then it always resulted in me being the centre of the negative spotlight. Luckily for Peter who also *exited centre stage right'* I hadn't realised what his barbed comment referred to so thankfully it did not go into a full-blown row. However, it did result in both parents storming out thus leaving their children to maturely deal with the situation.

'I think what Mum was trying to say was that she just wanted to feel that she was paying Grandad a personal tribute,' Graham said maturely and peacefully.

'I understand that Graham and like I said ordinarily that would be a fitting choice but not under these circumstances your grandma does not feel that her choice is appropriate,' I offered.

'I do not think it was as much what you said as how you said it,' Charlotte remarked quite sharply in the same manner as her parents.

'I am sorry?' I asked thinking who the hell do you think you're speaking to, little girl?

She said, 'I think Mum understands the concept of what Grandma was saying but you were quite rude how you spoke and she has just lost her dad.'

'I have lost my father too and Grandma has lost her husband; if anyone is being rude in the way they are speaking, I would suggest that is you right now,' I told her firmly.

'I just think you could have put it differently,' she said surly.

'Hold on a minute, Charlotte. 1, it has nothing to do with you and 2, your mum has been told on several occasions the answer is no. She might not like it but coming here and carrying on like this is not going to change the fact,' I told her.

'I think that Charlotte is just trying to stick up for Mum, Auntie Lois. I don't think she meant to be rude or cause any offence and yes, we should be respectful to both yours and Grandma's loss too,' Graham said to pacify the situation.

'Thank you, Graham, but with that in mind please understand that I am only sticking up for my mum too. Grandma came upstairs and requested I speak up for her because your mum would not listen to reason,' I spoke.

'I understand how things must have come across with us all turning up but honestly we did want to see Grandma and to ensure she was alright,' he looked towards Charlotte for confirmation, but she was sat stoney-faced, so he continued, 'Well, I did anyway.'

'Thank you love and I am sure Grandma really appreciates your support,' I stated as he stood, walked to his grandma, put an arm around her shoulder and kissed her lightly on the head. At that point, Peter and Kelly *entered centre stage right*.

'Right, are you ready guys,' Peter asked his children.

'I am sorry if we came across in the wrong way, I did not mean to upset anyone and if you need anything of course we are here to help.' Kelly said then approached me to hug me which was very uncomfortable given the immediate conversation and the circumstances with regards to Timothy. She held me at arm's length her hands on my elbows. 'We have just lost our dad so the last thing we need to be doing is falling out right now,' she said. I allowed her theatrical embrace, but no way were these her words, she had obviously been coached outside by Peter to behave so compliantly.

Inevitably we were glad when their car was seen pulling out of the drive and we could get back to what was really important sorting out Dad's affaires and writing the piece for the funeral. Later that afternoon when I had finished, I called both Mum and Ruby together to read it aloud for the first time. When I looked up at them at the end, they were both blubbering and agreed it was a perfect tribute depicting Dad's life, his loves, his family and his humour. All I needed to do now was to commit to read and re-read it every day until I could do it all the way through without crying in order to do him proud.

Over the next week, we were exceptionally busy obtaining Dad's death certificate for the various professionals who required a copy of it, meeting with friends, family and the minister. There was a function room to secure, flowers to order and numerous other things associated with a funeral that seemed to keep on growing. Towards the end of the second week, we were all spent emotionally the boys in the thick of everything yet kept on the periphery whilst I did my best to take as much pressure off Mum as possible. I felt spread in so many different directions trying to juggle all the responsibilities to save Mum, but I had lost my dad too and I was being given no time at all to come to terms with it.

I continually checked in with Jack as I could see he was doing his best to swallow his hurt and fight off the grief in the exact same way as me, for Joe. How hard it must have been for them to be submerged into the organisation of their beloved grandad's funeral without knowing what on earth was going on. Their loss so abundantly profound yet as little people within our world they are so often overlooked due to the adult desire to keep busy at such times. This is why I instantly agreed to a surprise proposal from my camping friend Barry.

'Hiya Lois, I know you are in the thick of things making plans for Jeff's funeral, but I wanted to run something by you, feel free to say no I won't be offended,' he spoke.

'Ok, now I am intrigued,' I said jovially.

'Obviously we had all planned to go camping again for the bank holiday weekend,' he said.

'Oh, I am sorry Barry that was this weekend wasn't it, I can't possibly go at the moment I need to be here to support Mum,' I said honestly.

'That is what I thought but we were talking about it last night and I wondered how you would feel about the boys still coming?' he said.

'Sorry,' I really wasn't expecting that at all.

'We were just thinking that the boys are in the centre of everything and it might do them power of good to get away with us for a couple of days and also take the pressure off you a bit,' he said thoughtfully.

I really was taken aback; no one had ever stood in the gap for me and here was Barry not only seeing my predicament but the boys too, I was immensely touched by his kindness. I think I was quiet for a bit too long and he took my silence as my not being in agreement.

'It's ok, Lois, if you don't feel comfortable with us taking them, I won't be offended I just wanted to offer that's all' he finished.

'It isn't that at all, I am literally blown away; thank you for demonstrating such love, care and concern for Mum, the boys and myself. If you don't mind taking them then yes, I would readily agree. I think it would be good for them,' I told him.

'Really? Oh, that is fantastic we will pick them up Friday lunchtime if that is, ok?' he enquired.

'That's perfect,' I said absolutely chuffed my boys would at least have some fun in the midst of all the sadness, hurt and upset.

When Friday came and Barry arrived to collect the boys, they were like cats on a hot tin roof jumping about and excited at being able to escape and enjoy an adventure with their mate Barry. When I had secured them into Barry's Range Rover, Jack was a little more subdued as he realised the implication of them going alone meant I was still in the thick of it. A wave of sadness crossed his sensitive little face.

'But Mummy, what about you, you need a break too,' he said thoughtfully.

'I know darling but right now it is important that you get out and enjoy some fun in the fresh air with your camp mates,' I told him.

'But we will miss you,' he said earnestly.

'Yes, we will miss you,' Joe chimed in.

'I know you will, but you have each other, and Barry and the gang will look after your every need,' I reassured them.

'Yes,' said Barry, 'You are going to share a pod together in our large tent, we are going to cook on the barbie, I am going to teach you how to ride Sean's motorbike Jack, and Joe, I am going to teach you how to fish.'

'All in a weekend! Wow you won't have any time to miss me,' I told them, 'Now go on have a great time and Jack make sure you look after Joe alright?'

'Alright Mummy, we will have the best time just for you,' Jack said smiling his beautiful, dimpled smile.

'Yes, we will have the best time just for you Mummy,' Joe copied.

I kissed them both goodbye and with a little tinge of sadness that I wasn't going too, I waved them off knowing it was in their best interests for them to go.

By the Sunday, Mum, Ruby and I decided we too needed to have a little break and planned to go out for some lunch until Mum received a phone call.

'It's me,' Nick said. 'I am on my way to Grey Gables, and I am bringing Timothy with me,' he stated, not asked.

'Oh, right,' Mum said a little taken aback by his brisk manner.

'He has lost his dad too so he has a right to be there!' he dictated then put the phone down before Mum could argue the fact.

To be honest it would have been far more amenable to have asked if it was alright, explained the situation and exercised the same concern for his abused sisters. Over the years I have failed to understand where their elevated rights and sense of entitlement have derived from to assert themselves above other's needs. Perhaps Dad employing them throughout their lives has given them a false sense of superiority that sometimes being the boss's son affords however it has unwittingly spilt over into every other aspect of their lives. Personally, I was going to leave, it was one thing being in Kelly's company, but it was altogether different being forced to be in *his*. However, Ruby was adamant, that I should not allow them to push me out, so I compromised and shut myself off upstairs instead.

After receiving the call, Mum was becoming increasingly anxious not knowing what demeanour to expect from them given Nick's attitude on the phone. She also recalled Dad's words on finding out about Timothy's behaviour stating that he was no longer welcome at Grey Gables. She was beginning to feel vulnerable and powerless when thankfully Dad's brother Simon and his wife Lesley arrived. Mum quickly briefed them on the situation and explained about feeling threatened by Nick's abrupt manner, so they willingly agreed to stay to give Mum their support. This then enabled me to retreat upstairs without having to come in to contact with either one of them.

I tried to use the time wisely to take some rest in order to replenish myself having been running on reserves of reserves for the past couple of weeks. I tried clearing my mind by listening to some soothing meditational music, but one voice seemed to keep penetrating my brain like a phlebotomist's needle. I could not counteract it no matter what I tried it was like an array of machine gun bullets repeatedly hitting its target without mercy.

In the rawness of my grief, I was powerless to stop the panic or impending doom that was rising up with Little Lois and so I began to feel hemmed in unable to get away. As the psychological torment of helplessness increased it perpetuated the usual emotional reaction of rigid fear. Subsequently the physical response was breathlessness, feeling hot and clammy, then digging my thumbnails into my adjoining fingers and I knew I had to make it stop. I got my house key and some other things together and then as discreetly as possible I crossed the room; they were all in focusing on the door to the kitchen and once through it I was out. I stayed at home for a good couple of hours in order to restore my equilibrium and maintain a safe distance, this was my home and here I decided who was welcome. Then my mobile rang.

'Hiya love are you coming back over tonight?' Mum asked.

'Yes, I was just waiting for them to leave. I am sorry, Mum, but I just could not stay there knowing *he* was downstairs,' I said honestly.

'It is probably a good job you did go. Nick was quite menacing and threatening towards us,' Mum revealed.

'What, in front of Simon and Lesley,' I asked.

'No, we all sat and chatted everything quite relaxed with both Nick and Timothy seeming to be ok,' she paused, then continued, 'Simon and Lesley were really good they stayed right up until Nick and Timothy said they were going so that is when they got up to make a move too.'

'Ok' I said wondering how this appeared to be menacing behaviour it seemed as though it couldn't have gone any better and there had been nothing for Mum to have worried about.

'Lesley, Simon and Timothy walked out followed by Nick, I was just saying bye and thank you for calling when Nick turned round, locked the door and said I am not going anywhere,' Mum informed me with a shake in her voice.

'What do you mean, he locked you in?' I asked really worried for them.

'He just locked the door and refused to leave until he had found out what had gone on,' she spoke.

'Gone on with what?' I asked unclear of what he could have meant.

'He wanted to know what had happened with your dad,' she answered.

'That is fair enough but surely you told him that 2 weeks ago on the day he passed away,' I said befuddled at this strange behaviour and why he had felt the need to make his sister and mother feel so uncomfortable by locking them in. That was a threatening act of assuming power and control over them.

'He wanted to know every little detail Lois he was like a dog with a bone making me repeat it over and over again wanting me to demonstrate exactly where he was laid on the floor,' Mum said getting upset.

'But that is monstrous why on earth would he put you through having to relive that?' I asked equally getting upset at the cruel treatment of my poor mother.

'That wasn't the end of it Lois he wanted to know thread through needle of what the decorator had done to save him, the paramedics, why the police were here and what they had said,' I was so upset I just wanted him to leave, and he wouldn't.

'You should have called the police Mum that is your house and basically, he was holding you hostage and making unreasonable demands which is all the more barbaric under the circumstances,' I told her now kicking myself for having left her and Ruby to endure this situation.

'In the end, I walked away from him and refused to discuss it further, so I went upstairs and when I came back down, I could hear him in the laundry threatening Ruby,' she said.

'Threatening her in what way?' I was getting riled the more Mum revealed about Nick's disgusting behaviour.

'You will have to ask her exactly what he said but I walked in to hear him sneering at her "you can say what you like but I will deny everything and then it will just be your word against mine, you will not be able to prove anything," Mum revealed. "He was saying it up in her face and threateningly with Ruby beside herself in tears."'

'What the hell is wrong with him she has just lost her dad for goodness' sake!' I said protectively.

'It was awful Lois he terrified both of us with his behaviour,' Mum said understandably shaken and upset.

'Why didn't you ring the police Mum, no one has the right to terrify you in your own home I don't care who he thinks he is,' I said expressing my feelings.

'I told him it was time he left and he just sniggered at me menacingly, unlocked the door, shut it behind him and went. So, I quickly locked it to make sure he couldn't get back in,' she said shuddering at the thought of this encounter.

'I am sorry you have been subjected to this Mum but you must promise if you are ever in a predicament like this again you either ring the police directly or call my number and keep the line open so I can hear and call the police on your behalf.'

We ended the call with her feeling safe in the knowledge that I was immediately setting off for Grey Gables. I was absolutely mortified that this vulnerable elderly lady who had just become a widow was being bullied in her own home by her son. I wondered what he could have been saying to Ruby and pondered the thought perhaps the Nick that did not stir had in fact stirred after all. What was he guilty of that he needs to corner Ruby for and threaten her to maintain her silence.

Ruby was not forthcoming with any specifics she only echoed Mum's feelings about the situation and her fear at his menacing actions towards her. She did reveal that he had been confrontational, so she had turned way and left the laundry in tears but that he had pursued her inches from her face until Mum had returned. What on earth did he have to hide I wondered I mean he couldn't have been threatening her to keep quiet over Timothy as this was all out in the open. He clearly did not want to approach the subject in front of Simon and Lesley but why would he not do it with Timothy unless it was something about himself, he wanted to keep under wraps.

The plot was definitely thickening, and I needed to be on my guard especially with the funeral due to take place in 5 days. I considered for a moment the uncomfortable and challenging prospect of being in the same company as them all and at the same time. I concluded none of them would behave badly in front of guests they only seemed to do this behind closed doors. Therefore, I felt safe in the knowledge they wouldn't upset the apple cart not at Dad's funeral, or would they?

Chapter 31
Saying "Goodbye"

The boys arrived home the next day, which was the bank holiday Monday, refreshed from having had a break, their faces slightly tanned by the sun, fresh and alert from enjoying the great outdoors. Barry was exceptionally complimentary on the boy's exemplary behaviour and astounded at the care Jack provided for his younger brother.

'Seriously Lois, I have never seen a kid like young Jack and how he took care of Joe. He would take him to the toilet block each night and morning, shower him, get him some breakfast then go for a shower himself whilst Joe ate. He was a right little dude serving Joe first and catering for his needs before his own, he had it all worked out like a well-oiled machine. We all marvelled over him and Joe did exactly what Jack told him to do, no arguments; they were amazing,' he said.

'I am so glad to hear that because I would have been mortified if they hadn't behaved,' I told him.

'Behaved?' he began. 'They were like little grown-ups who didn't need any of our help at all they simply mucked in and got on with it.'

I felt so proud that my boys had been on their very best behaviour and able to demonstrate how independent and smart they both were. 'Thank you, Barry,' I said.

'No thank you for letting them come it was ace spending time with them although there is one thing I should mention,' he said gravely and my heart sank, 'what the hell are you playing to these kids?'

'What?' I asked confused.

'On the way over there, they knew all the words to The Smiths "This Charming Man", Mika's "Lollipop" and The Cure's "Caterpillar Go"; what are you playing these kids?' he laughed.

We thanked Barry again before waving him off and then the boys rushed in to see their grandma to tell her all about their adventure. Over the next couple of days, we welcomed many of Dad's old employees who visited Mum to pay their final respects along with finalising plans for the funeral. As the time drew closer, I took the opportunity to sit and chat to the boys so I could brief them on what to expect. Jack had already been to a treasured neighbours funeral the year before, so he had an idea but inevitably this was Joes first experience.

'Do you have any questions,' I enquired, 'or is there anything that you are unsure about?'

'There is one thing, Mum,' Jack said tentatively but paused seemingly not able to find the words to express himself.

'What love, what is it,' I asked concerned.

'You, Grandma and Ruby have been to see Grandad, well I want to go too,' he blurted out.

'Oh, Jack love I really don't think that is a good idea,' I ventured.

'But Mum, I never got to say goodbye, and this is something I need to do,' he told me.

'You will be able to do that at the funeral, Jack,' I told him lovingly.

'No Mum I need to say goodbye to him on my own without everyone else there, he was my grandad, and I wouldn't be able to forgive myself if I didn't,' he told me.

'Jack, I think you are a little too young love, you should remember him as he was, I would hate to think how it could upset you,' I said trying to convince him to rethink his request.

'It would upset me more if I missed the chance to see him one last time. It is something I need to do so please let me he was my grandad, my hero and he deserves my respect,' Jack persisted the tears beginning to wet his eyelashes and then dripping down on to my hand.

I took him into my arms that brave, determined and amazing little boy oh how my siblings could learn dignity from this 9-year-old young man as I ushered my agreement for him to say his goodbyes. Then we sobbed together at the loss of our hero. I waited until the day before the funeral which happened to be Kelly's birthday to ensure everyone else had been given the opportunity to pay their respects, in privacy. I also felt that it would give Jack the time and space to think about his decision to be sure he was doing the right thing. I rang the undertakers and explained his tender years to seek advice of what time to book ensuring no one else would be around. The last thing I wanted was for Jack to undergo any further stress than he absolutely needed to endure. So, to be sure of absolute privacy I also requested that the undertakers maintain our confidentiality.

On the Thursday morning, I was tense and nervous wondering if I had done the right thing agreeing to Jack visiting the Chapel of Rest. He on the other hand was as chirpy and determined as ever.

'If you have any reservations at all Jack, just tell me you have changed your mind and we will leave. It is no problem and do not think it will reflect badly on you if you do not feel up to it when the time comes,' I reassured him.

'It is ok Mum I have got this, I need to say goodbye,' he told me.

About an hour prior to setting off, Mum's house phone rang and then she called me to say it was Ruby for me.

'Hiya,' I said.

'Just wanted to give you the heads up, Kelly's just rung me to say she can't go to the Chapel of Rest this morning as there was someone else going. She asked if I knew who it was and without thinking I said that you were taking Jack,' Ruby revealed.

'As long as she doesn't come interfering, I am not bothered because we will fall out if she does,' I stated imaging her usual theatrical performance.

'She actually said that she wanted to book in afterwards, but the undertakers wouldn't allow it then she got mardy about why should you be the last person to see Dad.' Ruby said.

'That had never even crossed my mind but obviously it did hers which is why she was trying to get the last viewing probably to lord it over us afterwards. I hate the fact that she judges everyone by her own very poor standards. Our appointment merely reflects the relationship Jack had with his grandad and with all due respect to him he should have the privacy to remember him without any drama,' I shared.

'I thought I would just let you know,' Ruby said triumphantly.

I tried to put what Ruby had said to one side but when I got off the phone, Mum could see the annoyance on my face, so I explained to her what Ruby had said.

'And here we go again; Miss Nosey Knickers wanting to know everyone else's business, why the hell does she think it has anything to do with her who is going or who the last person might be. It's ridiculous,' Mum spouted.

'I couldn't agree more this is about Jack and nothing else,' I stated.

When the time came for Jack and I to leave for the Chapel of Rest, I asked him again to confirm his decision and he was happy to pursue it so we set off. I decided to park the car on the gravelled forecourt of the chapel of rest that way if Kelly did happen to pass it wasn't on the street or equally if she did see my car, she would know to leave us alone. Whilst we sat a moment in the car, I think I was more nervous than Jack. I did not want this to scar him in any way, but I couldn't help noticing he seemed as cool as a cucumber. I decided to give him a rundown of what to expect starting with the layout of the entrance area and the room itself that Dad was in.

I explained to him about the coffin which was raised up on blocks with the lid lent at the side of it propped against the wall. I then had to explain what Dad looked like—the pallor of his skin, what he was wearing and the fact that his eyes and mouth were glued shut. I felt it was important to be abundantly open and honest with him so there were no grim surprises to knock him off guard and ultimately give him nightmares. Again, I enquired if he was absolutely sure he wanted to go ahead now that I had relayed all the relevant information. He was absolutely adamant this was his last time to see his grandad and nothing and no one was going to stop him.

'Ok love, if you are sure we will do it but remember you can turn around at any time,' I said.

'I know Mummy, but this is my last chance and I am not going to back out no matter what,' he said bravely.

We turned away from each other to open our respective car doors both primed to face the challenge ahead until a crazed woman came screeching and banging at the driver's window.

'I knew it was you,' Kelly delivered like she had just found out the answer to some cryptic clue.

'What?' I responded in disbelief.

'I knew when the undertaker wouldn't say who was coming that it would be you,' she said all self-righteous.

Jack suddenly burst into tears shocked and scared by her erratic behaviour and demeanour. The poor kid had sat there for 10 minutes plucking up the nerve to go in only to have the rug well and truly dragged from underneath him at the very last second like a reprieved prisoner on death row. He was literally panicked by her high-pitched tone and overly animated expressive gesticulations.

I did what any parent would have done in that situation and got my child as far away as I possibly could, what the hell was she thinking. She must have been sat waiting for us to arrive so she could scare the living daylights out of the poor kid, what an absolute idiot. I raced off towards Grey Gables the sight of me flying into the drive at speed inevitably alerted Mum to the fact that all was not well. Jack was out of the car and running in to find Grandma before I could get to the door.

'Is that right what Jack has just said, Kelly turned up screaming at you in the car?' Mum enquired.

'Yes, I was building Jack up to get the courage to go in and we were about to get out of the car when she suddenly appeared at my window,' I told her.

'What the hell is wrong with her?' She asked and then the phone rang so I went to answer it whilst Mum continued comforting Jack.

'Hello,' I said.

'What did you rush off for? I was only trying to tell you that he didn't look that bad,' Kelly said.

'Are you for real? I was sat there with my 9-year-old son who was plucking up the courage to say his final farewell, why on earth would you approach my car banging on the window and screeching like that?' I challenged her angrily.

'I was just trying to reassure him he would be ok because he didn't look that bad,' she said.

'Don't you think I have already been in to find out for myself so that I can advise and support my son? Or that we might have been sat in the car so that he could brace himself to go through with it?' I raged.

'Well, I didn't know that it was you who was going or that Jack would be in the car with you, how could I have known,' she tried deflecting any responsibility.

'Oh, my goodness, you are such a liar, you did know because you rang Ruby this morning to find out who the person going was because the undertaker wouldn't tell you,' I said.

'But I didn't know that Jack would be in the car with you!' she stated adamantly.

'Yes, you did because Ruby specifically stated it was going to be Jack and myself,' I revealed, 'and this is the reason I asked the undertaker to maintain our confidentiality because I knew full well that you wouldn't be able to stop yourself from pulling a shit stunt like this!' I said furiously and slammed the phone down.

The phone rang again but I knew it would be her, so I let it ring as the one thing Kelly hated was not having the last word. When I went back into the kitchen, I must have had a face like thunder because Mum suggested Jack get Joe and himself a drink with a biscuit. We then went into the lounge so I could relay to Mum the whole episode at the chapel of rest along with the telephone conversation.

'What a nasty bloody trick to pull,' Mum said.

'Seriously there is something wrong with her she knows exactly what she is doing then feigns innocence. Ruby told me that she already knew we would be there,' I said shaking my head in disbelief.

'The poor kid,' Mum began, 'he would have been all prepped up to go inside and then at the last hurdle, bang.'

'She knew it would be hard for him to get the nerve up to go through with seeing his grandad in death, how could she be so bullish and insensitive,' I raged.

'You know she has done it on purpose to hurt you Lois, don't you?' Mum stated, acknowledging what I already knew.

'Yes of course I do but to emotionally scar Jack in the process is unforgiveable,' I said, 'but there again it is not her child so what does it matter; isn't that her attitude?'

'Anyway,' Mum started, 'didn't she want us to change the day of the funeral because she didn't want to be reminded of it every year on her birthday?' Mum reminded me.

'Yes, and because she didn't want the funeral to spoil this birthday yet here, she is on her birthday just a walking contradiction,' I stressed.

At this point, Joe and Jack came into the lounge where we had been talking so I suggested they put the tv on as it would help Jack to calm down. After about 20 minutes of being quite restless, he wanted to know what we were going to do.

'About what love?' I asked.

'About saying goodbye to Grandad,' he asked solemnly.

'I think perhaps we should leave it love you have been through enough today and we still have the funeral to get through tomorrow yet,' I reminded him.

'It is more important now than ever that I go see Grandad mum,' he said surprisingly, 'Auntie Kelly may have tried to ruin it for me, but I will not let her rob me of saying goodbye.' I looked at his sad little face and the anxious plight of his eyes as they burrowed into me hoping for a favourable reply.

'If Jack gets to say goodbye, then I want to too,' Joe bravely delivered.

'I am sorry darling, but you are far too young to go into the Chapel of Rest,' I said putting my foot down.

'Why is he, Mummy? Joe has a right to say goodbye as much as me, you, Grandma and everyone else, Grandad loved us both equally. So, if I go then I think Joe should be able to go too,' he said defiantly. I turned to Mum for support.

'He is right love they were both very close to your dad and if we are there to support them through it then we should do it together,' she said unhelpfully.

After much deliberation, we rang the undertaker to make sure there was no one else expected and confirmed that we were on our way. Again, on arrival I went through the procedure and the get out clause if at any point either of them had second thoughts. I really did not have a good feeling about it, but I remembered not being allowed to go to the funeral of my auntie Lena when I was 8 and the devastation stayed with me for years. I decided to sit in the entrance area where I explained the layout of the room with the coffin again then informed them, I would leave Joe sat with Mum whilst Jack and I went inside. Afterwards I would take Joe in whilst Jack sat with Mum that way, I could give each child the individual support they required without causing the other any unnecessary distress.

'Are you ready?' I asked Jack.

'Yes,' he said with a smile on his face secure in both the decision he was making and the people who now surrounded him.

I slowly and carefully opened the door and glanced down at Jack who was gripping my hand like a vice, 'we go at your pace, mate,' I told him.

He looked up at me producing a thin weak smile his eyes beginning to smart and his face paling at the sight of the open coffin. He tentatively took a step into the room and I asked if it was ok for me to close the door, he nodded. As we neared the coffin, more of Dad coming into Jack's view, he hesitated so I stopped.

'Are you ok?' I asked him.

'Yes Mummy,' he nodded then unwaveringly and bravely he continued on until he was up close and able to peer into the coffin itself. 'Oh Grandad,' he sighed.

I stood for what seemed like an eternity whilst my young son examined the full length of his beloved grandad until his eyes rested upon his face and he began to blubber. The last two weeks of unspent grief trying to be the gallant older brother now culminated in a deluge of tears not at the sight of the coffin nor the physicality of his grandad in death, but at his personal loss. The loss of a great man, the loss of his mentor, his grandad and his all-time hero. Those were the tears of absolute love and of respect for a relationship both he and his grandad had fully invested into and which he would now miss forevermore. I tried so hard to refrain from expressing any emotion not wanting to break the spell of his right to grieve, his right to privacy. When he had finished, he simply looked up at me and murmured, 'thank you.' Inside my heart was literally breaking the void my elderly father had left behind was simply catastrophic.

We made our way back into the entrance area to where my mother and Joe sat patiently. As I caught her eye, I shook my head and breathed out heavily to let her know that it had been traumatic. Jack immediately sat down next to Joe, but he wasn't subdued; quite the contrary.

'If you want to go in and see Grandad Joe you should, it is not that bad he just looks like he is sleeping,' Jack told Joe.

'If you think it is ok for me Jack then I want to go in and say good-bye to Grandad as well,' Joe said.

'Are you sure, Joe?' Grandma asked as Joe swiftly nodded.

Before proceeding, I decided to knock on the receptionist's door just to gather their thoughts regarding Joe's age. To my surprise, they agreed with the boys that a child with such a deep-rooted connection to the individual should be allowed as it was a cathartic experience for them in the long run. If refused, they explained it could have an equally adverse negative affect. So, I conceded in allowing him to go in and pay his respects to his grandad in exactly the same way has I had conducted it with his brother, only this time I had to lift Joe up as he was too small to see over the edge of the coffin. Joe dealt with it differently he didn't cry maybe because he had been able to shed many tears throughout the last two weeks. He looked at his grandad with his bottom lip protruding and just said 'I am sorry you had to leave us Grandad, I will miss you very much.'

On returning to the waiting area, I put Joe back down and as soon as his feet touched the floor he ran past his grandma and straight round to Jack.

'Are you ok mate?' Jack asked tenderly Joe simply nodding in response burying his head into his brother, 'see it wasn't so bad, was it?' Joe just shook his head.

'Do you want to say a last goodbye on your own now Lois?' Mum asked me knowing full well I had put my children's needs first and that perhaps I might require a couple of moments.

'I think I would, thank you,' I told her.

I went back in to see my father to remind him that I would keep my promise to look after Mum and in return asked him to watch over us too especially with regards to how the others were behaving. I asked him to keep us safe and I told him I would forever miss him, love him and honour him. I then went back outside to collect "our" little family so we could all be together one last time before leaving Mum alone to share her last moments with him. Until Kelly had made the accusation that I was wanting to be the last person to see Dad I hadn't even given it a thought. However, I was now able to turn her bitterness into a positivity by encouraging the rightful person to be the last person to see Dad and that was the love of his life, Mum.

Before leaving, she requested that the coffin lid be secured, and that no other person be granted access to him and rightly so. We were then able to leave with peace in our hearts knowing that although we had suffered an intense loss we had also loved greatly and that was why our hearts ached so much. The depth of our grief was a reflection of and a testimony to the power of love we held for this amazing man. All that we needed to do now, was to get through the funeral.

Chapter 32
The Final Farewell

When I awoke the next morning, dread literally flowed through me and I instantly felt nauseous. I closed my eyes as though that would make it all disappear, but it was only momentary, I knew I had to face the day ahead though there was nothing within me that motivated me enough to want to. It would be hard enough having to face seeing the coffin in the back of the hearse a mark that the end was near without having to do it surrounded by them. I was absolutely sick of putting on a brave face of putting up with the snide comments and put downs not to mention the misguided superiority complex.

I had kept my mouth shut all these years to keep the peace at my dad's request for his sake but after today as far as I was concerned, I could walk away and be done with them forever. They brought absolutely no value to my life and never had, they may have been blood relatives but in reality, they were nothing to me. The only person hurting me was myself at allowing them a platform to continue to voice their unwanted comments and give their unwelcomed opinions. They seemed to think they had a right to dish out whatever measure of negative bile that spouted out of their mouths and that I should be a willing audience. The effects of their destructive behaviour or punitive words were of no importance to them just as long as they could disembowel their innards on to their verbal punch bag. I'd had a lifetime of it which was more than my fair share so after today they could all go to hell as far as I was concerned.

Yes, I would be as pleasant as I possibly could, but I was not going out of my way to pretend we were one big happy family. The reality was we never were, I had just kept laying down for them all to walk over me like some doormat to wipe the shit from their feet. Today I decided was the last time I ever needed to be in their company so with that in mind I smiled to myself in the knowledge I could face the day. I did not need to wallow in self-pity I needed to hold my head up high and remember what Dad's sister had told me 'You have been a very good daughter,' and she was right. Today was about giving Dad the send-off that he so richly deserved it was about celebrating his life, his achievements, the man that he was, the beloved husband, cherished dad and grandfather. Today my children and I would do him proud because that was what he deserved and that was the only aspect of today that mattered. Whatever they chose to say or however they chose to behave was for them to decide their actions were their responsibility as for me my power was in choosing not to react. My children and I would give my dad's funeral the respect that it required by behaving with dignity, poise and gratitude. Energised I was ready to face the day not by trying to control it but by allowing it to unfold naturally and accepting it graciously.

The morning became a hive of activity everyone in and out of the shower the boys dressed in their three piece suits a flat cap upon their heads like miniature grandad's. I wore a stylish grey dress nipped in at the waist that accentuated the recent dramatic weight loss with a long black coat. We arrived at Grey Gables at 11.30 way before the commencement of the service at 13.00 hours. Inevitably Mum was anxious so both Ruby and I assessed how we could support her and actively released as much pressure as possible. The first to arrive were Kelly, Peter, Charlotte, Graham and Haley. As I greeted them in the kitchen, I was immediately bowled over by their taste in attire they were a formidable force of elegance.

'You look amazing,' I said greeting them as a group, 'Charlotte, your hair is beautiful.'

'Thank you,' she smiled the ice broken from our last distasteful interaction.

'Where is Mum?' Kelly enquired.

'She is in the middle room,' I answered as Mum walked through into the kitchen obviously having heard their arrival.

'Urrgh, what have you done to your hair,' was Kelly's immediate admonishment towards Mum and so it had started already!

Here was the newly widowed matriarch of the family about to head the funeral of her husband being openly vilified in front of everyone, how humiliating and disrespectful. No gentle ease to one side or offer to assist Mum to look her best as Kelly had obviously done for her family there was just the inducement of self-consciousness at not being good enough. I looked at Kelly crossly shook my head then glanced towards Ruby noticing Charlotte examining our response. If she didn't think her mother's behaviour was appalling that was her problem but I certainly wasn't going to be made to feel self-conscious at my provoked reaction. Without a word Ruby lead Mum out of the kitchen towards the mirror in the middle room at the bottom of the stairs where she totally revamped her hair.

'What are these doing here?' Kelly spitted out scornfully in my direction.

'I don't know, what is it?' I asked regarding the battered brown envelope she was holding up at shoulder level.

'I gave these to Mum,' she said spilling out the contents to reveal a mass of old music sheets, 'they were supposed to be for the tables.'

'Kelly, I have absolutely no idea. I haven't even seen them before, for what tables?' I remarked honestly.

'I find that hard to believe; haven't you been planning everything?' she chided accusingly.

'Believe what you want,' I said then noticing Charlotte's dog look again I specifically voiced towards her, 'I am past caring.'

It was 5 minutes before the service was due to start before Nick turned up with Timothy albeit slightly intoxicated. Inevitably by then Mum was like a coiled spring wondering why they hadn't turned up having to hold the funeral cars back until the very last minute. Even on this particularly important occasion devoid of any support for their mother it was just the usual display of disrespect and lack of care or concern for anyone else. They walked down the drive and entered the house as though they were attending an after-hours party rather than their father's funeral.

'What the bloody hell do they think they are doing not turning up until this time,' Mum said bitterly.

'Deep breath,' I told Mum. 'Ignore what anyone else is doing just focus on Dad.'

'That is easier said than done,' she retorted.

'You are not responsible for their behaviour only your reactions to their behaviour,' I reminded her, 'I will not let their disrespect stop me from honouring Dad and neither should you.'

'Ok love, I will try,' she said.

'Right,' I started cupping her face in my hands and directly gazing into her eyes, 'I am going to get the boys in to the car because I don't want either of them being upset unnecessarily, this day will be hard enough for them,' I said and lightly kissed her forehead.

I walked out on to the drive to take a deep breath glad to get out of the pressure cooker that the kitchen had suddenly become and called to the boys who were sat on one of Dad's benches. As I turned back round Nick was suddenly in my face demanding to know which car, he was supposed to be in.

'What?' I asked.

'So which car am I supposed to be in then?' he demanded.

'That is something you should have found out before now it has nothing to do with me, I am just responsible for my boys and myself,' I stated and turned away from him the conversation clear and succinct with no room for continuation.

Ruby's two children Jake 11 and Aleigha 9 had been sat with Jack and Joe on Dad's bench also probably trying to escape the tension of the house so followed when I called them. I ushered the children in to the awaiting principal car that we were sharing with Mum and Ruby in the hope we would be setting off soon. The journey to the church was marred by the remnants of discord my siblings had induce when even on a day like this they failed to conduct themselves in harmony. However rather than assault my mind with negativity I chose to focus on the pleasure of witnessing the conductor from the undertakers walking in front of the hearse leading us round the corner towards the church, now that was the respect Dad deserved.

I was pleased to see an abundance of mourners gathered to share with us in the service to honour Dad's life and acknowledged the smartly dressed elderly gentleman that Dad regularly shared a pint with. It warmed my heart as I allowed their love for him to heal the wounds created by the barbed words and lateness of his other children. We filtered into the wide entrance hall awaiting the placement of the coffin to lead us down the aisle. We stood in place in absolute silence Mum directly behind the coffin the boys and I behind her, Ruby, Jake and Aleigha the others following though I paid no attention in what order. The music started to play as the doors began to open revealing a church packed to the rafters every seat taken apart from the ones marked "reserved" at the front. People were stood 3 deep all around the edges and many more even occupying the designated stalls used for the choir. I quickly tapped the boy's shoulders to get their attention.

'Remember boys, hold your head up high, everyone's eyes will be on you so let's do your grandad proud,' I said desperately trying hard to gulp back tears.

'We will do our grandad proud,' they chimed together.

'Quick, remove your caps before we walk into the church,' I guided them.

As Jack looked towards the packed church, he suddenly realised that his grandma was alone, so he dropped my hand and glided in beside her then linking her arm he whispered supportively, 'I've got you, Grandma.'

The pride I had for that little boy at that moment was overwhelming and I could no longer hold back the floodgates of tears. Her own sons lingering at the back somewhere ashamedly her needs disregarded but then Jack's actions mocked, that did not go unnoticed. We walked slowly and deliberately towards the front observing the sea of faces each hoping to catch our eye to share nods of acknowledgement and support. The minister welcomed everyone and shared with us each chapter of Dad's life from his early childhood, army days, being a singer, his work life, his marriage and family. We sang hymns and I was glad that we had chosen well there is nothing worse than a service where people do not know the words.

It was then time for Charlotte as head of the grandchildren to share a few words about the grandad she knew. She held herself well, she delivered an array of memories that depicted her account of Dad as her grandad. We looked lovingly and supportively towards her wishing her well due to the difficultly of delivering such heart-warming words at these occasions. I pondered at the fact her mum must feel really proud of her and rightly so. And then it was my time to read the poem I had written to depict my father's life.

I forced my jellified legs to navigate their way towards the lectern my hands shaking terribly with a mouth as instantly parched as the Sahara. I swallowed slightly and automatically attempted to wet my lips with the dryness of my tongue, it didn't help. I looked out amongst the crowd each one waiting with bated breath in anticipation of the words I would use to describe and characterise my dad. Then I made a mistake and looked at the front where Timothy, Nick, Kelly and their families were sat. An accumulation of stares darted at me as sharp as a pool of piranha's teeth. No encouragement spurring me on to do well just the disdain of hatred looking to devour, hoping I would crash so they could ridicule me afterwards. I turned away glancing to my left and saw the eagerness of my boys, mum and Ruby who knew the quality of my poem were urging me on and then I looked towards my father's coffin and gave him a nod. *I am here for you, to make you proud dad, to honour you,* I thought, *and I turned back to begin.*

Trucks a rattling, dark long nights,
Roping and sheeting, the cold wind bites,
You did your best, you worked all day,
A heavy burden for such small pay.
Out in the wagon all alone,
Well in those days there weren't mobile phones!

Tensions rising, wagons need loads,
Drivers stuck on busy roads.
Robbing Peter, just to pay Paul
Banging your head against the wall.
Rising costs, legislations imposed
How much longer can we keep afloat?

Then it was home for a bite to eat,
Gravy, two veg and a piece of meat.
Got to scrub off all that dirt,
Find yourself another clean shirt.
Up and out to entertain and sing
For now, it's time for Johnny King.

You never stopped you worked so hard,
Without recognition, toiling in that yard.
Your love didn't end, it just kept on flowing,
To provide for a family that kept on growing.
We needed a bigger house for our table,
So we moved across town, to Grey Gables

When you retired you didn't stop,
You cooked and cleaned and went to the shop.
Chatting to many along the town,
Always a smile, never a frown.
You'd deliver a joke with a dry sense of humour,
You brought such joy to those around you!

You encouraged, uplifted when others were down,
You'd guide and direct us and turn things around.
You taught compassion, gave insight no end,
A dad, a grandad, loyal husband and friend.
To Jack a hero a man he could trust,
With Joe you would chuckle and cut off his crusts.

Today I am sat here so full of pride,
With heartfelt sorrow that's difficult to hide.
I love and I miss you more than words can say,
You touched us all in so many ways.
I gave my heart and soul to you,
And in return you gave yours too x

But now there's no searching for your glasses,
No flat cap, or hospital dashes
No seaside trips, just for a paddle
Oh, by the way "you were right about that saddle".
No more talking until it's dark,
Or a McDonald's ice-cream in the park.

You've left behind a whole lot of love,
But I know you will still send it, far from above,
There is one thing for certain, there is no mistake, Jeff,
To have you back, I'd give my last breath!

I read carefully and consistently, ensuring I projected my voice so that those at the back would hear and feel the love in each and every word. He was not the body now laid in the coffin, nor was he the photograph on top of it he was my dad who had lived his entire life with integrity, love and devotion. When I came to a close, the scornful looks were still firmly in place but not on the faces of anyone who mattered so I took my seat with thanks that I had made my dad proud.

As the service drew to an end and we retraced our steps behind the coffin down the aisle, I was thrilled to catch the sight of Cerys accompanied by Sarah. I above everyone knew how hard it was for them to be in the vicinity of Timothy so I couldn't help but blow them both a kiss to acknowledge their presence and to thank them. On our way-out, Leanne also managed to catch my eye although seeing her blubbering weakened my resolve immensely especially when she murmured, 'Well done.'

The slow laborious journey to Dewsbury crematorium seemed to take forever and I was glad to pass Joe on to another school friend who took him into the adjoining park to let off some steam whilst we concluded the ceremony. Again, we waited for the coffin to be unloaded and then we filed into the church behind it to take our seats. I had Jake and Jack at either side of me with Ruby and Aleigha supporting mum. As people followed us into the church our attentions were abruptly drawn to Timothy who seeing a crowd was unable to recognise his responsibility to exercise decorum.

'Hey up, you alreet,' he said gesticulating with his right hand behind us to whoever he was addressing. 'Good to see yeah' to another with his left hand, then whilst stood up right at the front facing the back of the church he carried on 'Hey. Alreet.'

It was a complete fiasco even at his father's funeral he had to make yet another spectacle of himself whilst showing the rest of the family up. I was irritated but knew Mum would be getting upset it was a shame they didn't have bouncers who could discreetly remove disrespectful people. The minister embarked upon the formalities of the service before the time would come to finally leave Dad behind. As he drew to a close, the Frank Sinatra song "I did it my way" began to play. The minister then stepped down from the pulpit and as requested invited Mum to step forward in isolation to attend her husband's coffin.

Mum's fear had been that her children would charge forward to rob her of this final act of respect, so the minister stood guard to bar anyone from approaching her. And then something within her broke and she surrendered to the surge of emotion exacerbated by the tension her children had generated. As she held on to the coffin she began to crumble as her outpouring expediated and I knew she needed assistance, so I glanced at the minister to show my concern. He stepped back gently to affirm his support and so I moved forward to aid my grieving mother in her distress.

'Come on my darling, that's enough we have to let him go now,' I said gently guiding her to the head of the coffin. I turned her around, 'don't forget Dad's last request,' I reminded her nodding to the coffin.

She smiled with thanks, kissed his coffin and said, 'Goodbye for now my darling until we meet again.' Then we turned to walk out.

Frank was still singing away and as he came to the crescendo of 'I did it my way,' the idiot on the front row spontaneously bellowed it out at the top of his voice as Mum and I drew level with him.

'Is it really,' Mum wept glaring at him and then we made our way out of the door.

'Let it go,' I said to her calmly, a phrase that she had used many times when insignificant things had tried to derail me from what was important.

'That goes for you too,' the minister smiled.

'Thank you,' I mouthed to him as Mum burrowed herself into me.

Everyone spilled out of the little chapel inevitably greeting Mum and offering us both their condolences. Behind me Kelly was huddled with her family hearing her arguably disgruntled 'mmm they didn't offer me their sympathy.' So, I decided to take Jack away from the crowd and the negativity surrounding us in case Joe was back from his impromptu visit to the park. I steered Jack towards the row of wreaths and displays of flowers reading the expressions of love by well wishes. Some were for Dad, but others had been left behind from previous funerals. Nevertheless, I took the time to absorb the meaningful words people had taken the time to scribe for their loved ones taking comfort in the heartfelt words.

I was suddenly snapped out of my heavenly daydreaming thoughts by an all too familiar acidic voice.

'Look Peter, the silly little bitch doesn't even know they aren't Dad's flowers,' Kelly ridiculed with a fake laugh.

I did no more than turn myself around, glare at her and shook my head pitifully; she really was a very bitter, acidulous person but thankfully I could walk away, and I did. Once we were in the cars on our way to the wake the conversation was rife with regards to Timothy's behaviour and several other barbed comments that the others had been subjected to. By the time we arrived at Dimple Well Lodge, we had drained the negativity from our system and were able to compose ourselves once again. As we walked through the beautiful cottage style garden into the expansive reception area, we were greeted by a crowd staring up at a humungous tv on the wall. It was playing a slideshow loop of our favourite photographs that my siblings, mum and I had supplied of Dad that the owner Marcus had kindly created for us. I had pre-empted it would give us all a much-needed boost after the committal service and thought it would be a nice surprise to showcase them putting Dad back in the centre of us all. But apparently you cannot please everyone.

'Who's that over there with Kelly and Peter?' Mum's neighbour nudged me.

'Haley?' I asked.

'Who is she?' he asked.

'That is their youngest daughter,' I said quizzically.

'I thought they only had Charlotte and Graham, I've never seen her before,' he said honestly 'but there again we hardly see any of them visiting either.'

I was really surprised at his declaration because Haley was about 16, it wasn't as though she was a newborn or anything but like he said they very rarely visited so why would he know.

'She was none too happy about it,' he continued, nodding towards the TV screen.

'Who?' I asked not grasping his sudden change of conversation.

'Kelly, as soon as she came in, she scowled up at the TV and said to Peter I wasn't told about this! She was really pissed and then got all uppity at him,' he told me.

'I collated the photos together trying to include everyone because I thought it would make them smile after the upset of a service and the crematorium. Clearly no matter what you try to do it is never right with her but hopefully after today I won't need to look at her ugly mug again,' I stated and before he could press for more information, I turned away to enjoy the photographs displaying my dad in happier times.

The wake was a lot less heated where we could relax out of their glaring stares because there were lots of little rooms to chat to people and vacate if they entered. The only issue as such was when Joe and Jack went through into the bar area where Kelly and Peter were sat at one table with Haley at another. Haley called Joe over, throwing her arms open to him which he readily ran into, and she inched him up on to her knee much to the distaste of her mother who scolded Joe and sent him away.

'That wasn't very nice,' Jack told Kelly. 'He was responding to Haley; he did not do anything wrong!'

'I just didn't want him to dirty her dress with his shoes,' Kelly stammered, totally busted.

'It still wasn't very nice,' Jack said walking away.

When Jack came and told me, I congratulated him on not being afraid to stand up for his brother but also reminded him to maintain his manners no matter what as it showed the adults up for what they were, as he said not very nice!

It was the early evening by the time everyone had vacated the lodge with only Mum, Jack, Joe, and Nick's best friend Keith left in the bar. I had just been to order us both a coffee when I returned to the table they were sat at.

'I was just telling your mum Lois that she needs to be careful about Nick,' Keith said addressing me.

'Careful, why is that?' I said interestedly.

'He is not a very nice man and he won't be happy until he has everything that belonged to your dad,' Keith delivered.

'I am sorry I don't follow you.' I was confused at why Nick's best mate would be warning Mum to be careful; surely his allegiance would be to his best mate.

'All I am saying is she needs to watch her back; he conned your dad out of the garage, then he stripped his business and sold everything. I am telling you he won't be happy until he has everything else,' Keith said.

'What more is there?' I asked.

'He is a greedy man who is only out for himself, he thinks to obtain everything that was Jeff's insinuates that he is as great as the man himself, but he isn't fit to sniff his shoes let alone walk in them,' he suggested.

Mum and I stared at each other in bewilderment, 'so what else does he want?' Mum asked directly.

'The house!' he stipulated. 'Just watch your back Emmeline because he will do anything to get a hold of Grey Gables,' he said standing, 'anyway it is time I went too, it was a beautiful service look after yourselves.' Keith concluded and left.

Mum and I sat there for a few moments barely even acknowledging the waitress as she delivered our coffees. When we thought that we had got through the worst of it, there always seemed to be another challenge to face, another problem to solve, another threat to ward off and now apparently Dad's legacy was in jeopardy. When you didn't feel like things could get any worse, they seemed to plunge further down the bottomless pit of no hope. For the time being, we would take refuge in the strength of each other because today we had not just overcome the transgressions and iniquities of others together, we had conquered the enemy.

Chapter 33
It's Not My Fault

The next day I was collecting our belongings together to return home when Mum's phone rang, I wasn't taking much notice of the call because I had begun making the beds and so could only hear murmurings. That was until Mum started to raise her voice and become quite irate with the caller.

'Lois, Lois,' she called up the stairs.

'What is it?' I asked nearing the top of the stairs.

'Will you come down here and tell her I don't want her here,' she shrieked.

'Who?' I queried.

'Kelly!' she snapped. 'Yesterday she spoils my husband's funeral and today she is all sweetness and light. Tell her I don't want her here,' she said sharply.

'Have you forgotten what happened last time you made me do this?' I asked her.

'I don't care, she is not bloody listening again and seems to think she knows it all as usual, well she doesn't! I don't want her here and that is final,' Mum yelled turning on her heel and walking off in the direction of the tv lounge.

I had no other option but to go downstairs, pick up the telephone Mum had left on its side with the line still open and reiterate what Mum had said. I knew full well that Kelly could hear every word Mum had said because she was closer to the telephone than she had been to me.

'Hello?' I said short and sweet.

'Hi, I was just telling Mum that I was thinking of having a ride over tomorrow or if that was inconvenient maybe next week sometime,' she said ignoring the obvious elephant in the room, Mum's irate response.

'I think we both know Mum's feelings on that Kelly you heard exactly what I've just heard,' I said plainly.

'I don't know what is wrong with her or why she would respond like that,' she said innocently.

'Let's start with maybe the fact that you were supposedly "sitting on the fence" with regards to Timothy but then you jumped down encouraging him to lie dragging Mum into the investigation. Or perhaps it is about challenging Ruby about getting involved because after all "they are not her children,"' I said firmly.

'It wasn't like that at all,' she feigned innocence, sighed then pompously continued, 'Why do people always misinterpret what I say instead of asking me directly?'

'I don't think there is anything to misinterpret; it's Mum's children and her grandchildren that are affected so why wouldn't she be angry at your response and lack of responsibility in the situation. Maybe you should have stayed up there on the fence instead of getting involved in things that were nothing to do with you,' I said calmly and to the point.

'That is still no reason for her to talk to me like that and tell me she doesn't want me at the house,' she said ignoring any of the points I had made.

'Well, maybe it has to do with the fact that we were forced into telling Dad about the investigation because you're encouraging Timothy to lie and then 10 days later, he passes away from a broken heart. Or the fact that you all completely ruined his funeral with your snide comments and hostility.' I sucker punched her.

'It is not fair to blame me. I didn't tell him,' She dismissed.

'No, he had to be told due to you getting involved and encouraging Timothy to lie!' Seriously was she still not listening. 'That put pressure on the situation because both Mum and Dad were going to be interviewed and if it went to court, they would have to testify against him.'

'Yes, but it won't come to that, will it?' she dismissed.

'If he does not own up, everyone will have to testify in court and that is something that the children should not be put through. As I said they may not be Ruby's children as you say but they are Mum and Dad's children and grandchildren,' I told her.

'I was just meaning that Ruby didn't need to get involved as he was her brother and she should be standing up for him,' she said weakly.

'What, in some misguided pretext of tell the police nothing and it's a them and us situation?' I asked disbelievingly.

'Yes, I guess.'

'But neither of us can do that, Kelly, we are involved because your brother sexually abused your sisters when we were children,' I said hitting the nail on the head.

'I didn't know that' she said.

'Maybe you didn't but you do now and as for Ruby not getting involved because they are not her children why are you getting involved when it has nothing to do with you? They are not your children,' I asked.

'Because he is my brother,' she said.

'Your brother; well, we are your sisters whom your brother has committed crimes against,' I stipulated so it was easy enough to understand.

'But why is Mum being so angry with me and saying she doesn't want me at the house?' she seriously wasn't taking anything in.

'Your interference resulted in Dad having to be told which resulted in him having a massive heart attack and then you ruined his funeral with your snide comments and behaviour,' I said ultra slowly so she could take it in.

'How did I ruin his funeral, that's a bit dramatic, isn't it?' she said.

'From the moment of being told he had passed away, you bullied her to sing despite her telling you on numerous occasions she did not want it you went on and on about it. You even threw Haley under the bus trying to make out it was her suggestion which was a lie, then getting Peter to ring Mum to pressure her and when this didn't work coming over with everyone else. The only reason I came down was because Mum came upstairs to beg me to intervene on her behalf because you wouldn't listen. And what did I get? Bloody Peter going off on one that me and Mum are not joined at the hip what is that all about?' I spoke.

'I don't know I think he just thought you were talking for Mum and you should let her say it for herself,' she stated.

'You're right I was talking for Mum, but I was repeating her words at her request because you were talking over her trying to bully her to give the only answer you were willing to hear. She felt bullied by you so had to come get me because she knows I not only listen but will stand in the gap and fight for her not against her,' I finished.

'I just wanted to sing that's all,' she said sheepishly.

'Maybe, but you refused to understand that other people did not want to hear you or as the minister had stipulated that it was not appropriate,' I told her.

'So why would she accuse me of ruining Dad's funeral?' she asked.

'The first thing you said to Mum was to criticise how she looked, you were then arsey about the music sheets, though I have no idea why bits of old paper littering tables are so important. There were snide remarks throughout the day, no support given and then now you want to be here. Too little too late I would have thought,' I said having had enough of talking to her now and of not getting anywhere.

'I do not know why she would think I wasn't being supportive, and I certainly didn't make any snide remarks that you are accusing me of,' she said.

'I cannot comment about the ones either Mum or Ruby heard, but you went out of your way throughout the day to make us all feel uncomfortable. I personally heard you criticise Mum's hair, then get on at me about the music sheets, you sat glaring at me in the church when I was delivering the poem for Dad, your annoyance that no one was paying you any condolences outside the church, smirking about me looking at the flowers and reading the cards at the crematorium, your annoyance at the photographs at Dimple wells and then shooing Joe away like he was some stray dog. You never take responsibility for anything, but Mum is right you went out of your way to be non-compliant and did everything you could to ruin Dad's funeral.' I paused.

'But, but' she stammered.

'No, I have had enough of this crap, you told Mum that if anything happens to *him* or if he goes to prison, you will cut all three of us off. Well, touché. I don't need to wait until then as far as I am concerned consider yourself well and truly cut off!' I said replacing the receiver.

I took a deep breath and exhaled with a smile on my face knowing that the time had finally come to start cutting away the dead wood; enough was enough. I went into the TV lounge where Mum had taken herself off to and relayed my conversation with Kelly to her.

'Well done, it is about time she was put in her place I am sick of her self-righteous rubbish she behaves like that in front Nick and Timothy and then sheepishly rings today like nothing has happened. No, I don't want her here she has overstepped the mark trying to bully me to get her own way and then doing her best to ruin yesterday with her idiot of a brother,' she decided.

'You please yourself what you do or how you proceed with your relationship but as far as I am concerned, she is dead to me,' I began, 'her attitude and interference through this investigation broke my dad's heart and yesterday she was nasty and hostile not only to me but to Joe as well. She does not get to treat my kids like that and think it won't be addressed. Jack stood up for Joe and I am standing up for both of them,' I finished.

'I forgot to tell you about something else she was going to do at the funeral,' Mum said as I raised my eyes wondering how it would compare to the singing bullshit, 'she wanted everyone to wear a fez.'

'What the hell? Is she right in the head; why would we want to do that?' I asked astonished.

'Apparently because Jeff liked Tommy Cooper,' she said shaking her head.

'Maybe instead of using a hearse, we should have roped and sheeted his coffin on a flatbed truck as well,' I said sarcastically.

'I know, I thought it was ridiculous it seemed all she wanted to do was make a mockery of his funeral as though it was one big joke,' Mum said tearing up, 'and she wonders why after the way she has behaved I cannot abide her.'

During the next week, our last one of the summer holidays, we were focused on securing school supplies and uniforms and then before we knew it, we were back into the humdrum of everyday life. Each morning as soon as I had dropped the boys off at school, I called to see Mum either having a walk in to town, going out for breakfast or shopping. I was surprised to see how quickly she adapted to life on her own but did consider whether Grey Gables would be too imposing for her now. So, whilst having a coffee at the local café I decided to broach the subject to get some clarity.

'Here's yours,' I told her placing the buxom cup and saucer onto the beige coloured tabletop. 'A cappuccino with plenty of chocolate.'

'Oh, thank you love is that a large one?' She asked.

'Enormous I would say, can you actually pick it up?' I giggled.

Using two hands she picked up the bowl-sized cup and tentatively lifted it towards her mouth for a sip when she removed it, there was a white frothy trail upon her top lip. Before she could wipe it off, I snapped a photograph of her and showed her it.

'Oh, my goodness,' she said taking the serviette from beneath the cup that the waitress had placed on to the saucer for any excess drips or spillages.

'I was wondering how you were feeling now it's been a few weeks since the funeral?' I enquired.

'Alright love, well I have to be don't I,' she said.

'I know there is nothing you can do about it but all the same I wanted to make sure that you were ok, like when I leave to pick the children up from school you have the evening and night on your own. How do you feel about that?' I enquired.

'I am fine love honestly,' she assured me.

'I just wanted to make sure you were ok being at Grey Gables as I would hate to be there on my own,' I told her.

'Don't you start,' she said with a twinkle in her eye, 'Nick turned up last night saying a similar thing.'

'What do you mean?' I asked puzzled.

He dropped in on the guise to see if I was alright but really Jenny (his daughter) had a dancing lesson, so it suited him to wait here rather than have to go home and come back again. Anyway, he was looking at the bronze plaque above the mantelpiece in the middle room and he says, 'I have always loved that plaque it would look nice over our fireplace,' she said.

'You are joking, what did you say?' I asked.

'I told him it looks nice over my fireplace,' she said with a giggle. 'Then he informed me that they were looking for a new piano and how he would like to get a pianola like we have.'

'What?' I asked in disbelief.

'Oh, it gets better,' she said, 'he then says he would rig it up so that he could make it play on its own by remote control. Apparently, it would be a centre piece, a joke element for when they have visitors around.'

'So, what did you say,' I asked.

'I said there would be no point because you don't invite anyone to your house and when we did come you never made us feel welcome,' she spoke.

'You never did,' I laughed.

'It's true we've had one invite and that was to Jenny's first birthday party that was it! When he realised, he wasn't going to get anywhere with the plaque nor the pianola, he moved to your dad's car,' she said enjoying my look of horror.

'Why would he want to know about Dad's car?' I asked.

'Apparently, Maggie needs a new car and your dads would be perfect for her!' Mum threw in.

'I cannot believe the audacity of rocking up with a shopping list of your belongings that he wants! What is it, Dad has gone so he is putting his name down on the items he wants to inherit, the cheek of the man,' I said in utter disbelief.

'I don't know about waiting for an inheritance, Lois, he then moved on to the house,' she said.

'What!' I exclaimed almost spitting my coffee at her. I glanced around to make sure I hadn't disrupted other customers; a couple of people did look up due to my raised voice but quickly resumed their conversations.

'Yes, first of all he started telling me that he thought the house was too big for me on my own and then that he and Maggie are contemplating buying and selling houses to do up!' she exclaimed with a grin on her face.

'So, what did you say?' I wondered.

'Oh, I knew his game I told him straight I was fine where I was thank you very much,' Mum retorted.

'So, Keith was right then, he is after the house as well as the business and everything else, wow!' I said in disbelief.

After I had left Mum, Ruby called me for a catch up.

'Lois I was wondering if you and mum would come with me to see Sophie, Cerys and her mum?' she asked.

'Why?' I asked.

'I have just found out that the police have taken her statement now and I think it would be beneficial to let her know that we are supporting her,' she said.

'I am happy to go but only if she is happy for us all to go over, I would hate for her to think we are going over mobhanded,' I said thinking the last thing they needed was their biological fathers family turning up after not seeing them for such a long time.

'I will contact Lilly their mum and ask her to see what she says,' she told me then rang off.

A few minutes later she rang me back, 'Lilly says that Sophie is apprehensive about seeing us because apparently Kelly found her on Facebook and has had a right go at her. But both her and Cerys are happy for us to go over,' she said.

'Kelly has had a go at her?' I repeated.

'Yes, pressurising her not to tell lies to the police about Timothy,' she revealed.

'Oh, my goodness so she is intimidating a witness now. Poor Sophie I make no wonder she is apprehensive,' I spoke.

'So, what do you think we should do?' she asked.

'I think that by adding that little nugget of information to the mix you are right we should definitely go over to show our support,' I told her and rung off so she could make the necessary arrangements.

On the day we had made plans to see Lilly, Sophie and Cerys, I collected the boys from school and went straight over to Grey Gables where the boys changed out of their school uniforms and we waited for Ruby, Aleigha and Jake. Mum travelled with us whilst I followed Ruby's car on the 20-mile journey to the pub the family now lived in. Lilly greeted us with fondness and introduced us to her two other children Josey and Amy. Cerys was exactly as I had remembered her a very strong, assertive young girl warm and welcoming. Sophie stayed in the kitchen where she was prepping meals with her father the chef and owner of the bar. He came out to meet with us to let us know that Sophie was feeling a little unsettled, but he seemed sure she would come out in her own time.

I was immediately struck by how friendly and self-assured he was not to mention handsome Lilly had done well. We decided to order drinks and peruse the menu then everyone sat about chatting excitedly catching up with each other. Once we had eaten, I went outside to let Poppy out of the car for a wee and to give her the titbits from the dinner. Cerys decided she wanted to accompany me but after a few minutes when she followed me out, I was astonished to see that Sophie was with her.

'Hello darling,' I said greeting her.

'Cerys said you had your dog with you, I love dogs,' she said.

'I went into the kitchen to tell Sophie that everyone was lovely and there was nothing to be worried about and that we were coming outside to let Poppy out,' she informed me as Sophie stood awkwardly not knowing what to say.

'Well, I am glad you felt that you could come out and say Hello even if it was only to Poppy,' I joked.

'I wanted to say hello to you too,' she said.

'Can I have a hug?' I asked.

'Yes, of course you can,' she said stepping forward and embracing me.

'How have you been?' I asked.

'Not good, I knew as soon as the police turned up what it was all about,' she began, 'I have been expecting it since he got married to Sarah.'

'I am so sorry this has happened to you Sophie but please know we are backing you 100 %,' I told her earnestly.

'I was just worried why you all wanted to come over that's why I stayed in the kitchen because I thought you might be on his side like Kelly.' She sniffed.

'No love, absolutely not! I will tell you now just so you know that he abused me as a child, so I have given a detailed statement to the police and so has Ruby,' I informed her.

'I told the police it only happened that one time,' she said fading off, 'but it wasn't there were others,' she opened up.

'You know the police will want to know everything don't you Sophie?' I said softly.

'I know it's just that when they came to talk to me it was when I was at school and I didn't want anyone knowing so I only said about the time in the wagon when he made me lay down on the bed then he masturbated on to my stomach,' she told me.

I was trying so hard not to react to the new piece of information of him masturbating on to her stomach that Timothy had interestingly omitted from his story when missing Sarah.

'He rubbed it into my stomach saying it was good for my skin then acted like nothing had happened. There was another time when he was babysitting and I had woken up so went to the toilet. He was laid naked on his bed playing with himself and called me in, but I ignored him and just went to the bathroom. On my way back, he called me in again then got up off the bed and pulled me in wanting me to touch him,' she said getting upset.

I drew her to me and held her until she had stopped crying before reiterating that the police needed to know about this incident and any others that had occurred as part of their investigation.

'I know, I haven't thought of anything else since,' she said weakly, 'I will tell them because it is eating away at me,' she said resigning herself in defeat.

'Just so you know love that because you have revealed it to me, I also have a responsibility to let them know, is that ok,' I asked.

'Yes, I know I just wanted to tell someone,' she said with tears in her eyes.

'I appreciate that was very brave of you it is not easy saying it out loud, now come on shall we go back inside, and you can say hello to everyone?' I asked locking the car and putting my arm around each of their shoulders.

We enjoyed the rest of our evening together reconnecting, taking photos, re-establishing our relationships and strengthening our bonds until it was time to take the long journey home to get the children to bed. If there was anything good to have come out of this fiasco, it was that we had restored our contact with each other, and nothing would keep us apart again.

Chapter 34
Pressing Forward

Over the coming weeks and months, we were kept up to date with how the investigation was progressing with the all-important consideration for prosecution taking place just before Christmas. I was in the middle of wrapping up some last-minute presents in Emmeline's bedroom at Grey Gables when the call came in.

'Hiya Lois, this is Melissa Maya; how are you?' she enquired as my blood suddenly ran cold.

'Hello Melissa, what's wrong?' I asked dread in my heart.

'The CPS have deliberated over all the information and have determined that we have sufficient evidence to charge him on four counts of child abuse,' she said as my head began to spin.

'Four counts?' I asked.

'Yes,' she said, 'the two incidents that Sophie has detailed the one in the wagon and the second which she later revealed to you,' she advised me.

'And the other two?' I asked wondering if they were to do with Danny and Elena.

'The other two are the incidents of when he abused you as a child and the one when you were older,' she revealed much to my relief. 'It will still be a long process and due to the nature of the case it cannot be held at a magistrate's court so it will be opened there but then sent to Crown Court. Don't be surprised if you don't hear from me for a while we are still working hard behind the scenes although I will be in touch if there is anything further to tell you. Do you have any questions for me?' she asked.

'No, I don't think so,' I said weakly my mind in absolute turmoil and when I came off the phone, I wept tears of relief mixed with fear at the coming year.

I didn't hear from Maya again until 11 January 2012. I remember the date vividly as Mum, the boys and I were at the Tropical Butterfly House in Sheffield, and it was the day before Joe's 5th birthday. She rang to let me know that he had been formally charged with all four counts and that a date was being set for it to go to the magistrates. I already knew from our previous conversation that it would then be sent straight to Crown court, so it was now a waiting game.

Inevitably, I informed Mum and then I rang Ruby but as the line was engaged, I assumed Maya was relaying the same information to her too. I did not feel that there was any victory to be had quite the contrary I pondered the fact that he would now be wishing he had come clean instead of lying. As Mum always said, 'the truth will out' meaning whatever happens the truth will be revealed in the end. I also contemplated the reaction Kelly may be having now the investigation had stepped up a gear and wondered if she was reconsidering her position. Maybe she wished she had stayed on the fence instead of interfering because she had caused far more harm than good.

Neither Mum, Ruby nor I had spoken to her since the funeral and although Nick had been around a couple of more times it was only to enquire about the plaque, the pianola, Dad's car and Mum leaving Grey Gables. Much to Mum's avid amusement.

I only saw Nick once and that was when he happened to call at Grey Gables when I was there. He seemed to be making an exaggerated effort of appearing to be laid back which just made him come across at being all the more uncomfortable. I also found his conversation bizarre as he was jibing at Mum and taking digs at her for no reason. He was ridiculing her about when he was around 11 years of age and a neighbour used to take him to school and he said, 'Just imagine having to arrange your own transport at 11 so you can get to school because your mother cannot be bothered to take you, what kind of a mother is that' he declared.

'Do you mean the Evans up the road in their little van?' I asked.

'Yes,' he sneered as though he thought he had an ally, 'so you remember it too.'

'I remember a lot from my childhood,' I said menacingly staring directly at him daring him to have a go. 'And what I remember is you wanting to go with your new buddy, we were all attending the same school so it wasn't that Mum couldn't be bothered to take you, you didn't want to travel with the rest of us.'

There was obviously some undercurrent that was irritating him because he clearly had a bee in his bonnet about something yet failed to address it directly using nonsense like this to try to score points. I remember thinking that for a 50-year-old man he was exceptionally immature. Perhaps the Nick that didn't stir had finally stirred and maybe he had been brought in for questioning too either way I didn't care he had made his bed and like the rest of them, he could lay in it for me. From the day of the funeral up until the end of April, Mum recalled him attending Grey Gables only 5 times and, on each occasion, mentioned the plaque, the pianola, the car and the house much to Mum's amusement. It was around this time that we were notified a court date for trial had been set for Thurs 21 June 2012 and then all contact from Nick suddenly ceased. Timothy desperately tried to maintain some semblance of normality throughout seeking his mother's approval, but it was not forthcoming.

So, a new countdown had begun to the date 21 June 2012, and we were ticking the days off as they went by, hoping that Timothy would change his plea and that our family name would not be publicly shamed. The clock was ticking, and the time was beginning to run out, would Timothy come clean before the trial date, or would he force everyone to stand up in court? And if he did, what would the verdict be?

Chapter 35
No More Shenanigans

As the trial date neared, we were inevitably becoming more and more nervous hoping against hope that he would eventually do the right thing and take responsibility for his actions. However, I think deep down everyone knew what a spineless person he was and if there was an easy way out, he was going to try and take it.

'Have you heard?' Ruby asked screeching at me down the phone.

'Heard what?' I asked with a veil of dread immediately clothing me.

'The trial has been put off for another 6 months; it will not be heard now until December,' she said very irate.

'Why?' I wondered.

'I don't know, hasn't Melissa Maya rung you to inform you,' she told me, 'I cannot believe this, how can they put it off for another 6 months?'

'No, she hasn't but don't worry about it, it will all be ok,' I said calmly, 'and it will go ahead.'

'How can you be so calm about it?' she yelled.

'Because I have faith and I know it will go ahead as planned; you wait and see,' I reassured her.

'I hope you are right but according to Melissa she has just said there is no way it will be going ahead this week and it has been rescheduled for December,' she continued.

'All things are possible for my God, and I have absolute faith it will be going ahead as planned despite what tantrums he has or what stunts he pulls. This is just him trying to delay the inevitable,' I told her.

'I hope you are right!' she said.

About an hour later, I received a phone call from Melissa Maya. 'Hello Lois, have you spoken to Ruby by any chance?' she asked.

'Yes, she rang about an hour ago saying you had informed her that the trial had been postponed until December,' I informed her.

'That's right, when I couldn't reach you, I contacted Ruby,' she told me.

'So, what is the new update, is it going ahead after all?' I played devil's advocate.

'How did you know?' She asked surprised.

'I just had a gut feeling he was throwing the teddy out of the cot or something hoping to elongate his freedom,' I stated.

'Well, you're not far wrong,' she began, 'he actually sacked his entire legal team this morning which sent everyone into a frenzy.'

'It doesn't surprise me, and it is probably a case of they have evaluated the evidence against him along with the number of witnesses so advised him to plead guilty,' I said casually.

'That is the exact conclusion our team arrived at,' she said triumphantly.

'So, what is going to happen now?' I asked.

'Well, he sacked his team just before it went in front of the judge to open the trial, but the judge directly told him he was having none of his antics. The Judge addressed Timothy stating his right to have legal representation, but he needn't think that just because he had chosen to dismiss his team that the trial would be delayed. Timothy has been appointed another team who have been told quite sternly that they had better get up to speed on the case over the weekend because it will be going ahead as planned Monday morning regardless of any shenanigans,' she told me.

'Wow, so he was well and truly put in his place then?' I spoke.

'Most definitely and as instructed by the judge, it will go ahead on Monday; can you contact Ruby and let her know?' she asked.

'Yes, not a problem,' I told her and then she ended the call.

'Hi Ruby, just had an update from Maya,' I began.

'So has she confirmed to you that it has been put off until December then?' she wondered.

'No, on the contrary, it is going ahead on Monday!' I said amusedly.

'No way, how the heck did you manage that?' she asked stunned.

'It was nothing to do with me but like I said I have faith because my God can move mountains!' I told her, 'Maya has just rung me to explain Timothy had sacked his legal team but the judge was having none of his shenanigans he has been appointed a new legal team and given them strict instructions they have to be ready by Monday. So, the trial is going ahead.'

'Any other predictions?' She asked flabbergasted.

'Yes, I am supposed to be fourth on the list to give evidence. I think they will move me to the number one spot to see how I fare and decide then whether it is worth proceeding,' I told her.

'I can't wait to see if that comes true,' she said.

'I hope not but I have a feeling that is what this new team will do, so no pressure on me if they do,' I spoke then we said our goodbyes and I sat a moment to take stock of the new information.

So, the day before the proceedings were due to begin, he suddenly sacks his legal team either it was a last-ditch attempt to prolong his freedom or perhaps it was because they'd advised him to plead guilty. Who can say? One thing was for sure I needed to get my head together because if they did change the order around, I was going to be cross examined within an inch of my life.

Early on the Monday morning (25 June 2012), I dropped the boys off at Jenny's so she could drive them to school then I went over to Grey Gables where Ruby was meeting me. I do not know who was more nervous Mum, Ruby or myself. Ruby and I had to arrive at Leeds crown Court early and park in their secure car park at the back. As the barrier went up and I drove through I felt more trapped than safe as I saw it settle back down in its cradle. We found the allotted side door and pressed the bell to await a court official to let us in.

The door was opened by a man who looked to be in his late thirties; he was rotund and wore a shirt that was gaping at its central buttons. His black tie clung to his shirt like a sticker on a car bonnet and his shiny iron marked trousers had seen better days. He was a man of few words. Having given our names and identifications we were shown to a small room that was more like a holding cell it did absolutely nothing to calm our nerves. I felt imprisoned the anxiety building within me already and yet it was only 08.35 hours.

There was a fixed wooden counter type top protruding from the wall opposite the door it had no cupboards below just a small old monitor on top, the type with the big backs. There were no posters adorning the walls just a laminated script used to swear witnesses into court. On it's reverse was a note informing the reader that it was a crime to lie in court and the possible sentence if a person committed perjury. Talk about trying to psyche a person out! I placed it on top of the monitor and sat at one of the two seats Ruby sat at the other then we waited and waited.

After a couple of hours, I really needed the toilet, so I rang the bell that told us to ring if we needed attention, but it was some time before the same man of few words attended.

'I need to use the toilets,' I told him.

'This way,' he said walking off presumably expecting me to follow.

'Do you know what's happening or how much longer we will be left down here?' I asked.

'At the moment, the solicitors are in talks with the judge so we will not know anything until those talks are concluded,' he said officially.

I used the toilet then followed Mr Helpful back along the nondescript corridor to our dungeon cell, we were literally beneath the whole court in what appeared to be unoccupied old offices. It was drab, depressing and I suddenly needed air if I was to be locked back in the tiny room again.

'I need to get some air. I am beginning to go stir crazy down here,' I told him.

He walked past the "holding cell" that we had been in making his way towards the door we had entered through to reveal daylight, although the car park in Leeds city centre failed to offer the clean air I had hoped for. Disappointed I reluctantly allowed him to close the door and lead me back to the room where Ruby was awaiting her turn to use the toilet. I sat in the seat Ruby had vacated hoping there would be something different to observe from this angle but of course there was a whole lot of nothingness.

'What do you think is going on?' Ruby asked when she returned and Happiness had closed the door again.

'I don't know; he told me that the solicitors were in talks with the judge so it could be anything from changing his plea to throwing the teddy out of the cot again,' I spoke.

'It would be good if he was changing his plea then we could get out of here,' she said.

'Somehow I do not expect him to do that at this late stage,' I told her.

You never know; he could be shitting himself now, she thought.

'He hasn't come all this way to suddenly change it, he is a paedophile and generally they do not think they have done anything wrong. Seemingly, they make themselves believe that the child either came on to them or they were asking for it,' I told her.

'I don't get how an adult can find a child sexually attractive,' she shrugged.

'No, me neither but to them it is normal, so they don't think they are doing anything wrong,' she spoke.

'But why is it they abuse boys and girls do they have suppressed gay tendencies or something?' she asked.

'I believe they see the innocence of the child not the gender and this is what they are attracted to, maybe their perversion makes them so black on the inside they want that child's innocence. Perhaps some have been abused and had their innocence stolen so they follow the same pattern. Either way I do not think they see the gender of the child because they objectify them not even observing them as people possibly to excuse their behaviour to themselves,' I deliberated.

'I hope they put him away and throw away the key,' Ruby said unapologetically.

At that moment, the door opened, 'I have news regarding your case,' Happiness said as Ruby and I stared at each other, 'we will begin in about 15 minutes.'

'Does that mean it is going ahead then?' Ruby asked surprised.

'Yes,' Happiness said looking confused at her then turning to me, 'I have been given a new running order and they will be hearing your evidence first, Ms Rodgers,' he checked his sheet, 'followed by yours, Ms Williams. If you would like to come with me, Ms Williams,' he said and turned to leave. Ruby looked at me with wide eyes then obediently left.

So, I was right; they had changed the whole running order and I was now first. It was a daunting experience not knowing what was going on and I thought that if this is how they treated the witnesses for the prosecution I would hate to be a defendant. Happiness returned a few moments later, it was now 11.30 hours.

'The jurors have been sworn in and once the court is in session the courtroom will be played your video interview this will be fed directly through to this monitor,' he said pointing to the one on the makeshift desk. I gulped at the thought of not only having to see myself on the tape but the thought that more than a dozen strangers would be sat upstairs scrutinising it. 'Once it has finished playing, I will escort you to the holding area upstairs,' he finished then closed the door.

So, I was to sit alone now in this bleak soulless room in the bowels of Leeds Crown court to watch the interview I had completed 12 months ago for the very first time, I felt sick. When the monitor began to flicker, my heart shot straight up to my throat like a starting pistol the anxiety erupting like Vesuvius and then the video began. I stared into the face of the person held on the screen; her eyes were sad, she looked worn out and afraid resigned to the fate of having to reveal her innermost self. I could feel her anxiety, her hurts, the truth behind the recollections of her memories and the deep pain she still suffered. It was more harrowing watching her account than it was of having been filmed giving it. Although this was me speaking, I had always felt disconnected but at that moment watching myself on that impersonal old monitor, I suddenly felt very connected to her and angry for her.

Inevitably, I was fearful of the path I was now compelled to walk being unable to calm the fear of the unknown however I was angry at the merry dance *he* was having everyone jump to. As my dad had described, this "weasel" was not going down easily and apparently it hadn't been enough for him to perpetrate those crimes against Sophie, Danny, Elena or I, he was now causing our humiliation by forcing us to testify. At that point, the tables turned, and I decided the court would definitely hear the truth, the whole truth and nothing but the truth, so help me God.

Chapter 36
The Shield of Faith

As the video concluded, the screen began to flash black and white when the door opened to notify me that Happiness had returned. I wondered if he had been stood in the corridor this entire time, it didn't matter, I was ready.

'If you would like to walk this way, Ms Rodgers,' he said turning swiftly back down the corridor towards where the toilets had been. He unlocked a door at the end where I was then escorted out into the hustle and bustle of the courtroom before being ushered through another door to a quiet corridor again with officers at either side. 'If you would like to wait in here,' he said stepping aside to allow me into another small room.

'What the heck?' I said seeing Ruby who was sat there waiting.

'What happened?' she enquired.

'They played my video interview on to the monitor in that room we were in whilst it was being simultaneously played into the courtroom,' I told her.

'Oh, my goodness; what was it like having to watch yourself,' she asked.

'Harrowing to say the least,' I said truthfully, 'I now have to wait for them to conduct some preliminaries and then I will be called into court.'

'Bloody hell Lois are you alright?' she enquired.

'No but at the end of the day this is the path I have been forced to walk so I am taking it,' I told her.

'I cannot believe they changed the running order; any more predictions?' she asked.

'Only one, I am being given the number 8 for some reason,' I told her.

'Ooh I hope he gets 8 years,' she spoke.

'I do not think it is that, but the number 8 is relevant for some reason.' I reiterated.

'How are you staying so calm?' she enquired.

'I am not, inside I am bricking myself, but this is the last time he gets us all to dance to his tune. We are here, he wants a fight so he will get one I am just focusing on the endgame as far as I am concerned enough is enough and after the trial this stops for me,' I said clearly.

'So, let's get the bastard,' Ruby declared as the door was opened by a kindly looking lady in her mid-fifties.

'Ms Rodgers?' she queried looking from me to Ruby.

'That is me,' I told her.

'Are you ready?' she asked.

'As ready as I am ever going to be,' I informed her, and she smiled supportively.

I waited for her to close the door behind me leaving Ruby alone in the room and then she said, 'you will be fine, just remember that the solicitors are unimportant they may ask you the questions but look towards the jury when you answer. The jury are the ones who decide who is telling the truth so make sure you look directly at them then they can see your face,' she said helpfully.

She led me back out into the buzz of the court foyer then up two flights of stairs to an open expanse with several doors into individual courtrooms and private booths for solicitors and their clients. I was taken through two double brown fire type doors emblazoned Court Room 8, I smiled wryly 'if God was for me then no one could be against me.' Romans 8 v 31. I was led into the open court room which had a small area for the public directly in front of the door beyond this in an elevated position was the defendant.

Although I did not look in *his* direction, I mused that he would get a kick out of looking down on everyone else. I kept my eyes fixed on to the back of the kind lady as she led me towards the front of the court to my far left to the witness box which had a thick heavy curtain draped around it. The Judge sat above me to my left an elderly gentleman with a heavy-duty wig and glasses that sat upon the bridge of his nose. The solicitors were opposite the judge to my right in front of the elevated defendant with empty benches directly opposite me and to the solicitors right, the judges left.

'Can you hold the bible in your right hand and read out the affirmation upon the card please,' the kind lady instructed.

I held the bible in my right hand as requested and declared, 'I Lois Rodgers do solemnly declare and affirm that I will tell the truth the whole truth and nothing but the truth.'

'Thank you,' the judge said to me and then addressed the court clerk to invite the jurors back into the court room.

The door opened and 12 random members of society filed their way in one by one along the jurors' benches. I probably looked like the proverbial deer in the headlights as I watched each person as they took their seats reflecting that they had just watched my interview, and these were the ones who would be considering all the evidence at the end. My mouth was not just dry it was positively as coarse as sandpaper.

'Would you like a drink of water, Ms Rodgers?' the judge asked.

'Please Your Honour,' I said truthfully, and he nodded to the clerk who immediately disappeared returning with an ice-cold drink of water. I was thankful it was in a glass and not the thin plastic disposable cups often found at drinking stations as my hands were shaking so much, I don't think I could have held it.

He asked the solicitors if they were ready and then he commanded the proceedings to commence. The solicitor nearest to the jurors stood and introduced himself as being the solicitor for the prosecution 'don't look so scared I am on your side,' he smiled. Firstly, he asked some very basic questions just wanting me to confirm my name, address and occupation before setting out the case with more detailed questions and then he abruptly stopped. It was very quick and painless so when he came to an end, I actively felt my body relax until the judge spoke.

'Thank you; right, we will break for lunch and then afterwards you will be questioned by the defendant's solicitor,' the judge stated, slamming his gavel down then the clerk asked everyone to stand whilst the judge left.

The kind lady's face appeared around the curtain then she guided me back out of the court room, down the stairs to where Ruby was waiting in the little room.

'That was quick; what happened?' she asked stunned.

'Nothing the prosecutor just asked some basic questions to open it up and then they broke for lunch,' I told her dismayed, 'I have to go back in after lunch when it's his solicitor turn.'

'Do you think they have done this on purpose to put even more pressure on you?' Ruby enquired.

'I don't know but it has definitely worked,' I said as the door opened and Maya entered.

'How are you doing?' she asked us both, so I explained what had happened up to press. 'Do you know who it was that was sat in the gallery?' she asked me.

'To be honest I didn't even notice anyone was there,' I told her. 'What did they look like?'

'It was a short fat woman with long, straggly grey hair tied back in a ponytail,' she said.

Ruby and I looked at each other and said in unison, 'Maggie, Nick's partner.'

'She has probably come to gather as much information as possible to tell Nick and Kelly,' Ruby said.

'The whole point about giving evidence in turn is so that no one holds information about what has been said beforehand,' Maya stated.

'That might be the case but they will definitely have sent her so they know what they are up against and can prepare accordingly,' I stated.

'She should be removed,' said Ruby.

'The only problem is she will have already seen my video interview,' I said dismayed, 'how embarrassing.'

'Don't worry about it Lois you could also look at it from the viewpoint that she will now have a clear picture of just what Timothy Rodgers is guilty of,' Melissa said supportively.

'Yes, you're right, Melissa,' Ruby said encouragingly, 'do you know of anywhere we can get some lunch? I am absolutely starving.'

We walked outside then followed the building around the back towards a busy little street that contained several eateries and sandwich shops. We got a light snack not being able to manage anything else though needing something and then sat out on a piece of grass at the front of a nearby church to eat. We had little to say both of us lost in our own thoughts whilst absentmindedly people watching. As we entered the courts, this time from the front we were required to remove our belts and shoes together with emptying our belongings into a tray for it to go through a scanner. We walked through an airport type metal detector before being scanned with a hand-held wand and then physically given a rub down search. There were two court personnel sat behind a desk in the middle of the foyer and above their heads to the right I noticed several framed lists containing the details of each court proceedings.

'Just hold on a minute, Ruby,' I said veering over to the display and began locating the relevant information, 'look at this.'

'What?' she asked uninterested then her eyes nearly popped out of her head, 'courtroom 8!' she glanced up disbelievingly.

'Told you the number 8 was significant,' I stated making my way back towards the locked corridor which one of the two seated personnel opened for us so we could continue our wait.

Maya arrived, 'how are you feeling, Lois?'

'Nervous, like I have been called in front of the number one governor to give evidence,' I stipulated.

'You will be fine, listen to each question, think before you speak and do not allow his solicitor to rile you because he will try,' she said doing nothing for my nerves and then she left wishing me luck.

I knew I needed more than just luck so as we were in a courtroom, I decided to search the area for a bible and told Ruby I needed to prepare myself for the afternoon ahead. I sat reading scriptures of where God had provided strength in times of difficulty and came upon Ephesians 6: 10–17.

The Armour of God

[10] Finally, be strong in the Lord and in his mighty power. [11] Put on the full Armour of God, so that you can take your stand against the devil's schemes. [12] For our struggle is not against flesh and blood, but against the rulers, against the authorities, against the powers of this dark world and against the spiritual forces of evil in the heavenly realms. [13] Therefore put on the full Armour of God, so that when the day of evil comes, you may be able to stand your ground, and after you have done everything, to stand. [14] Stand firm then, with the belt of truth buckled around your waist, with the breastplate of righteousness in place, [15] and with your feet fitted with the readiness that comes from the gospel of peace. [16] In addition to all this, take up the shield of faith, with which you can extinguish all the flaming arrows of the evil one. [17] Take the helmet of salvation and the sword of the Spirit, which is the word of God.

https://www.biblegateway.com/passage/?search=Ephesians%206%3A10-18&version=NIV

I was energised into seeing the task ahead of me as being merely the work of the enemy whereas through God who is so much more powerful and mighty I could conquer anything. I wasn't naïve enough to think that I was untouchable or that being called to give my evidence was going to be easy on the contrary my faith in God made all things possible. And then there was a tap at the door to reveal the same lady in her mid-fifties with the kind face waiting to escort me to courtroom 8.

Each step I took was like being back on the bus in my dream the year before where I'd had to fight an invisible force to push forward to get to the top of the stairs. When she led me through the doors emblazoned with "courtroom 8", I pushed down the fear knowing once I walked back through those doors it would all be over. On entering the physical space of the court, I noticed that it was Maggie sat in the public seating area along with Paul an old friend of Timothy's. What was this a spectacle for all to come and savour.

As I entered the box with the curtain around it, I noticed the solicitors sat aimlessly around before the jury arrived and then we were required to stand before the judge took his seat. The defendant's solicitor introduced himself and then he started thick and fast with an array of questions barely giving me time to answer before firing out the next. Obviously, he was trying to catch me off guard attempting to muddle me up so I would come across as an incompetent witness but then I remembered what the kind lady had said.

Each time he asked me a question I paused, looked away from him towards the jury and addressed them with my answer, much to his annoyance. Inevitably he asked me specific and detailed questions about my recollections as a child and queried whether they could be relied upon due to the number of years that had passed. So, I closed my eyes, pictured the room and described it carefully and precisely to demonstrate my photographic memory. As I described the brown wooden bed that I had used in the boys' room, he queried why no one else had a recollection of my bed ever being in that room.

So, I pressed the point that what stood out to them as gravely important in their childhoods but did not to me doesn't mean it didn't exist. My bed in that room had no significance to anyone else but it was engraved on my brain like a permanent tattoo. You may be able to cover them up with new designs over the years, but the fact remains it is still there underneath.

He then questioned my integrity and suggested that I had a grudge against Timothy and that I was fabricating a story to get back at him. So, I told him that if it had been a story that I had fabricated I wouldn't have needed the years of therapy that I'd had to undergo due to the abuse I'd sustained. I delivered my answers with absolute confidence and determination adamant of my truth despite the solicitor trying to knock me off course at every turn.

And then it came the accusations to try and devalue who I was as a person depicting me as the bully throwing pieces of Kelly's lies in that I had assaulted her. Rather than getting distressed I focused on the facts thus being that I was the youngest of five children with 10 years separating our ages and periodically I would have to stand up for myself after being beaten, bullied and belittled. I reiterated that as the victim in this case my siblings were using the court to continue to bully me. He then moved to Sophie and her disclosure of further abuse accusing me of colluding with her to coax her into manifesting new evidence to twist the knife further. He pushed the fact that I was alone with her, so it was my word against hers. Inevitably though he didn't like it when I told him he was wrong and in fact Cerys was also present and that she had encouraged Sophie to come outside. He tried to make out that I had used the fact of having the dog in the car as an incentive like the dirty old man to 'come see my puppies.'

So that was how they were playing it an attempt to discredit the validity of my evidence by depicting me in the role that they had followed my entire life. I was suddenly the instigator, the bully having to defend myself exactly as Mum had predicted they would do, they had ganged up against me. I then remembered Ruby telling me that Kelly had effectively bullied Sophie via Facebook's messenger, so I brought this to the court's attention. The judge asked me to explain so I described the moment Ruby had mentioned it, of us going over to see the girls arranged by Ruby as I didn't know where they lived, nor did I have a contact number. I then went on to say about how Sophie had been reluctant to come out of the kitchen and was quite a timid young girl worried about our responses towards her as Kelly had apparently told her to stop telling lies about her father. The judge thanked me and made some of his own notes.

The solicitor then accused me of "interrogating" Timothy the time Mum had forced me into meeting him in the park not the truth that he was weak, and she was scared of him doing something stupid. I was crushed that I had let Mum talk me into meeting that piece of shit because she felt sorry for him and now here, they were again using my good nature against me. Not only had Kelly jumped off that fence but she had fallen straight through the gap to the pit of hell as far as I could see with her lies and slanderous comments. They were not just trying to get him off, both her and Nick were decimating my good name from every angle with the slant of a different lens. And boy were they grating the cheese as close to the bone as they could regardless of the lasting damage it may cause.

His solicitor then ran down a completely new path totally dragging the bottom of the barrel to a time that Timothy had stayed at my house, again another example of using my kindness against me. He was trying to make out that I couldn't be so scared of him if I allowed him to stay at my home. The incident in question had been the result of a drunken altercation with his wife Lilly where the police had removed him from the premises. Mum and Dad did not want him at their home in case it escalated further and so he was fobbed off on to me again being the closest living relative. The difference this time was that I wasn't a child or a teenager I was a prison officer, and he knew he didn't stand a chance against me especially as I had given him the Scarborough warning beforehand.

I was in the witness box for the whole of the afternoon and by the end of it felt nothing less than battered and bruised. It was hard to know how I had come across or if I had successfully managed to answer his barrage of questions adequately before he had jumped to the next. All I knew was that I had been put through the wringer, I felt utterly exhausted but there was no doubt I now did not care what happened to him and as far as I was concerned, they were all dead to me.

As I walked out of the door with the "Courtroom 8" above it, I was relieved that for me my part in it was over but then immediately felt devastated that Mum would have to undergo the same grilling with Ruby tomorrow. Although it wasn't usual practise for people who had already testified to be able to converse with those yet to give evidence, Ruby and I were permitted to travel home together. We both solemnly vowed not to discuss the trial in any way, and we didn't. I have to be honest there were some pieces I would have loved to have chewed over with like reminding her of my bed being in the boy's room for instance but for me it was important to come to court with clean hands.

As we left the court building all I wanted to do was get home, have a long hot soak and wash the day off me but directly outside the court staring straight at us was the ever-smirking Kelly. I could have walked straight over and wiped the floor with that lying bitches face the sneer of someone who had orchestrated the ordeal that I had just suffered.

'Just look at that,' I said to Ruby nodding in Kelly's direction, 'nothing like rubbing salt in the wounds.'

'Ignore her Lois she will have known the running order had changed she is only here to wind you up,' Ruby said grabbing my elbow.

'So, Maggie is here to watch my interview and to gather information for when Nick and Kelly have to give evidence, but we are not allowed to discuss what went on during my questioning. Its corrupt the whole lot of it no wonder people pull out or crumble under the pressure,' I said deflated.

'Don't worry Lois you have done your bit and tomorrow I intend to do mine,' she said as we made our way to the car to head for home.

That night as I lay in bed contemplating the day's events, I felt exceptionally alone not only couldn't I chat to Mum or Ruby, but I had no one to come home to talk it over with either. All along this sordid journey I had maintained some semblance of decorum but today I left the court feeling violated and dishonoured once again. I so wished my dad was here to give me words of encouragement to keep me steadfast and strong to ensure the "weasel" was made accountable for his actions.

I couldn't believe that Kelly's support of him was at such a huge detriment to me. I could understand her feeling obliged to support him with an ear to listen to or a shoulder to cry on but to twist situations to actually stick the knife into me to get him off crimes she knew he had committed was evil. He wasn't a clever man he had a memory like a sieve and couldn't lie for toffee, so I knew the allegations that had been made had come from her mouth. I could not fathom where the depth of her hate had arisen from, but it seemed to have poured out like a natural spring and then she was there waiting for us to emerge with victory upon her face.

I am not sure if it was her payback about not singing at Dad's funeral but either way it appeared my passage from Ephesians was correct, I had to put on the full armour of God because I was up against the devils scheming. It hadn't been easy to get through it but that was not what God had promised, my faith in Him had made it possible now all I needed to do was pray for Ruby, Mum, Sarah and Sophie. The days ahead were going to be as equally as testing so I would continue to submerge myself in the armour of God to try and support everyone else going through it.

Chapter 37
A Poor Show

The next morning, I had to make my way to the court alone whereas both Ruby and Mum could travel together as they still had to give evidence. No longer was the waiting room downstairs available as I had given my evidence now. I walked independently through the security check point and made my way upstairs to the massive expanse outside the court rooms. There were numerous bodies going in and out of the independent rooms to chat privately with their solicitors along with people cluttering the seats down the outer parts or leather backless couches down the middle.

I decided to grab a coffee from the canteen and then took a seat nearest the entrance to observe my surroundings. As Timothy was not on remand, he was free to wander around at leisure which he exercised with great delight and swagger. I noticed that Ruby had arrived before me, and she was talking to a couple at the far end of the huge hall like expanse. After a while, she approached me but keeping her distance so that no accusations could be made.

'You see that couple over there that I was talking to?' she said shamelessly pointing them out.

'Yes,' I said.

'I know them from school; she was telling me that he was here on a drink-drive charge worried that he was going to lose his licence,' she told me.

'Right,' I said not knowing what on earth this had to do with anything or why she would feel a need to come over to tell me that as I didn't know them.

'Apparently,' she continued, 'the guy said that he asked Timothy what he was doing here and the explanation he gave was that it was "to do with some jumped up charges because Ruby and Lois are being bitches."'

'Jumped up charges?' I began, 'has he actually made himself believe that he is not guilty now?'

'He is just an idiot have you seen how he is lording it past us every two minutes then going in and out with his solicitor, he probably thinks he is some kind of celebrity,' Ruby described.

'As long as he stays away from me, I don't care,' I told her.

Then a tannoy announcement called for the solicitors and defendant to attend courtroom 8, Ruby and I looked at one another like athletes weighing each other up at the start of a race and so day 2 in courtroom 8 was about to begin.

'Are you coming in?' she asked excitedly.

'No, I do not think I could face it,' I told her.

'But you have given your evidence, Lois, so you are allowed to sit in and hear everyone else's,' she said triumphantly.

'I know Ruby, but yesterday I could have done with someone out here to catch me when I came out feeling dishevelled. The ordeal was immense, so I have decided to wait out here to provide that support to everyone else, if you don't mind,' I declared.

'Please yourself,' she said loftily, 'I can't wait to go in and hear everyone else's evidence.'

'That is fine, Ruby, but as far as I am concerned, I do not want all that information running through my brain. When this comes to an end, I want to walk out and leave it behind me,' I told her as she was called in as the next witness.

I kept my seat wondering where Mum could be because I hadn't seen her yet and was worried about how she was feeling. Not only was it a massive undertaking giving evidence but against your own son and at the age of 80 made it an arduous task for her. After Ruby had been in the courtroom for some time, Mum appeared escorted by the nice lady who had accompanied me the day before. She guided Mum towards the two seats directly outside the door of courtroom 8 and sat down with her.

To my dismay, Mum looked in absolute shock, terrified at the prospect of what she was being driven to do all because her son was a coward. She glanced towards me, so I attempted to convey with my face what my heart was saying. I hated the fact that she was sat in front of me in that state and I was forbidden to make any contact with her. I wanted to reassure her that everything would be ok to just let her know I was praying for her. My heart was literally breaking whilst her other children thought they were so clever at manipulating the judicial system to bully the innocent. And then Ruby came out walking right past Mum as she strode purposefully towards me.

'How did it go?' I asked.

'Fine, his solicitor tried to insinuate that we had made it all up like we had some vendetta against him, but I told him straight he is a pervert. I relayed everything that I said in my statement although he did ask me about when we were younger and if I remember you ever having a bed in the boys' room which I didn't,' she said.

'I knew he would ask you that, I so wanted to remind you about it yesterday because it hinges on the bedrock of my testimony, but I didn't want to coerce you in any way,' I told her.

'You should have said something when we went home in the car, Lois, no one would have known,' Ruby spoke.

'Maybe not but I would have known and when he gets convicted, it will be by his own hand not by any underneath stunts that I have performed. That might be how they are choosing to play their hand, but I have more integrity,' I explained.

'You know they will probably ask Mum about the bed thing too,' she began, 'have you seen anything of her yet?'

I nodded towards Mum who was having a quiet word with the nice lady and then they both got up and walked out towards the stairs.

'You don't think she is bottling it do you?' Ruby queried.

'No, she will probably just want to use the toilet before she goes in,' I said.

The court clerk came to the door and called for Mum so we advised him she had gone to use the toilet but before she returned Ruby decided to slip back into the court so she could hear Mum's testimony.

'Are you sure you don't want to come in?' she asked me, but I couldn't bear to witness Mum going through such an ordeal and not be able to stand with her or support her.

Instead, I remained outside avidly praying for her to have a sound memory along with sending her good vibes and strength. It seemed like an age before she came back out that I was beginning to get worried about her. As she walked out, I threw my arms around her then held her as she wept tears of relief that it was over. The court broke for lunch so Ruby, Mum and I decided to go for a walk along the street we had meandered through yesterday to sit in a café and eat. We sat to eat Ruby dissecting every exchange that had occurred during both hers and

Mum's testimony, comparing things that they had said then sharing her thoughts on how things were progressing. I knew that she might need to do this to process all the information, but I did not want each and every word engrained in my brain as I wanted to be able to walk away and shed it like a snake's skin.

During the afternoon it was Sarah who was giving evidence relating to Elena and Danny who were far too young and traumatised for a statement to be extracted. She detailed how their behaviour had changed when they had gone for overnight stays with Timothy, the issues that teachers had addressed and Elena's reaction to seeing the social worker. She also recalled a telephone conversation from Sophies mum Lilly just after she and Timothy had got married. Lilly had apparently said she wanted to talk with Timothy regarding something that had occurred with Sophie when she had gone out in the wagon with him. Timothy's damning response was 'well that's me getting locked up then.'

Again, I stayed outside the courtroom to pray and to offer Sarah support when she finally emerged, but Ruby was hot on her heels wanting to deliberate what had been discussed. I knew it may be helpful for them, but I took myself off to the canteen because I really didn't want to embark upon a thread through needle account. I was not getting any joy out of being there at all but felt it was my duty to see things through to the end because that was all that was important to me that it was concluded.

The 3rd day of the trial Wednesday was when Sophie and her family were attending court and I could see how beside herself Lilly was trying to stay composed. I honestly could not have imagined how difficult it must have been to support your child in giving evidence about the abuse they had sustained against their biological father. It had been hard enough to do it myself. I was just glad that their real dad was there to support them although how he didn't lose it and lamp Timothy one is beyond me. At lunchtime, Ruby, Mum, Lilly, Sophie, her dad and myself all went to a bar around the corner to chat about how we were all feeling. Sophie sat quietly flanked by her mum and dad the poor love shell shocked from having to detail in open court the abuse her biological father had carried out against her, she was 16. As soon as they had eaten, they left for home.

During the afternoon, Timothy was being interrogated so as people began milling back in towards court 8, Melissa Maya asked me if I was going in to hear Timothy being questioned but again, I declined. She didn't seem to understand that I wasn't here for retribution I was only there for closure. I could hear Ruby telling Melissa about the prediction of the trial going ahead, the change of the running order and of the number 8 being significant so she came over to hear more.

'So, any more predictions?' Melissa asked.

'Not at the moment because there is a question mark,' I said.

'A question mark, what do you mean?' Melissa asked.

'There are 4 counts that he has been charged with 3 are guilty but one has a question mark over it, at the moment I don't know which one that is,' I informed her.

'Ooh that's interesting but to be honest I would settle for 3 guilty verdicts,' she said as the solicitors were called into courtroom 8.

I was sat in the large hall area for most of the afternoon mooching around to stretch my legs and with Maya periodically popping out to check on me. When court finally dispersed for the day, I was glad to get out of there and walked with Ruby and Mum back to the car.

'The judge was amazing, Lois, he tied him up in knots, didn't he, Mum,' Ruby said.

'Not half, he made him look a right fool,' Mum agreed.

'Well to be honest he did that to himself,' Ruby said cryptically.

'Why?' I said unable to not engage.

'Timothy was asked about the abuse regarding Sophie, but he said that she was lying and it had never happened the way she had stated. So, he was asked to explain the way it did happen and he obviously made up a cock and bull story, didn't he, Mum,' Ruby said looking for Mum's input.

'Yes, it was ridiculous he was humming and hawing and flapping about like fish out of water,' Mum said laughing no longer stressed about being in the court environment.

'Anyway, our solicitor then asks him about the earlier things to do with you, but he wouldn't answer a direct question he kept making out that he couldn't remember. So, the solicitor said, 'well if you can't remember whether they happened you cannot testify to say they didn't happen, can you?' Timothy was digging his hole and the solicitor was burying him in it,' Ruby said laughing at the sight of him squirming under oath.

'Yes, Timothy then stated that the other offence against you when you were older never happened, but the judge said to him "hold on a minute your mother has testified to say that Lois did stay at your house that night and she was not herself on her return. She also stated that Lois told both herself and Ruby about the abuse, you were here when that happened, weren't you?" To which Timothy replied, "yeah, yeah I was here." But you have just said that it didn't happen, either you're a liar or your mother is,' Mum told me.

'Never! So, what was his response to that?' I enquired.

'He didn't say anything so the judge pressed him further and said, "come on Timothy are you the liar or is your mother a liar?" and he said, "well yeah she must be then,"' Ruby finished.

'I cannot believe that he actually stated that you were the liar, really?' I was stunned.

'Funny thing about it was that the judge shook his head in disbelief as well,' said Mum.

The tales went on all the way home and I have to admit I kind of felt sorry for him and his stupidity at thinking he could enter a court room, lie and actually get away with it.

The next day it was the turn of Kelly who brought her husband and eldest daughter Charlotte to watch her perform as though the courtroom was her stage a lot like Dad's funeral would have been. It made me laugh because she thought she was smart by downloading sheets of the conversations she'd had with Sophie over Facebook. Inevitably I had brought it up during my testimony so to counteract this little titbit knowing she would get questioned upon it she had come prepared. All she proved was that they were colluding with one another undermining the legalities of confidentiality by sharing key pieces of evidence not to mention the conversation provided could have been doctored. I was sat outside the courtroom at the far right of the door because Nick was sat at one of the two seats awaiting his turn.

Apparently, the judge had asked her to step out to a little room within court 8 to decide whether to submit the sheeted information as evidence. He had told her specifically to sit in the room and not to talk to anyone as she was still under oath. However, she couldn't resist the temptation to brazenly share her perceived shrewdness and opened the door to share with Nick how clever she was that the court had come to a standstill. He kept his eyes down as she popped her head through the door to him giggling. He did his best to alert her to me sitting out of her peripheral vision, but she was too consumed by her cunning intelligence to see her own stupidity. I glared at them the epitome of disgrace thinking they could pull a fast one on the judicial system.

Apparently, she told the court that I had bullied her all her life and that I had always been an angry child. The judge called bullshit in a roundabout way by getting her to reiterate our 10 years age difference. He then queried if she expected the court to believe that I bullied her when I was 6 and she was 16? He also stated for the courts attention that if I had been an angry child maybe it was due to the fact that my adolescent brother had been sexually abusing me. He theorised that this was enough to make any child angry. From the feedback, both Ruby and Mum shared it seemed Kelly's only achievement was to make a laughing stock of herself.

In fact, whilst giving evidence the judge interrupted her to directly ask if she was an actress because there were no authentic words coming out of her mouth. Inevitably when she had finished her piece of drama, she sat down with her family for the congratulatory applause of a pat on the back for how brave she had been. Although to everyone else, she had been the joke offering and had ended up doing much more damage to the case than even Timothy had done.

Lastly it was the turn of Nick, which was neither here nor there really, he just took the coward's way out of not knowing anything and of having nothing of any importance to say. We had been informed that over the months leading up to the trial Nick had attempted to get several people to write a character statement on Timothy's behalf. However, from what we'd heard every single person contacted had refused whether these had been family friends, work colleagues or associates. Not one person had a good word to say about Timothy at all. In fact, many voiced their opinions of him as "not being quite right" or "something being off with him" that they couldn't put their finger on. So apparently no matter whom they tried to coax or manipulate not one person came forward so in the end Nick had written a character reference that couldn't have been further from the truth.

Nick depicted Timothy as being a "pillar of the community" he was an "older brother whom he looked up to" and he "admired him as a father". I think he must have forgotten that his pervert brother was on trial for interfering with his children so to say you "admire him as a father" could evoke all manner of thoughts. Nick was the man who couldn't stand Timothy, he openly ridiculed his life choices, he hated working with him, he belittled him as being a poor achiever, of amounting to nothing and of living in a caravan.

At the end of the trial, when the judge read the statement out to the court, he equally disregarded it by stating that the evidence that is given will not all be truthful. He stated that some people will come to court and tell the truth, the whole truth and nothing but the truth and then there will be the others who will lie through their teeth. He addressed the jurors to tell them he was sure that they were smart enough to distinguish the wheat from the chaff. He then summarised the facts of the case and told the jurors their legal obligations upon reaching a verdict before dismissing them.

As everyone began filtering out of courtroom 8, the fire alarm suddenly screeched into life and the whole building was evacuated. No doubt some trickster thinking it was funny to pull such a childish prank. I stood outside in the cold air noting our opposition and became transfixed at how clearly Peter looked out of his comfort zone.

Seeing my gaze, Mum reflected, 'surely after hearing Kelly's ridiculous performance Peter has got to be assessing the lies, she has been feeding them,' she said.

'You would think so but after his performance regarding her singing at the funeral I would say it takes one ham actor to know another. They deserve each other,' I said without any feeling at all.

Once we were allowed to go back in, Maya came over to me to ask whether I had any new predictions.

'There is still a question mark over one of the charges, but he will be found guilty of the other three, the jury will come back with their verdict today and he will be sentenced,' I said.

'There is no way that will happen!' Maya stated, 'in all my years at prosecuting, the defendant has never been sentenced on the same day.'

'Yes, I get it, usually there are presentence reports and a whole host of other paperwork to be filed but I am telling you he will be found guilty on 3 charges, and he will be sentenced today,' I affirmed.

I decided to take myself away from the hustle and bustle of everyone going back upstairs and elected to sit in the room we had been held in just before giving evidence. I found the bible I had used before and intently searched through it praying now for my brother Timothy. I felt that his fate had been sealed so I prayed for him, for his mind and the turmoil he must be going through right now despite the bravado he was displaying. I thought about the new inmates that I had received and on recalling how they had felt on their first night incarcerated I prayed for his protection. I no longer felt any connection to him other than pity because Kelly and Nick had done him a great disservice interfering where it had got absolutely nothing to do with them. They would be going home tonight but their brother wouldn't and by not owning his acts of depravity in favour of listening to their ideas at getting him off they had done him more damage than good. Worse still was the fact that they had forced poor Sophie to testify along with Mum and the rest of us. My dad would have been mortified at their dishonesty, their complete disregard for his children, grandchildren and wife and had he not already disowned them he would have surely done so on this day.

When I had prayed for their souls until I could pray no more a dread fell upon me like the black cloth of death worn by judges who used to pass death sentences and I knew it was over. I walked back up the two flights of stairs to courtroom 8 where there was a flurry of activity.

'Where have you been? I have been searching for you everywhere,' Ruby said.

'Why, are the jury back?' I asked genuinely feeling sad for him.

'Yes, they have called everyone back,' she said as the solicitors tore through the entrance towards the courtroom.

'Are you coming in, Lois?' she asked.

'No,' I said calmly, 'I will wait here all I want you to do is tell me the verdict then let me go.'

'What do you mean, let you go?' she asked.

'I have stayed here throughout I have prayed for each and every person over the past four days but as soon as the verdict is revealed I want to be left alone to deal with my own feelings,' I told her. 'I do not want to talk to anyone, and I never want to discuss this again, today I walk forward free of the blame, shame and guilt.'

As everyone piled into court, I had no doubt that if it went Nick, Kelly and Timothy's way there would be over expressions of "told you so" etc but that was not the way I needed to express myself. What I needed to do was to leave it all behind. I sat in the quietness of the expansive hall completely alone the tension so acute a pin could have been heard dropping on to the carpeted floor. And then the door eased open to reveal Maya.

'I cannot believe it,' she said stunned, 'he has just been found guilty on 3 out of the 4 charges but a question mark hovered over the four which pertained to one of Sophies. Lois, he has been found guilty on both of the crimes he committed against you,' she paused 'and I don't believe this, but the judge is going to sentence him today!'

I closed my eyes but could not stop the barrage of tears cascading down my face from the utter relief that it was finally over. I stood up so Maya turned thinking I was going to follow her into the courtroom, but I didn't. I fled down the steps and out through the building. I had no idea where I was going or what direction I was taking I just left and walked. The brisk wind was biting at my bear arms and passers-by were staring at me, but I kept going with the tears continuing to fall. I had stood in the gap for the children, I had told the truth, the whole truth and nothing but the truth and in doing so the liars had been exposed. They may have thought they were clever in their scheming and plotting to stab me in the back, but my God had shown me that when he was for me no one and nothing could stand against me. I had not only been vindicated but he was now known for exactly what he was a paedophile who had abused his sisters and his children and thankfully I would not have to see him, Kelly or Nick ever again.

I took my phone out of my pocket and rang Laura and Leanne my childhood friends who had offered their continual support to give them the news as I continued to weep. Once I had cleansed myself of the residue of past emotion, I made my way to the steps across from the court to wait for Mum and Ruby. Then the doors flung open, and Ruby ran across to me.

'What the hell happened where did you go,' she yelled.

'I had to get out of there Ruby I am sorry,' I told her.

'We did it Lois, we got him, and he was found guilty on 3 of the 4 counts, exactly as you predicted,' she said in astonishment holding me and weeping herself.

The thing is I didn't see it as a victory how could it be? I was still damaged by the abuse, and I would still wear those scars for the rest of my life. Not like some people do as medals no, they would be there loitering under the surface waiting to remind me. Like when Tracy, Ruby and I would play 'What time is it Mr Wolf' on the tennis court sized lawn at Grey Gables it might be behind me, but it would creep back up to tap me on the shoulder. This will always manifest if I feel I am not being listened to or if someone is continually talking over me or ridiculing me. It might evoke a trauma response to recoil, switch off or one of anger that has nothing to do with the imminent situation but a symptom of supressed emotional development.

No, there was no victory for me; he may have got 2 years for each charge, but he would only be imprisoned for 2 years in total and then he would be out on licence. My life had been profoundly affected for 40 years compounded by the secrets, the lies, the weight of the blame, the shame, and the guilt that had not been mine to carry in the first place. He may have been found guilty, he may have to do 2 years in prison and then have to sign on the sex offenders' register for life, but he could then move on.

I have to now unpick the effects of the past 40 years before I can be completely free of what my head tells me. I am quite categorically unashamedly me, and I will never seek anyone else's approval for my existence ever again; love me or hate me that is your choice, but it will never change the amazing person that I have grown to become.

Although I have to be aware that there is Little Lois and she is still hurting, still uncertain, lurking in the background seeking reassurance, love and tender care. For me to be healed, she also needs inner healing; otherwise, in those uncertain times of fear and tension it will stimulate her appearance and then generate anxiety and stress. It can be a vicious cycle but then that is the result of childhood trauma; we learn to respond in a certain way which can then become unhelpful coping mechanisms as adults.

Unfortunately, there is a lot of learnt behaviour that needs unlearning but hopefully, now that I have cut all the deadwood out of my life, I can find the plan and purpose God had for me all along. Maybe writing this book about my experiences in order to help you and to change your life was why it had to happen to me first. If so, just know that you were worth it…xx.

Printed in Great Britain
by Amazon